LITERATURE AND POLITICS IN EASTERN EUROPE

SELECTED PAPERS FROM THE FOURTH WORLD CONGRESS FOR SOVIET AND EAST EUROPEAN STUDIES, HARROGATE, 1990

Edited for the International Council for Soviet and East European Studies by Stephen White, Professor of Politics, University of Glasgow

From the same publishers:

Roy Allison (*editor*)
RADICAL REFORM IN SOVIET DEFENCE POLICY

Ben Eklof (*editor*)
SCHOOL AND SOCIETY IN TSARIST AND SOVIET RUSSIA

John Elsworth (*editor*)
THE SILVER AGE IN RUSSIAN LITERATURE

John Garrard and Carol Garrard (*editors*)
WORLD WAR 2 AND THE SOVIET PEOPLE

Zvi Gitelman (*editor*)
THE POLITICS OF NATIONALITY AND THE EROSION OF THE USSR

Sheelagh Duffin Graham (*editor*)
NEW DIRECTIONS IN SOVIET LITERATURE

Lindsey Hughes (*editor*)
NEW PERSPECTIVES ON MUSCOVITE HISTORY

Walter Joyce (*editor*)
SOCIAL CHANGE AND SOCIAL ISSUES IN THE FORMER USSR

Bohdan Krawchenko (*editor*)
UKRAINIAN PAST, UKRAINIAN PRESENT

Paul G. Lewis (*editor*)
DEMOCRACY AND CIVIL SOCIETY IN EASTERN EUROPE

Robert B. McKean (*editor*)
NEW PERSPECTIVES IN MODERN RUSSIAN HISTORY

John Morison (*editor*)
THE CZECH AND SLOVAK EXPERIENCE
EASTERN EUROPE AND THE WEST

John O. Norman (*editor*)
NEW PERSPECTIVES ON RUSSIAN AND SOVIET ARTISTIC CULTURE

Derek Offord (*editor*)
THE GOLDEN AGE OF RUSSIAN LITERATURE AND THOUGHT

Michael E. Urban (*editor*)
IDEOLOGY AND SYSTEM CHANGE IN THE USSR AND EAST EUROPE

Literature and Politics in Eastern Europe

Selected Papers from the Fourth World Congress for Soviet and
East European Studies, Harrogate, 1990

Edited by

Celia Hawkesworth

Senior Lecturer in Serbo-Croat
School of Slavonic and East European Studies
University of London

St. Martin's Press

First published in Great Britain 1992 by
THE MACMILLAN PRESS LTD
Houndmills, Basingstoke, Hampshire RG21 2XS
and London
Companies and representatives
throughout the world

This book is published in association with the International Council for Soviet and East European Studies.

A catalogue record for this book is available
from the British Library.

ISBN 0–333–55324–1

Printed in Great Britain by
Antony Rowe Ltd
Chippenham, Wiltshire

C
C

First published in the United States of America 1992 by
Scholarly and Reference Division,
ST. MARTIN'S PRESS, INC.,
175 Fifth Avenue,
New York, N.Y. 10010

ISBN 0–312–07991–5   6 oo 36747 o7

Library of Congress Cataloging-in-Publication Data
Literture and politics in Eastern Europe / edited by Celia
Hawkesworth.
p.   cm.
"Selected papers from the Fourth World Congress for Soviet and
East European Studies, Harrogate, 1990".
Includes index.
ISBN 0–312–07991–5 C
1. Europe, Eastern—Literatures—History and criticism–
Congresses.   2. Politics and literature—Europe, Eastern–
Congresses.   I. Hawkesworth, Celia, 1942–   .
PN849.E9L52   1992   92–2749
809'.8947—dc20   CIP

Contents

General Editor's Introduction

The Fourth World Congress for Soviet and East European Studies took place in Harrogate, Yorkshire, in July 1990. It was an unusual congress in many ways. It was the first of its kind to take place in Britain, and the first to take place since the launching of Gorbachev's programme of *perestroika* and the revolutions in Eastern Europe (indeed so rapid was the pace of change in the countries with which we were concerned that the final programme had to incorporate over 600 amendments). It was the largest and most complex congress of Soviet and East European studies that has yet taken place, with twenty-seven panels spread over fourteen sessions on six days. It was also the most representative congress of its kind, with over 2000 participants including – for the first time – about 300 from the USSR and Eastern Europe. Most were scholars, some were activists, and a few were the new kind of academic turned part-time deputy: whatever their status, it was probably this Soviet and East European presence that contributed most directly to making this a very different congress from the ones that had preceded it in the 1970s and 1980s.

No series of volumes, however numerous, could hope to convey the full flavour of this extraordinary occasion. The formal panels alone incorporate almost a thousand papers. There were three further plenary sessions; there were many more unattached papers; and the subjects that were treated ranged from medieval Novgorod to computational linguistics, from the problems of the handicapped in the USSR to Serbian art at the time of the battle of Kosovo. Nor, it was decided at an early stage, would it even be desirable to attempt a fully comprehensive 'congress proceedings', including all the papers in their original form. My aim as General Editor, with the strong support of the International Council for Soviet and East European Studies (who cosponsored the congress with the British Association for Soviet, Slavonic and East European Studies), has rather been to generate a series of volumes which will have some thematic coherence, and to bring them out as quickly as possible while their (often topical) contents are still current.

A strategy of this kind imposes a cost, in that many authors have had to find other outlets for what would in different circumstances have been very publishable papers. The gain, however, seems much greater: a series of real books on properly defined subjects, edited by scholars of experience and standing in their respective fields, and placed promptly before the academic community. These, I am glad to say, were the same as the objectives of the publishers who expressed an interest in various aspects of the congress proceedings, and it has led to a series of volumes as well as of special issues of journals covering a wide range of interests.

There are volumes on art and architecture, on history and literature, on law and economics, on society and education. There are further volumes on nationality issues and the Ukraine, on the environment, on international relations and on defence. There are Soviet volumes, and others that deal more specifically with Eastern (or perhaps more properly, East Central) Europe. There are interdisciplinary volumes on women in Russia and the USSR, the Soviet experience in the Second World War, and ideology and system change. There are special issues of some of the journals that publish in our field, dealing with religion and Slovene studies, émigrés and East European economics, publishing and politics, linguistics and the Russian revolution. Altogether nearly forty separate publications will stem from the Harrogate congress: more than twice as many as from any previous congress of its kind, and a rich and enduring record of its deliberations.

Most of these volumes will be published in the United Kingdom by Macmillan. It is my pleasant duty to acknowledge Macmillan's early interest in the scholarly output of the congress, and the swift and professional attention that has been given to all of these volumes since their inception. A full list of the Macmillan Harrogate series appears elsewhere in the Macmillan edition of this volume; it can give only an impression of the commitment and support I have enjoyed from Tim Farmiloe, Clare Wace and others at all stages of our proceedings. I should also take this opportunity to thank John Morison and his colleagues on the International Council for Soviet and East European Studies for entrusting me with this responsible task in the first place, and the various sponsors – the Erasmus Prize Fund of Amsterdam, the Ford Foundation in New York, the British Foreign and Commonwealth Office, the British Council, the Stefan Batory Trust and others – whose generous support helped to make the congress a reality.

The next congress will be held in 1995, and (it is hoped) at a location in Eastern Europe. Its proceedings can hardly hope to improve upon the vigour and imagination that is so abundantly displayed on the pages of these splendid volumes.

University of Glasgow   STEPHEN WHITE

Notes on the Contributors

Richard Aczel is a British Academy Post-doctoral Fellow based at the School of Slavonic and East European Studies, University of London, where he teaches Hungarian literature. His special interests are twentieth-century Hungarian literature and culture, the Austro–Hungarian monarchy at the turn of the century, contemporary Central European literature and cinema.

Elka Agoston-Nikolova, MA University of Sofia, Doctorate University of Groningen, is a Lecturer in Bulgarian and Serbo-Croat at the Slavic Institute, University of Groningen, the Netherlands. Her main areas of interest are South Slavic oral poetry, twentieth-century literature and women's studies.

Bohunka Bradbrook, PhD Prague, DPhil Oxon. was formerly Lecturer in Education, English and Czech, University College of North Wales, Bangor. Her main areas of interest are Karel Čapek, Czech literature, George Eliot and the English novel.

Dobrica Ćosić, is a novelist and essayist, mainly concerned with the recent history of Serbia, whose works include a series of novels dealing with the First World War. In his recent works he has begun to investigate themes which were previously taboo.

Regina Grol-Prokopczyk, PhD State University of New York at Binghampton, MA Warsaw University, is Associate Professor of Comparative Literature, Empire State College (SUNY) in Buffalo. Her main areas of interest are East European Drama, Polish émigré literature and literary translation.

Celia Hawkesworth, BA Cantab, MPhil London, is Senior Lecturer in Serbo-Croat, School of Slavonic and East European Studies, University of London. Her main areas of interest are twentieth-century literature and women's studies.

Danuta Zamojska-Hutchins, BA Warsaw University, MA and PhD University of Minnesota, is Research Professor, Slavonic Studies, Buena Vista College, Storm Lake, Iowa. Her main areas of interest are Slavonic poetry and drama, comparative literature and semiotics.

Michael H. Impey is Associate Professor of Italian and Comparative Literature at the University of Kentucky. He has published critical studies of contemporary Romanian prose and poetry. He is also the translator, with Brian Swann, of *Selected Poems of Tudor Arghezi* (1976) and Tristan Tzara's *Primele poeme/First Poems* (1976). He is currently at work on a critical reappraisal of the work of Ignazio Silone.

Predrag Palavestra is a literary critic, author of several volumes of criticism and literary history. For many years he was Director of the Institute for Literature in Belgrade, and is now an active member of the Serbian Academy of Science and Art.

Norma L. Rudinsky, AB, AM Stanford, is Senior Instructor in English, Oregon State University, Corvallis. Her main areas of interest are the literature of the Slovaks and women's studies.

Myroslav Shkandrij, BA Cantab, MA and PhD Toronto, is Associate Professor of Ukrainian and Russian, Department of Slavic Studies, University of Manitoba. His main areas of interest are twentieth-century literature and literary debates of the 1920s.

Josef Škvorecký is a novelist who emigrated to North America after the Soviet occupation of Czechoslovakia. He teaches literature at the University of Toronto and runs a publishing house which he founded in 1971 with his wife.

Lydia Tarnavsky, PhD in Germanic Languages and Literature, is Assistant Professor in German, Modern Language Department, Siena College, Loudonville, New York. Her area of interest is Ukrainian themes in German literature.

Nina Taylor MA Oxon, is a freelance scholar, writer and translator. Her main areas of interest are Polish literature of the Eastern borderland, Polish émigré literature and Gulag literature.

1 Introduction
Celia Hawkesworth

A collection of papers from a conference where there is no binding
theme is inevitably to some extent disparate and arbitrary. This is
particularly the case when the potential geographical and historical
scope is open-ended as it was in the case of the non-Russian or Soviet
literature papers offered at Harrogate. In order to impose some coherence on the present volume the editor's intention has been to focus on
the twentieth century, particularly the period from the Second World
War up to the changes of 1989, and within that time-scale to give as
wide as possible representation to a broad range of countries and
cultures. Although the picture is not of course comprehensive, there is
sufficient common ground in the area's shared post-war experience for
it to be at least representative. It has also been decided to include some
mention of earlier periods, notably eighteenth-century Poland and
Ukraine. This decision was taken in order to highlight the extent to
which the notions of 'politics' and 'literature' have been inextricably
related throughout this part of Europe ever since its peoples began to
have a sense of themselves as national groups.

One of the complex questions facing writers in Central and Eastern
Europe under Communist rule has of course been whether or not to
remain in their homeland. The opening contribution in this volume by
the Czech novelist Josef Škvorecký, his plenary address to the Harrogate
conference, offers an account of some of the pressures he was himself
subjected to before he chose exile. Among the many Central and East
European writers who have achieved prominence in the West and
whose names are frequently mentioned in this volume are Miłosz and
Kundera. The choice of exile, removal from the wellspring of inspiration in their native language, which has been made by so many writers
from these countries, is of course far from easy. The altered circumstances of the writer's life may entail a complete reappraisal of his or
her work. Regina Grol-Prokopczyk offers a detailed study of the effects
of exile on the nature of the Polish playwright Mrożek's subject-matter
and style. Equally, the prominence achieved by some writers in the
West by virtue of their dissident status may lead to distortions in
reception. In his short reflection on literature and politics, the Serbian
novelist Dobrica Ćosić touches on some of the negative effects of
exaggerated attention to 'dissident' writers and thinkers. This distortion

1

of the value of a given writer works in two ways: it can also lead to false neglect of gifted writers whose work does not qualify for the label and hence are of no interest to publishers in the West. This other kind of 'exile' – confinement within the borders of their homeland – is considered by Michael Impey in his essay on three contemporary Romanian novelists, mentioning in passing that a contributing factor to this neglect is the problem of inadequate translation.

For the majority of Central and East European writers under Communist rule, of course, the question was not how to achieve prominence in the West, but how to continue to write honestly within the constraints of the system. One possible device was the use of Aesopian language, a concept frequently referred to in the pages of this volume. Škvorecký gives an example of a simple allegory of this kind in his story 'The End of Bull Mácha'. Norma Rudinsky treats two possible procedures, dissent and disguise, as they relate to two Slovak women writers.

The writers discussed so far all share a common rejection of ideological oppression. But for many intellectuals in Eastern Europe, including some of the contributors to this volume, the path has not necessarily been so clear-cut. This was perhaps particularly the case in Yugoslavia, where Communist rule was not imposed from outside, but grew out of a revolution inseparable from a successful war of liberation from the occupying Axis powers. For many young people coming to maturity in the immediate post-war years this was a heady atmosphere. Several of these essays identify a turning point, an 'awakening', referred to by Elka Agoston-Nikolova as a 'rite of passage', a moment of separation of the individual from the prevailing values to which she or he has previously subscribed. One way or another, the political context is thus foregrounded to an obvious degree in Eastern Europe, demanding that each individual's public and private position depend on conscious decisions.

A different kind of reappraisal of the individual's situation is considered in two essays focusing on women's consciousness. Norma Rudinsky suggests that women writers in the Czech and Slovak lands are beginning to think of themselves in terms of a separate women's consciousness and Celia Hawkesworth traces a similar process in women's writing in Yugoslavia, based on the example of an auto-biographical work by a Croatian woman writer. Women have been strikingly absent from the literary histories of many East European cultures, with some notable exceptions such as the prominent Bulgarian poet Blaga Dimitrova, whose novel is the subject of Elka Agoston-

Nikolova's study. This does not apply so much to Czech, Slovak and Polish women writers who have been more in evidence than their colleagues in the South Slav lands or Romania. Nevertheless, the consciously 'feminist' dimension that characterised women's writing in the GDR, and notably the work of Christa Wolf, is only now beginning to emerge in other East European literatures.

A woman poet who illustrates one of the central functions of mainstream literature throughout the territories of Eastern Europe is the Polish–Lithuanian poet, Iłłakowiczóvna, whose work is described by Danuta Hutchins. In circumstances of occupation and annexation which have been so much a part of the history of these nations, the function of literature has often been to keep alive and foster a sense of separate nationhood. Iłłakowiczóvna, with her dual allegiance to both Poland and Lithuania, offers an example of the way questions of national identity have demanded a response from individuals in these territories throughout their history, very much as questions of political allegiance have in more recent times.

In the years of Communist rule, the relationship of writers to history has been a complex one. On the one hand historical contexts have been used to disguise treatment of contemporary problems, and on the other hand where it was possible, notably in Yugoslavia, literature has been used to expose historical truths suppressed by the official ideology. Richard Aczel discusses another aspect of this relationship, notably a sense of 'loss of history' that pervades much contemporary Hungarian fiction. His essay explores the way this sense of loss coincides with postmodernist attitudes in Western culture.

One of the consequences of the changes in Eastern Europe for people in the West has been the increased visibility of certain territories, which were more or less anonymously absorbed in the vast mass of the Soviet Union, and which are beginning now to achieve some measure of autonomy. Among these are Lithuania, the other Baltic states, and Ukraine. Some sense of the history of much of Eastern Europe is given in Lydia Tarnavsky's essay on Ukrainians under Austro–Hungarian rule. Myroslav Shkandrij contributes to the process of reappraisal of the culture of these areas in his essay on the Ukrainian avant-garde. The other excursion into the history of the region, Nina Taylor's treatise on eighteenth-century life at a Polish magnate court, encapsulated in a balloon trip, conjures up an age in which politics and art were also interwoven, in intricate patterns of privilege and patronage.

The final essay in this volume, Bohunka Bradbrook's discussion of Karel Čapek's relations with prominent English writers of his age:

Chesterton, Wells and Shaw, harks back to a time when literature was discussed and evaluated on its terms alone. The relationship of all four writers to politics and the scientific discoveries of their age was certainly an important aspect of their work. But it was a relationship which depended on individual temperament and choice, rather than resistance to non-literary pressures.

As the countries of Eastern Europe emerge from the distortions of the years of Communist rule, we can expect major changes in the function of literature throughout the area. We may begin to look forward to a time in which politics will undoubtedly play a part in literature, no longer as criticism of an imposed ideology as described by Predrag Palavestra in this volume, but in the manner suggested by Ćosić: no longer as a restricting, distorting force making artificial demands on individuals, whether as writers or ordinary citizens, but as a natural dimension of human life.

2 Reception: An Authorial Experience

Josef Škvorecký

The soundest advice ever given to a writer is Hemingway's: a writer should never read his critics. If he believes them when they praise him, he must believe them when they say he is no longer good. That undermines his self-confidence, the prerequisite for a job well done.

It is excellent advice but very few writers were able to take it to heart and act accordingly – although some were. There is a story in the émigré Czech novelist Egon Hostovský's memoirs *Literary Adventures of a Czech Writer in Foreign Lands* (*Literarní dobrodružství českého spisovatele v cizině*, 1966), about an experiment conducted by Linscott, Faulkner's editor at Random House. *A Fable* had just come out in France, and the author, in New York at the time, had an appointment with his editor who wanted to introduce Hostovský to him. As they waited for Faulkner's arrival, Mr Linscott, to Hostovský's puzzlement, covered his desk with clippings of French reviews of the new novel, and arranged them in a certain pattern. 'Let's remember the pattern,' he told Hostovský, 'so that we can see whether he touched them'. When Faulkner entered his office, Linscott excused himself and the Czech writer for ten or fifteen minutes since – he said – they had some business to see to, told the novelist to take a seat at his desk and, in their absence, amuse himself by reading the reviews. A quarter of an hour later, when they came back, they found Faulkner sitting in the editor's chair with the pattern of reviews undisturbed.

In the end, Hemingway did not follow his own rule, and literally devoured reviews of his books during the last and bitter phase of his life when reviewers were almost unanimous in their opinion that the star of the 1920s had written himself out. After several years of such reading, the star of the '20s blew away his head with a shotgun.

It is simply dangerous to read one's reviews. But, then, until the arrival of modern American democracy where even defecating on the Stars and Stripes is permitted, writing had always been a dangerous profession. Increasingly so in our own century, and in that part of our world whose literatures are the subject of this volume.

However, some specifications should be made.

5

You may have noticed that I used the word 'critics' only when I paraphrased the quote from Hemingway: otherwise I talked about 'reviewers'. That is, of course, a very basic distinction to be made if one wants to discuss what happens to the mind of an author contemplating things written about his artefact. Only the negative verdict of a critic should be deadly: the reviewer's scathing remarks should be dismissed as irrelevant.

Should be, but very rarely are.

In my vocabulary a critic is someone who does his homework. He won't write about an author until he has familiarised himself with at least the most important parts of his *oeuvre*, until he has spent some time thinking about it, and only then come up with an opinion. If that opinion includes no redeeming qualities and passes the unequivocal verdict of 'No good at ALL!', then the writer should reach for his shotgun. But such situations, these days, are fortunately rare, at least in the West. Since the times of Marx there have not been too many critics filled with enough Marxian meanness peppered with heavy irony and caustic sarcasm, to invest the long hours of work and great amounts of mental energy necessary to write a substantial book of criticism in a scathing attack on a novelist they dislike. Most critics, fortunately, seem to share Anthony Burgess's feelings about their profession. 'In my capacity as critic,' wrote Burgess, 'I never stab anybody, for I know how life-denying it is to be stabbed. Writing a book is damned difficult work, and you ought to praise any book if you can.'

Therefore, nowadays critics pose little danger to the novelist.

Theoretically, reviewers should pose even less danger. They work in haste; they base their judgement on a first impression rather than on at least a pretence at analysis; often they have not read anything else by the author but the book under review; and how thoroughly they've read even that one work is open to question judging by the frequent misquotations and interpretational contortions one reads about in 'Letters to the Editor'. The tendency to show off, moreover, to demonstrate the brilliance of the reviewer's mind at the expense of the misquoted author is also well known. All in all: authors really should not read reviews, and if they must, they should dismiss their opinions as mostly inadequate, often ridiculous, sometimes malevolent, and generally invalid. After all, there have been too many categorical dismissals of great books by reviewers to bother about the views of those frustrated and underpaid gentlemen. The man, for instance, who wrote about *Madame Bovary's* author that 'Monsieur Flaubert is not a writer' could not have spent too many hours reading the book, or else he was devoid of any sense of aesthetic beauty, and of any understanding of life. Similarly, the reviewer of the *Odessa Courier* who searched in vain for 'a page that [contained] an idea' in *Anna Karenina*, and labelled the book 'sentimental rubbish', was hardly qualified for his job. And so, since it is another well-known fact that negative reviews do not affect sales, and, if they do, then – more often than not – it is positively, the author should not lose one minute of sleep over bad reviews.

He should not, but . . .

Many years ago I wrote a short story 'The End of Bull Mácha'. In 1953, to be precise. I'm still quite proud of that story, although being proud of my literary efforts is usually not one of my sins. However, I have good reasons to be proud of this one. At a time when almost everybody wrote soc-realistic fairy-tales, I concocted a story about a zootsuiter who, at a Sunday matinée dance, tries to do a jitterbug, is led off the dancing floor for 'eccentric dancing', and when he protests against the treatment which, he says, insults human dignity, the cop makes him show his identity card, takes down his name and address, and throws him out of the premises. I'm sure those of you who have 'been there', to paraphrase Mark Twain, or have studied the times, will agree that whatever else this story is, it is not a fairy-tale.

In the early 1950s I showed it to a good friend, Dr Ludvík Šváb, a psychiatrist and the guitar player of the Prague Dixieland Band of classical fame, who liked it. He liked it to the extent that, in a private apartment somewhere on Pohořelec, he read it aloud to a midnight gathering of underground intellectuals. There was a literary critic present; I did not know who he was, and never found out since. But he must have been one of us, the unsung dissidents of the early 1950s when the word didn't even exist: otherwise he would not have been there, and Ludvík would not have dared to read my highly subversive stuff to the gathering. When Ludvík finished reading, the company remained quiet for a few minutes which I happily interpreted as a symptom of the deep impression my story had made on this circle of the like-minded. Then the critic got up and asked Ludvík whether the author was present. Before we went to the gathering, we agreed that Ludvík would not identify me as the bloke responsible for 'Bull Mácha', and so he said: 'No'. 'In that case,' said the critic, 'I can be frank.' And he launched into an improvised but fluent diatribe against 'Bull' which, I felt, lasted an eternity. He dissected and aborted my brainchild without mercy and with what seemed to me then great scholarship and deep critical acumen. In his final remarks he compared my, in his words, shapeless and aimless attempt at literature to a story by, of all writers, Jack

London, a favourite of the Stalinists. And yet, he was an underground
critic. Or was he a police spy just posing as one of us? In any case, the
comparison demonstrated that, unlike London's, my story was a
complete artistic disaster for it failed to produce an unpredictable
climax. And sure enough, he was right. The consequences of
jitterbugging in the '50s were quite predictable. Many years later I
learned that London had been buying ideas for such stories from the
young and penniless Sinclair Lewis, for hard cash. I also realised that
the tale was a typical example of the rather debased genre known as the
twist-in-the-tail.

But on that terrible night so many years ago I had no such knowledge. Ludvík, the good friend that he was, sensed the catastrophic state
of my mind and walked me home, all the way from Pohořelec which is
on the hill west of the Hradchan castle, to my sub-let room on the hill
above Smíchov, although he lived in Malá Strana, only about fifteen
minutes brisk walk from Pohořelec. He tried to give my badly
punctured ego a boost. Without any success at all.

That nocturnal literary execution felt like the end of my life, and I did
not recover from it for about a year. I was young, over-sensitive, over-
uncertain, too deeply submerged in writing for anything – friendship,
love, praise from friends – to give me the tiniest of consolations. Those
were most certainly the darkest, most hopeless, utterly horrible months
of my life.

This is no exaggeration, as all who know about the many similar
sufferings over the immaterial stuff of letters penned on a page of paper
will understand.

I wanted to begin the next paragraph with the phrase 'Strangely
enough' but then I thought better of it. There is nothing strange about
the fact that the avalanche of vicious criticism that followed the
publication of my first published novel *The Cowards* was not nearly as
pernicious to my soul as the midnight verdict of the unknown
underground connoisseur of Stephen Crane's 'clever school of literature'. The explanation is easy, and it has to do with the second
distinction I'd like to make here.

The first distinction, if you remember, was between critics whose bad
opinion hurts, and reviewers whose acerbic stabs should be dismissed
as unimportant. The second distinction is between aesthetic and
ideological condemnation. The first can be, and sometimes was, fatal to
the writer's soul: after the disastrous reception of *Moby Dick*, for
instance, Melville fell silent for nearly forty years. Ideological condemnation can be, and far too often was, fatal to the writer's social status,

financial fortunes, wellbeing, and even physical survival.

Surely I do not have to remind my readers of the tragic fates of many writers in the Evil Empire. But as far as the writer's soul is concerned, his artistic self-confidence and his sleep, ideological criticism is harmless. It may even often boost the ego rather than puncture it.

The nocturnal underground critic almost killed me, and caused me months of beastly suffering. Something similar, though not nearly as drastic, happened to me shortly before the Party gave orders for launching a campaign against *The Cowards*. I had read my friend Karel Ptáčník's new work *The Border Town* (*Město na hranici*), and the experience threw me into desperation. Compared to what seemed to me a rich, panoramic and superbly knowledgeable description of a very complex social situation, peopled with a stunning number of finely drawn characters, my own simple transcript of a week's adventure at the end of the Great War in a small Bohemian town seemed insignificant light stuff, telling the reader nothing about the complexities of life and society: in short, an embarrassing failure.

I was utterly desperate. It was not jealousy which is usually the word used to describe the state of mind of the writer who feels that his colleague and rival has written a better book than himself. Jealousy is a form of envy. But this is not envy. It has nothing to do with your colleague's brilliance and success. It has to do with your feeling of inferiority, not hatred. It is not a temptation to commit murder, but a veritable dark night of the soul. I do not believe that Salieri killed Mozart. He only went mad.

It's a platitude to say that authors are the worst judges of their own work, and I can only hope that the platitude is correct. In any case, the extremely well orchestrated campaign against my novel pulled me out of the abyss of desperation and made me feel that, perhaps, after all, I was not such an entirely lousy novelist as I thought myself to be.

Why?

Because the ideological critics of the Communist Party of Czecho-slovakia put me into very good company indeed, and painted my character in colours I very much wanted to display in real life, but never quite managed to. I was an introverted, shy youth who was unable to step knowingly on an ant, and who always offered his seat on trains to the elderly and to what was then known as the weaker sex. But to the distinguished Party poet-reviewer Josef Rybák, writing in the Party daily *Rudé právo*, I was a 'cynical photographer' who has 'shown his own low moral character better than anyone before him.' Surely, this was quite some praise in a field that was the playground of some very famous cynics known to the Czech literati in translation. And sure enough, their names popped up in connection with mine. Another Communist critic, Václav Behounek, commented disapprovingly that my hero and *alter ego* Danny Smiricky 'reads like a latter-day Sanin', the hero, of course, of Mikhail Artsybashev's novel, or like Smerdyakov from *The Brothers Karamazov.* The book, Behounek opined further, was out of the category of 'Céline's *Voyage au bout de la nuit.*'

Could there be better praise? Yes, there could, Céline was invoked also by Rybàk who compared *The Cowards* to *Mort à crédit* which, he wrote, was a book so despicable that *Voyage au bout de la nuit* 'was by comparison harmless reading for Girl Guides.' The dear old man! And what about the following wonderful assessment from the pen of one František Kejík, the reviewer of the Army daily *Obrana lidu?* '*The Cowards* is the methodological handbook from which the remnants of the Golden Youth draw their means of expression rather than, as was believed until now, getting them from the penny dreadfuls, illicitly distributed pornography, and even more illicitly circulating trashy American novels.' The latter category was made specific by the Slovak socialist realist Vladimír Mináč who, in *Kveĕten*, named Hemingway, Faulkner, Dos Passos, Joyce, Kafka and Proust as the alleged and dubious models for me and the likes of me.

And so on. As I said, I was in good company. They crowned me the spokesman of the zooters who, in my mind, were pleasantly associated with an old article in *Der Neue Tag*, the Nazi Party daily in the Protectorate of Bohemia and Moravia, in which they were held up for contempt as cynical and decadent American jazz fiends. The 'humorous' Party weekly *Dikobraz* printed a rhymed satirical poem about me of which the first line – spoken by a Prague lady snob – stuck in my mind: *Ten autor nudu zahání*, or 'This author dispels boredom,' One of my innermost ambitions, since my days on the tenor sax, was to become an entertainer. Well, perhaps I had become one.

So the smear campaign, although I lost my job, gave me at least some shaky confidence in my abilities as a fiction writer. It almost annulled the lingering dark night of the soul, the aftermath of that midnight on Pohořelec so many, many years ago.

3 Literature as Criticism of Ideology in Contemporary Serbian Culture

Predrag Palavestra

There is an important new cultural phenomenon in Eastern Europe. For a long time after the Second World War, many Slav literatures (for example, Russian, Polish, Serbian and Czech) were exposed to the influence of Marxist aesthetics and the literary ideology of socialist realism. But in the course of the last twenty years a new literary current has become established – a literature of critical dissatisfaction and resistance. It was from these parts of Europe that many important works of modern literature reached the West, complementing and at the same time modifying the poetics of postmodernism. In contrast to Western ideas of alienation, the absurd and the search for essential and enduring existential topics, cosmic anxiety and flight from politics into a self-enclosed world, radical thought in Eastern Europe has bred a subversive style: a literature of defiance and critical non-acceptance of the ruling ideology and Party culture.

The forefathers of such a literary style were the 'outsiders', writers rejected and banned by the Bolshevik revolution, the unrecognised and censored authors, read in secrecy. Their books, written in hiding and copied by laymen, were disseminated underground. Thus it happened that in Russia it was precisely those whom the official administration wished to destroy and eradicate who became the first true bearers of a critical spirit, the proponents of an alternative culture of resistance. Alexander Solzhenitsyn, Varlam Shalamov, Joseph Brodsky, Vladimir Voinovich, Alexander Zinoviev – these writers can be considered as natural heirs of the bourgeois moralism of Nikolai Berdyayev, Osip and Nadezhda Mandelstam, Anna Akhmatova, Marina Tsvetaeva, Mikhail Bulgakov and Boris Pasternak.

It was in Yugoslavia that this specific literary phenomenon – this *glasnost* in Slav literatures – first became apparent. The determined resistance of the Yugoslav authorities to Stalin and the Cominform in

1948 resulted in a bold duel with dogmatism. One aspect of this was the comprehensive rejection of socialist realism as it was reflected in artificial optimism, black and white values, crude, one-sided peda-gogical realism and rigid ideological indoctrination. Serbian literature, which had preserved a strong democratic tradition of aesthetic and stylistic pluralism from the period of modernism and the avant-garde of the early twentieth century, readily accepted this spirit of resistance and succeeded in rapidly melting away the icy layers of ideology. Although in practice it never completely rid itself of Stalinism and the pernicious ideological suspicion with which the ruling Party bureaucracy always 'welcomes' the cultural initiatives of the critical intelligentsia, at least for a time official policy supported creative trends towards freedom. It endeavoured to use the intellectual movement for political and pragmatic purposes. Thus the freedom achieved was not complete but it greatly strengthened Yugoslav alternative thought. The values and achievements of the arts and sciences were on a par with Western civilisation. As broader and freer vistas were opened, the Yugoslav cultures were able to function on virtually the same level as Western Europe.

Over the last twenty years Serbian literature has generated a new literary style: literature which is recognised as a new concept of aesthetic cognition, as a criticism of the mystifications of the ruling ideology. This *critical fiction*, or *critical literature*, represents an intellectual, aesthetic and stylistic resistance to totalitarian practice, creating an opposition culture as an alternative beyond unified ideo-logies. Serbian critical fiction is a creative alternative to every external normative ordering of the nature and function of literature, an alter-native particularly to the ideology and practice of socialist realism as a closed system of thinking, based on dogmatic concepts of art. With no illusions about its ability to put things right, literature has been obliged once more to search for its own identity. Like it or not, writers are in a position to develop new ethical values and a new philosophy. In a way, this new literary philosophy has been extorted from them: it is part of the critical disposition of the intelligentsia, oppressed by ideological monism, by the perfidious manipulations of the ruling system and by the ever diminishing possibility of developing alternatives. Literature strives to restore the balance of its aesthetic and ethical meanings, to expand our knowledge of the human condition and, in its own way, to help modify our consciousness. In other words, literature is creating new possibilities for a further liberation and transformation of the human mind. By contemplating themselves in the contradictions of contemporary history, Serbian writers are discovering, with horror and hope, that literature itself must be a form of ideology.

The intellectual scepticism of today which questions every faith, every dogma and eschatology – even itself – is a form of rebellion of the consciousness against the rule of force. By opposing ideology, art defends its very purpose. Whilst protest limits art, it is through resistance and criticism that art regains its meaning. This is what has happened in some Slav literatures including recent Serbian literature: literature became the protagonist of a critical consciousness, while official ideology locked itself into the bondage of dogma.

Similar phenomena have been noted in some other Slav literatures, especially Polish (Czesław Miłosz, Andrzej Kusniewicz, Witold Gombrowicz, Stanisław Witkiewicz), Czech (Milan Kundera, Václav Havel, Bohumil Hrabal, Josef Škvorecký), Hungarian (György Konrád, Peter Esterházy), and of course Russian (from Boris Pasternak and Mikhail Bulgakov to Vladimir Voinovich, Joseph Brodsky, Alexander Zinoviev, Varlam Shalamov and Alexander Solzhenitsyn) – that is to say, in those literatures which, for a shorter or longer period in post-war history, were exposed to dogmatic pressures from the normative aesthetic theory of socialist realism, and in which public opinion (*'glasnost'*) was suppressed by the monistic structure of bureaucratic power. Sources of critical energy and new forms of critical alternative art are being discovered wherever the social context of literature is tested. The American critic Gerald Graff, analysing the function of literary ideas in contemporary society, suggests that postmodern tendencies in literature represent a 'breakthrough of new energies of critical negation opposed to the dominant socio-cultural directions of the nineteenth and twentieth centuries'. [1] For the English theoretician Terry Eagleton, 'the history of modern literary theory is part of political and ideological history' and 'any "pure" literary theory is an "academic myth"'. [2] For the scholar Rosemary Jackson, even literary fantasy has a subversive function, representing dissatisfaction and frustration with a secular cultural order: 'modern fantastic is a subversive literature'. [3]

From the morphological point of view, it is interesting that critical literature has no genre limitations, although the commonest form is undoubtedly the novel. It has acquired particularly critical colouring in recent Russian, Czech and Serbian literature (Solzhenitsyn, Zinoviev, Voinovich, Kundera, Cosić, Kiš, Selenić, Pekić). However, Poles, Czechs and Serbs often use the grotesque and the drama as well (Witkiewicz, Havel, Dušan Kovačević). There are also some outstanding poetic contributions – from lyricists of great reflective and ethical concentration (Akhmatova, Miłosz, Brodsky), to the rebellious mass media poetry of Serbian rock singers and groups.

The critical fiction which is currently growing in the Slav world and represents the main current of Serbian literature, corresponds to human confidence in the increased possibility of self-realisation through art. The aesthetic function of critical fiction complements the ideological function of critical thought. The latter takes an active and critical stand towards all aspects of social practice and towards the whole historical epoch. This literature is the voice of the man who, through his practical and creative self-realisation in freedom, overcomes historical alienation. The critical spirit of scepticism and the aesthetic energy of catharsis are the main driving forces of critical fiction in modern Serbian literature.

In Serbian literature there are some characteristic examples of overt critical demystification of Stalinist ideology and practice in the novels of Dobrica Ćosić, *Sinner* and *Renegade*, [4] describing the background of the Yugoslav Communist movement and the destiny of revolutionaries in the Communist International. The same is the case with the novel *Instant 2*, by Antonije Isaković,[5] which paints the brutal reality of the Yugoslav *gulag* on a barren island in the Adriatic Sea, where the prison for followers of Stalin and the Cominform was located after 1948. The same critical note can be found in the volume of short stories *A Tomb for Boris Davidovich* by Danilo Kiš,[6] the satirical grotesque novel *Dictionary of the Khazars* by Milorad Pavić,[7] as well as in the novel *Fathers and Patriarchs* by Slobodan Selenić,[8] which describes the defeat and the downfall of the Serbian bourgeoisie in the course of the Communist revolution. In its own special way, the same can be seen in the grand cycle of novels *The Golden Fleece* by Borislav Pekić,[9] which is founded on a phantasmagoric history of the Balkans from mythical times until the Second World War.

Looking at its extreme variations in current Serbian literature, it is obvious that Serbian critical fiction cannot avoid being a form of ideological attitude towards reality. It releases the immanent ideological charge of critical thought. It has the dialectic function of transcending given historical reality with all its socio-cultural, ethical and spiritual contradictions. Critical fiction possesses a natural capacity for organising the imagination and for projecting – in itself and through itself – a new aesthetic reality.

This constructive function of East European critical fiction should be both aesthetic and social to the same degree. Critical fiction is both an aesthetic and a socially concrete form of negation of all dogmatic normativism by any over-ideologised mind. At the same time, it is an open creative projection of a different world and of different possibilities for mankind. It is a constituent part of the same general need of the critical mind to overcome the limitations and rigidity of dogma. It is an aesthetic form of critical thinking which strives to liberate modern man from tension, humiliation and alienation in confrontation with powerful ideologies and with the ever-growing tyranny of history over the individual. The literary struggle against every oppressive ideological doctrine, with all its open and hidden forms of censorship, pressure and manipulation of works of art, could not be fought forever by tame compromise with evil. Such a 'fight' would mean the preservation of the *status quo*. The struggle could not be fought either by enforced isolation, or by an artistic flight from the truth. The guerilla warfare of literature against the terror and violence of totalitarian power allows to some extent different tactical devices and camouflage but it does not accept that fear and hypocrisy need be the main virtues of the epoch and that lies and injustice should become the lasting conditions of human survival.

As an expression of the general need for an alternative, critical fiction in Eastern Europe does not conceal its intentions. It strives to broaden and purify that space in the spiritual culture of the epoch which belongs to literature. It does not demand the autonomy of culture against society, nor the autonomy of society against the state – this is not the realm of its influence. It calls for the ethics of demystification and serves as a form of aesthetic catharsis. It intercedes for the full and free interaction of all cultures in the world, for the autonomy of the creative spirit versus ideology, for the creative dignity of every human being against the alienated power of the ruling bureaucracy. Ivory towers and glass shades are no different from gaols and concentration camps along the road taking literature into isolation, into submission or into silence. Wherever ideology has become a form of pressure of the ruling classes, art emerges as an alternative: its very critical spirit tends to re-establish the lost space of freedom. In that sense, contemporary Serbian critical fiction proves the hypothesis that literature must have an ideology – even if this ideology is one that brings all ideologies into question.

Notes

1. Gerald Graff, *Literature Against Itself: Literary ideas in Modern Society* (Chicago and London: University of Chicago Press, 1977) pp. 31–2.
2. Terry Eagleton, *Literary Theory. An Introduction* (Oxford: Blackwell, 1983) pp. 194–5.
3. Rosemary Jackson, *Fantasy* (London and New York: Methuen, 1981) p. 180.
4. Dobrica Ćosić, *Grešnik* (Belgrade: BIGZ, 1985); *Otpadnik*, (Belgrade: BIGZ, 1986).
5. Antonije Isaković, *Tren 2* (Belgrade: Prosveta, 1982).
6. Danilo Kiš, *Grobnica za Borisa Davidovića* (Belgrade: BIGZ, Zagreb: Liber, 1976); *A Tomb for Boris Davidovich* (London: Faber & Faber, 1985).
7. Milorad Pavić, *Hazarski rečnik* (Belgrade: Prosveta, 1984); *Dictionary of the Khazars. A Lexicon Novel* (London: Hamish Hamilton, 1989).
8. Slobodan Selenić, *Očevi i oci* (Belgrade: Prosveta, 1985).
9. Borislav Pekić, *Zlatno runo* (Belgrade: Prosveta, vol. i, 1978 – vol. v, 1981).

4 Politics – Challenge and Temptation in Contemporary Serbian Literature
Dobrica Ćosić

In order to focus properly on this subject, I feel that I must first of all make a clear statement about politics as a literary theme: it gives rise to considerable misunderstandings, involving both theory and reception. The most common response is to deny politics any aesthetic value as a literary theme. Politics – that human activity which seeks to realise national, social, confessional, ideological, group and individual interests; that essential regulator of inter-state, international and social relations and the relations of the individual with society and the state; that human striving for freedom and the general good; that pernicious craft of governing and subjugating people and nations; that skill of assuming and retaining power; that right, legitimate or usurped, to do either good or foolish things publicly; that sinful power which grows as it spends itself – has been so compromised by tyrants and power-mongers, twentieth-century ideologies, political parties, leaders and political bureaucracy, that in the consciousness of readers, and also from some 'pure' theoretical standpoints, politics is seen as a literary theme of the lowest artistic order. Indeed, many do not consider it suitable material for a work of literature at all. And there is good reason for this attitude. What has discredited politics as the subject of literature is above all its use of any means to further its ends, its amorality and its ephemeral nature. In recent times this process has been exacerbated by 'ideological societies' and the many writers who have used ideological and political material in their works. In ideological societies, politics has been imposed, decreed, and as such is normative, controlled subject-matter, in the service of power and tyranny. At the same time, it is also the monopoly of tendentious ideological writers, whose works contain many lies, and little truth. In addition, in all societies, a political theme offers minor writers a chance of cheap success.

But it is hard not to see another truth as well: ideological societies have enhanced the social role and significance of literature both when it affirms and when it denies them, particularly if it denies them through freedom and truth. Writers and intellectuals in non-democratic states, in states under the rule of the Communist Party, have thus assumed the role of conscience of the nation and society, the role of prophet and spiritual saviour as they did in the age of national romanticism. Such a role is certainly not appropriate to the real function of literature. Writers who are critics of dictatorial and repressive regimes, writers who are dissidents or represent the opposition, heretics and renegades with regard to the ruling ideologies and faiths, that is, political writers, have today a social, cultural and moral importance which surpasses their true aesthetic value and the durability of their works and ideas. In this way, dissidents from the Stalinist tyrannies have become import-ant, powerful writers even when they are poor writers; second-rate dissident philosophers and scientists have become influential, para-digmatic, celebrated intellectuals. In other words, politics and ideology both destroy and elevate, glorify the social and intellectual role of literature and render it worthless. This fact has probably had a crucial influence on prevailing negative attitudes to political themes in literature. Such attitudes are, however, essentially ideological and political even when their rhetoric is anti-ideological and anti-political. And from a creative point of view, they are irrelevant. In order to demonstrate this, we must answer the question whether politics, political thought and political action can be creatively transposed into an aesthetically relevant work of literature?

As I understand the aesthetic, humanistic and historical meaning of artistic narration, politics has always been an important theme, a condition of human existence, a human activity of existential signifi-cance, the social, intellectual, moral preoccupation of most people, with fateful consequences. Causes and consequences in politics, politics as human suffering and joy, as passion and sin, as the idea and morality of social survival, as an endeavour to control individual, social, national destiny – that is, everything that may be designated politics – is potentially just as significant for the purpose of aesthetic transposition as every other human act and event, idea and feeling, every theme in literary works from Sophocles and Aeschylus to Malraux and Solzhenitsyn. Of course, every theme, including politics, is only the starting point. It is material which must be transposed through the creative imagination into intellectual, psychological, moral, temperamental, human attributes. It is only when political acts and events are transposed into fiction, and universalised in a dramatic form, that they become suitable material for art. The so-called political novel (although I believe that a more adequate label for the political novel as a genre would be the novel of ideas) is like the so-called romantic novel, family novel, war novel, social novel: its aesthetic value depends on the intelligence, imagination, talent of its creator. It is the creator of the literary work who gives significance and value to any theme.

With this theoretical hypothesis in mind, I shall present to you in as few words as possible my own view of political writing in contemporary Serbian literature, that is, the role and significance of critical-political thought in Serbian literature since the Second World War.

Under Communist Party rule, Yugoslavia joined the ranks of the ideological societies. And ideological societies have always been the unhappiest societies for literature, for in societies with limited freedom or with none, the truth about man and his world is also limited, as is the creative power of the writer. But, at the same time, unhappy societies and bad times are also the best times for literature. Both because human suffering is the most human material for art; and because in unfree societies and difficult times, authentic poetic discourse is the discourse of the highest ontological identity of man. In poetic discourse, however limited, the spirit and soul are preserved and man surpasses his social determinants. We would violate historical truth if we did not stress the fact that Yugoslavia was the most liberal of all the ideological societies under Communist Party rule. The liberality of the Yugoslav order in culture was expressed in the rejection of the Party's normative aesthetic of socialist realism and the adoption of freedom of artistic form as early as the beginning of the 1960s. This freedom of literary expression, style and language offered the possibility of deeper, more comprehensive truths about man and society. And, at the same time, it opened up a more complete range of creative activity for the writer. With freedom of choice of subject and artistic form, the potential subject matter of literary discourse was also enriched. The Yugoslav literatures [There are several official languages and hence also literatures in Yugoslavia (ed.)] enjoyed the objective conditions for psychological and lyrical, philosophical and moral themes. But, until the end of the 1980s, these creative freedoms were not complete; the Yugoslav national cultures were limited by numerous taboos, subject to repression, ideological campaigns of the ruling party and its 'self-managing' censorship. Books, films and theatrical productions were banned; there were trials and prison sentences for free thought and true words. Fortunately for Yugoslav writers, the repressions and non-freedoms in Tito's despotism were incomparably milder than those in the hard Stalinist regimes of the Soviet Union and Eastern Europe.

The relative liberality of the Tito order in some areas of social and civil rights was not only its own political and ideological trade mark, however. Many freedoms and rights in Titoist Yugoslavia were won through the persistent efforts of the creative intelligentsia. The role of a critical opposition, particularly among writers, in the ideological, moral and psychological dismantling of the Titoist inheritance, was huge. By fighting for creative and political freedoms, by condemning violence, lawlessness and inhumanity, immorality and ideological lies, by awakening civil and national dignity, by criticising social pathology, by speaking the truth about the past and present, by broadening intellectual horizons, by reintroducing enduring human values, the most gifted people in contemporary Serbian literature have been carrying out the spiritual rebirth of Serbian society. Our best poets, novelists, playwrights, literary critics, theorists and historians created works of great artistic value, precisely through criticism and negation of the social order – Titoism – and through the drama and tragedy of people and nations within that order.

The prominent Serbian critic and theoretician Predrag Palavestra has, with good reason I believe, designated this period of Serbian literature an age of 'critical literature'. In this phrase, ideologism is conditional and illusory; the category of critical literature comprises the primary prerequisite of literary creativity: the idea of freedom and humanity. Through the freedom of its ideas, imaginative form, the humanity of its subject matter and ideas, I believe I dare to say that contemporary Serbian literature has achieved the spiritual catharsis of contemporary Serbian society. If Serbian traditional poetry preserved and fostered the historical memory and historical self-awareness of the Serbian nation, carrying them into a new era, contemporary Serbian literature has brought about the spiritual revival of the Serbian nation, renewing its best traditions, leading it into contemporary European intellectual currents and a new age. And that is, presumably, the high existential meaning of literary thought and poetic discourse.

5 Sławomir Mrożek: Exile and the Loss of Mission
Regina Grol-Prokopczyk

The role of a satirist under a repressive regime cannot be over-estimated. Satirical works are not only outlets for socio-political criticism, they are also a means of psychological adjustment for the author and the audience alike. They serve as a vent for the writer's pent-up negative emotions and, simultaneously, allow for the expression of repressed emotions by the audiences, whether readers or spectators. In countries such as Poland until not long ago, specifically until the emergence of the independent presses (*wolny obieg*) in the mid-1970s, a message conveyed obliquely, indirectly, through humorous innuendo has often been the refuge of freedom. And laughter, or parodies of existing reality, or those in power, have been the ultimate and frequently the only weapons of opposition, as well as a powerful mechanism of psychological relaxation. Aesopian language was quite often the artist's and the intellectual's vindication. Audiences also derived a sense of intellectual alertness – or even superiority – through close observation of the manipulation of language or the satirical distortion of conventional situations on stage. Satirical works provided an opportunity for intellectual stimulation as well as comic catharsis. Satire was tantamount to a kind of medicine of the mind.

No one would dispute that a satirist such as Sławomir Mrożek fulfilled an exceptionally important social role in the Poland of the late 1950s or the 1960s. It was particularly his plays, which were staged in theatres throughout Poland, and continue to be staged to this day,[1] that provided evidence of the sanative power of satire. The common laughter of the spectators united them. The theatre transformed the audiences into communities which shared a contempt for their social reality as well as an appreciation of the exposure of the bureaucratic and ideological absurdities of daily life. The full meaning and impact of Mrożek's plays became transparent when exposed to audiences who were actively involved in unravelling his messages. As Jan Błonski correctly observed: 'allusions were born in the audience, not on stage.'[2]

Even visitors to Poland sensed the power of Mrożek's theatre to convey inflammatory messages and to relay them through oblique hints and humour. One foreign critic went as far as to declare that when he saw the performance of Mrożek's *Tango* in Warsaw, 'the tenseness of the atmosphere in the theatre' made him realise 'what it must have been like to attend a performance of Beaumarchais' *Le Mariage de Figaro* just before the French Revolution'.[3] Indeed, being a satirist in Poland amounted to a special social service, or a mission.

What happens, however, to the satirist upon his emigration? The freedoms acquired through emigration include the freedom of producing uncensored literature. That tends to remove the necessity of resorting to Aesopian language, or allegory, or other clever games within the satirist's arsenal of devices intended to reach an understanding with his audience, and yet smuggle messages past the ever alert censor.

What happens, in other words, when the walls of the metaphoric prison are removed? In the case of Mrożek the dramatist, the outcome has been a gradual erosion of his satirical bent and a drastic qualitative change in his writing. Mrożek's major trump card – his knack for political satire – lessened considerably after his emigration in the early 1960s and seems to have disappeared altogether in his drama since 1975. (Occasional glimmers of it surface from time to time in his short prose). Does it mean then that, paradoxically, the satirist's gain of freedom spells his loss of mission? Or are there other reasons behind Mrożek's transformation and his fading as a satirical playwright?

A brief review of Mrożek's literary career seems in order. He began work in the early 1950s as a journalist, caricaturist and writer of satirical short stories, but since 1958, the date of the appearance of his play *The Police (Policja)*, he has been best known as a dramatist. Until the mid-1960s Mrożek's plays were allegorical. In them he mocked cultural, literary and political stereotypes, yet he himself relied on stereotypical characters functioning merely as elements in an artificially concocted situation. The plays pointed out the absurdity of various aspects of life through allusion, metaphor or parable; they were dramas based on syllogistic humour, logical paradoxes and generous dosages of the grotesque. The hallmark of Mrożek's early drama was the technique of *reductio ad absurdum*. In *The Police*, for example, the security apparatus of an unspecified police state does its job so well that no one is left to be arrested. To preserve its *raison d'être* the police must generate criminals, and the play ends with policemen arresting each other. In *Striptease* (1961) Mrożek ridiculed Sartre's concept of freedom by placing two gentlemen in a locked room and having them profess freedom, while a giant hand appeared at various intervals and by pointing made them successively remove all their clothing. The effect of this male striptease was hilarious and the political message was unequivocal. To cite one more example, in *The Martyrdom of Peter Ohey* (*Męczeństwo Piotra Oheja*) a family man's turbulent domesticity (nagging wife, noisy children, etc.) is disturbed by the visit of an official who alleges that a man-eating tiger has made its home in the family's bathroom. That 'fact' triggers an escalation of external intrusions: a tax collector, groups of school children, the circus, even a hunter from the Siberian steppe all invade Ohey's privacy. To make matters worse, his wife develops an inexplicable attraction to the tiger. Finally to satisfy the wish of a foreign visitor, an Indian maharajah who enjoys hunting, Ohey has to take the place of the non-existent tiger and become the object (and by implication the victim) of the hunt.

As these few examples indicate, Mrożek used parody in his treatment of reality or topical intellectual issues. Most of his early plays were quite short (largely one-acters) and were travesties of literary models, often written in a stylised language. The culminating achievement of that early period was *Tango* (1964), a full-length play, which marked the first shift toward seriousness. *Tango* still contained characters of literary origin and with little room for emotion; there were still absurd stage situations and an abundance of verbal and situational humour. The play has a very rich textual and intellectual fabric. It deals, among other things, with the desperate need for values, with generational and class conflict, with cultural transitions, and the tyranny of crude social elements. Nevertheless, the grotesque wrapping was still in clear evidence and the satirical elements were abundant.

Yet in *Vatzlav*, a play written in 1968, when Mrożek was already in the West, the humour is much tamer and the title character, a slave who becomes a free man through a shipwreck, is merely pathetic in his inability to cope with his newly acquired freedom. Mrożek still used satirical elements in *Vatzlav*, even resorting to new artistic tricks, such as the literalisation of metaphors (such as 'naked truth', or bestowing the names of Mr and Mrs Bat on the capitalists in the play and having them literally suck the peasants' blood). He also relied on old techniques such as ridicule, literary allusion, the parody of peasants' speech or telling contrasts between high and low language. But psychological insight and sombre tones are much more pronounced in *Vatzlav*. The central character is no longer the stereotype of a slave. He is endowed with consciousness and the ability to make decisions. As Janina Katz-Hewetson observed, 'Vatzlav is humanised by his own defeat and degradation.'[4] One can certainly agree with the critic that *Vatzlav* is the 'first of Mrożek's plays that can be called a tragedy'.[5]

Indeed, Vatzlav experiences tragedy in the classical Hegelian sense of being confronted with two 'rights' – the 'right' of the West and the 'right' of the East – yet finding both lacking. Nevertheless, satirical elements and overtones continued to prevail in the play. Shortly afterwards, however, Mrożek seems to have stopped displaying his satirical *élan vital*. His plays become devoid of the grotesque, of humour, puns or paradoxes. More and more steadily their tone became serious and their conventions more and more realistic. Black humour and *reductio ad absurdum* were replaced by direct description and serious dialogue. Mrożek himself commented on the transition in a letter to Konstanty Puzyna, the editor of the journal *Dialog*. In that letter, subsequently published in the September 1973 issue of the journal as a commentary on Mrożek's play *The Slaughter House (Rzeźnia)*, the playwright stated:

> You can probably guess how I would have written the same play ten years ago: I would expand the metaphor to its outer limit; I would draw out of it the maximal number of contrasting, conflicting [. . .] situations; I would avoid tirades and direct lectures, I'd spice it all up maximally with the grotesque and the comic. The problem is that now, when someone talks to me about a metaphor, I don't understand what for and I ask: all right, but why won't you tell me directly what you mean? And grotesque bores me and saddens me. It's possible that what emerges out of my sensibility and my old habits is neither fish nor fowl [*ni pies ni wydra*]. But it appears to me [. . .] that nowadays people want to hear serious matters discussed seriously; they want to have the impression that he who speaks takes responsibility for what he is saying.[6]

Not only has Mrożek assumed that responsibility by writing more and more explicit and serious plays, but he has also made a significant shift from the dramaturgy of models and allegories, which explored above all social reality, to drama exploring the existential experiences of the individual. It is a transition from an orientation toward the outer social reality, or the 'without', to the orientation toward the personal 'within', to an investigation of the individual experience. Krzysztof Wolicki rightly observed that even the titles of Mrożek's plays suggest that change. *The Police* is a collective name and refers to the institution rather than its individual members. Mrożek's masterpiece *The Emigrés*

(*Emigranci*), however, refers to individual émigrés, although Mrożek certainly had the option of naming the play '*Emigracja*'.[7] Mrożek himself conceded, moreover, that '*The Emigrés* is about people and not just about issues or causes (*co ludziach, nie tylko o "sprawach"*).[8] The two characters in the play, an émigré intellectual and an émigré *gastarbeiter*, engage in an intense conversation highlighting the enormous gulf between them. Without resorting to allusions or symbols, Mrożek focuses instead on their mental constitution and points out that the source of their problems is not some anonymous external power. Rather it is their individual psyches and mental attitudes that constitute the source of their entrapment.

The Emigrés was followed by *The Hunchback* (*Garbus*) written in a conventional format and language. Then came a sequence of four dramatised philosophical fables featuring the fox as their main character, and finally in the last few years, Mrożek has produced several very serious plays totally devoid of grotesque, or humour, or any traces of satire. The play *On Foot* (*Pieszo*) (1980) is a series of vignettes reflecting very realistically the final days of the Second World War and offering a kind of selective illustration of attitudes under the circumstances.

His next play, *The Ambassador* (*Ambasador*, written 1980, published by *Kultura* in 1982), was clearly an outgrowth of the Solidarity era. Although the ambassador's country of origin is never specified, and nor is his host country, any Pole reading or viewing the play had no trouble guessing that the ambassador represents Poland and his host country is the Soviet Union. In the course of his diplomatic service, the ambassador is subjected to continuous surveillance and repeated intimidation. When he offers political asylum to an individual preoccupied with having a soul, his contacts with his own government are hampered; he is unable to establish telephone communication with the ministry of foreign affairs in his country, and ultimately is told that his government has fallen. In the absence of contacts with his country, the ambassador has to allow for the possibility that his government has indeed been disbanded. He is forced to rely on his own inner resources. His host country, to be sure, gives him the option of becoming a pro forma ambassador, in effect subsidised and manipulated by it. When he rejects the offer, he is gradually deprived of food and heat, and also abandoned by his staff. The play ends with the ambassador on a bare stage accompanied merely by his charge, the man seeking political asylum. He has refused to send the man away, despite pressure and staged demonstrations in front of his windows, and is now standing ready, with gun in hand, prepared to shoot any intruder.

The suggestion of establishing a fictitious embassy may be read by extension as the Soviets' attempt to establish a fictitious Polish government, manipulated by the Soviets. The play also hints at the nobility, and yet the powerlessness, of resisting a totalitarian power. It contains numerous ideological arguments rendered in the form of dialogues between the ambassador and the representative of his host country's government. In fact, it almost seems to follow the Shavian model of a play based on a clash of ideas. Repeated invidious comparisons are made between the ambassador's dignity and straight-forwardness and the sophistry of the ideological arguments spouted by his opponent. The manipulation of words and concepts, the fabrication of facts by the (Soviet) plenipotentiary clearly suggest Mrożek's awareness of the utmost cynicism of the Soviets, their Machiavellian ploys and moral corruption.

Another set of informative dialogues occurs between the ambassador and the man seeking asylum. In the course of these conversations, the ambassador begins to discover his own soul, his own human dimensions and responsibilities. These dialogues occasionally soar high into the realm of philosophical discourse. Note, for instance, this statement: 'If one has to believe in a president in order to be an ambassador, one has to believe in God to be a man.'[9] The play is also replete with psychological insights which surface primarily in exchanges between the ambassador and his wife. Questions of an individual's identity apart from his social role or function are explored closely. The dominant theme, however, is one man's, the ambassador's, intellectual epiphany and confrontation with a very new set of circumstances, a condition faced by many a Pole during the Solidarity period.

Mrożek's later play, *Alpha*, (*Alfa*), published in Paris in 1984, was the response to yet another recent event in Poland. The title character, Alpha, bears unmistakable resemblance to Lech Wałęsa. The play deals with the year-long detention of Wałęsa in a secluded villa somewhere in Poland. In the course of the play Mrożek presents the various ploys Alpha's captors resort to in order to corrupt him (food, drink, women, persuasion through select influential visitors). Mrożek concludes his play with a scene that proved to be an inaccurate prophesy, the scene of Alpha's (alias Wałęsa's) murder.

While comparisons between the East and the West were already present in *Vatzlav*, they become crucial in Mrożek's two more recent plays, *A Summer Day* (*Letni dzień*, 1983), and *Contract* (*Kontrakt*, 1985). In the former we are exposed to a confrontation between Ud and

Nieud (the names imply success and failure, respectively). Ud, the Westerner, accomplishes everything easily and finds his Eastern 'antagonist's' situation enviable, since Nieud can still strive, aspire and hope to enjoy success. The Westerner is too blasé, too spoiled by his continuous success to appreciate anything. Nieud, the Easterner, has a very different perspective, of course. The question raised by the play is: will the two sides ever understand each other? Although the political interpretation of the play tends to impose itself, a purely psychological interpretation is equally valid.

In *Contract* Mrożek presents again a confrontation of West European and 'barbarian' mentality. We are exposed to an ongoing dialogue between Magnus, an elderly gentleman residing in neutral Switzerland and representing the West, and Moris, an individual representing the barbarian culture. Their clash of ideas allows Mrożek to air his views on the inevitable gap between the East and the West, the inescapable prisons of one's experience, one's heritage and one's self. Likewise the values and ideals of old Europe for which Easterners tend to yearn so wistfully are clearly brought into question in the play. Joanna Godewska was quite right when she suggested that *Contract* can be read as 'one of the cruellest contemporary plays' and a 'text which undercuts all certainties, removes from under one's feet what appeared to be immovable foundations.'[10]

Mrożek's play *Portrait* (*Portret*, 1987) is perhaps psychologically his most probing, and, except for its preamble – a lengthy profession of love to what we later discover is a portrait of Stalin – most realistic. For the first time in Mrożek's career as a dramatist it is also structurally innovative in terms of the deconstruction, or decomposition, of action and shifts in time sequences. The two major characters in the play are Anatol, who is denounced, sentenced to death and later has the sentence commuted to many years in prison, and his 'friend' Bartodziej, who denounced him. Upon Anatol's release from prison due to an amnesty, the two meet. Their confrontation reveals not only the moral dilemmas of the two, but also the destructive nature of Stalinism and its insidious ways of corrupting minds. The play ends with Bartodziej expiating himself by taking physical care of Anatol who has suffered a stroke and is paralysed. The fully developed female characters in the play as well as the exposition of the marital relationships make this the most realistic yet of all of Mrożek's plays. The prominent critic Jan Klossowicz went as far as to say about Mrożek's *dramatis personae* in *Portrait* that they are endowed with 'a psychologism – both analytical and behavioral, almost as in some American play.'[11]

This cursory review of Mrożek's dramatic evolution, in which I have referred to his major works, but by no means all of his works, was intended to establish the major shifts in his writing. To sum them up they were:

(a)   a shift from stereotypical, flat characters to three-dimensional and more fully developed ones;

(b)   a shift from 'model' plays based on logical arguments to plays of more and more realistic convention and greater psychological depth;

(c)   a shift from humour, grotesque and parody to seriousness;

(d)   a shift from a light and impersonal tone (where a thin line of irony divided the author from the characters) to the author's direct voice being heard (albeit still through his characters).

Additionally, Mrożek's themes have become more and more moored in psychology and philosophical considerations. While the universal aspect of Mrożek's early plays derived from concrete provincial situations, in many of his recent plays the universalism stems from parallels between East and West.

Mrożek has clearly expanded his cultural and intellectual horizons since his emigration. He has immersed himself in Western reality, confronted and evaluated its values and has been able to focus on issues which, as Tadeusz Nyczek wittily observed, 'are greater and more serious than the election of the vice-chairman of the local Writer's Union or the market price of eggs in Southern Poland.'[12] Increasingly, therefore, Mrożek's plays reflect his sense of the illusory quality of truth. In a mini-essay entitled 'Before the Deluge' (*Przed potopem*), published in the April 1981 issue of *Dialog*, he inserted this bemused reflection:

> Let theatres of the absurd sneer at life, hey, those were the days when a man would make a sneering face before a mirror and it seemed to him that he was wise.[13]

These words reflect Mrożek's retrospective – and perhaps even nostalgic – view of the early stages of his career as a dramatist and author of satirical sketches. At the same time they are a testimony to his awareness of his evolution as an artist and an intellectual. In another recent statement he professed a similar sentiment: 'The older I get, the more I feel like laughing and the less I laugh. And I hardly tell any jokes any more.'[14]

Let us return to my original question – why has the dramatist taken his leave of satire?

One is tempted to consider a number of answers to this question. To begin with, perhaps Mrożek's enormous international success – and his recognition that he is in the West to stay – made him realise that he has to address himself to a much broader audience. He may have chosen, therefore, to write in a manner more accessible to the West. His early satirical plays, after all, relied on uniquely Polish social and cultural co-ordinates. Only a Polish audience could respond to the full range of his satirical devices, to his linguistic games, his parodies or stylisations. Only a Polish audience could catch echoes of lines and motifs from classics of Polish literature, or note the humorous distortions of Polish clichés or 'newspeak'. And yet, this does not appear to be a sufficient reason to abandon the satirical vein. Mrożek's early plays, particularly in view of their basis in logical constructs, had the chameleon-like quality of being understood in the West as well. Perhaps understood somewhat differently, or not fully, but understood and appreciated nevertheless. Common cultural legacy with the reader is not necessarily an essential prerequisite for a satirist. After all many satirists – Juvenal or Swift for example, to mention two of the best known – transcend that barrier.

Likewise, the argument that Mrożek's distance from Poland (he has lived abroad since 1963, first in Italy and since 1968 in Paris) has made him less sensitive to local matters, less attuned to the minutiae of political and social reality which had fuelled his satirical drive, must be rejected. Mrożek is very much in touch with Poland and Polish affairs and his writing clearly reflects that.[15] *Alpha* is about Wałęsa; *On Foot* contains a survey of strikingly Polish characters and attitudes; *The Ambassador* deals with the political realities of Poland during the Solidarity period, and some of Mrożek's prose is even more responsive to current events than his drama.[16]

Perhaps Mrożek sought new means of expression because he realised that satire or irony are, as Czesław Miłosz has put it, the weapons of the slave. Maybe that is why he defiantly chose to speak directly and seriously, from his mind and from his heart.

In my judgement, however, the primary reason for Mrożek's abandoning satire has a great deal to do with his emigration. Emigration often leads to a 'turn toward oneself' (*zwrot do ja*), a search for a mooring within oneself, and a descent to one's private underground. The pressure of cultural comparisons brings about a sense of the relativity of values and is intellectually unsettling. Thus the self becomes the ultimate anchor, or even refuge. Mrożek seems to have found his own grounding in himself. In an interesting little essay published in June 1978, the dramatist confesses apologetically to his love of hotels and his euphoria when he finds himself in a foreign land and among strangers. He alleges that it is in foreign lands that his senses and thoughts are at their sharpest. And he continues, 'I am aware that these are the confessions of a pervert. [. . .] Am I really a pervert?' He answers the question as follows:

> If I live without any ground under my feet, and still I don't fall through it, although I can't fly, that means that there is some ground on which I rest, although I don't see it. [. . .] If I feel so well in foreignness [*obcości*], although I should feel so miserable, it is not because my organism is perverted, but because my fatherland does not fit within the dimensions and the substances in which it is typically confined. One needs to be mightily within oneself, to be able to be among strangers.[17]

This is a rather explicit admission of his mooring within himself. The focus on self, on his interior, leads by extension to the individualised characters in his plays. Interestingly, much of Mrożek's recent writing (for instance, his plays *On Foot* and *Portrait*) is based on the re-examination of personal youthful experiences, and though these plays are historical in nature, they are also very distinctly personal retreats into the past. Such retrospective exercises also result in psychological revelations, at least in the confrontation of one's former and present selves.

Satire is a charged mode of writing; to a greater or lesser degree it is a form of militant irony, an expression of commitment to particular values. It has to result from a set of deeper beliefs. If it ridicules something, it is in the name of an ideal; if it criticises implicitly, it is out of a sense of outrage, or at least discomfort, at the distortions of an ideal. By pointing out evils, the satirist indicates implicitly that he knows what is right or good. Though not overtly, nevertheless the satirist is a guardian of ideals. Perhaps Mrożek's exposure to both East and West, his profound disappointment in both, and his increasing disbelief in any system of values, have deprived him of a sufficiently firm axiological basis to assume a satirical point of view. To put it crudely, if at first he believed that the socialist order is a perversion of reason, by now he has come to realise that in some ways all orders are flawed. Not only have many ideological and philosophical distinctions or differences become suspect to him, reality has become more and more cluttered by ideas, all of which claim an equal status and seek to be treated on a par. Mrożek wrote about this in the form of a quasi-anecdote:

[*Spotykają się*. . .] The following get together: a hero, a witness, a judge, a teacher, a sneerer, a squealer, a desperado. And also a madman, Santa Claus and Mickey Mouse. Others are on their way, they will be here soon.

The 'anecdote' begins very conventionally, but ends rather unconventionally with an ominous forewarning of more clutter to come. Mrożek is clearly befuddled, bewildered and confused by the proliferation of notions. He neither knows nor believes any truths. In his play *The Ambassador*, using, appropriately for the leading Polish dramatist, a theatrical metaphor, he observed: 'cognition is like a farce, the curtain goes up and one sees the truth which makes the past laughable'.[19]

Having lost his belief in any transcendental values, Mrożek, nevertheless, doggedly searches for some certainty, or some intellectual anchor. Perhaps that is why he engages in a perpetual process of axiological destruction. Hence also his artistic palinody, that is, his repeated questioning and repeated rejection, or transcendence, of earlier artistic accomplishments. Perhaps for him, as it was for Kafka, 'writing is a form of prayer'. Thus Mrożek the satirist has become the author of psychological portraits, a mournful philosopher and even a delicate lyricist. These are the new facets of his literary talent.

Of course, other factors may account for Mrożek's loss of satirical drive. My brief essay has no claims to being exhaustive. Nor do I claim that the loss of satirical mission necessarily implies a loss in absolute terms. What Mrożek has lost as a satirist may well have been compensated for in the depth and originality of his psychological and philosophical insights. What is more, the new artistic forms he has devised for their expression may be more appropriate.

Notes

1. See the extensive list of Polish productions in *Pamietnik Teatralny*, vol. 1, 1975.

2. Jan Błonski, *Romans z tekstem*, Krakow, Wydawnictwo Literackie, 1981, p.219. [All translations of quotations are my own, R.G-P.]
3. After John Weightman, 'Ideas and the Drama', *Encounter*, 27, September 1966, p.47.
4. Janina Katz-Hewetson, *Kultura*, 6/429, 1983, p.149.
5. *Ibid.*, p. 148.
6. *Dialog*, September 1973.
7. K. Wolicki, *Pamietnik Teatralny*, no. 1, 1975, p.49.
8. Jan Kłossowicz, 'Mrożek w teatrze Dejmka', *Literatura*, 5, 1988, p.63.
9. *The Ambassador*, Paris, Instytut Literacki, 1982, p.87
10. J Godlewska, 'Pytania o *Kontrakt*', *Twórczość*, 9, 1986, p.115.
11. J Kłossowicz, 'Mrożek w teatrze Dejmka', p.63.
12. T. Nyczek, 'Mrożek Epistolograf', *Dialog*, 10, 1982, p.135.
13. S. Mrożek, 'Przed potopem', *Dialog*, 4, 1981,p.143.
14. Mrożek, 'Kawałki', *Dialog*, 1, 1980, p.143.
15. E.g. Mrożek's note on his visit to Poland in June of 1987 in *Kultura*, 1–2, 1988, p.133.
16. E.g. the sketch on Jaruzelski, 'Pogadanki z historii najnowszej', *Kultura*, October 1982.
17. Mrożek, *Dialog*, 6, 1978, p.128.
18. Mrożek, 'Zdania', *Dialog*, 10, 1980, p.152.
19. Mrożek, 'Ambasador', p.120.

6 Postmodernism and its Histories: Representations of the Past in Contemporary Hungarian Fiction

Richard Aczel

This essay will examine one aspect of the concept of postmodernism in the context of contemporary Hungarian prose fiction. My use of the term 'postmodernism' is at once an act of bad faith and a gesture of heuristic exploration. On the one hand, I am aware that, as a descriptive literary historical construct, postmodernism begs questions of theoretical definition and practical periodisation which it is – even by its own admission – both ill-disposed and ill-equipped to answer. It both incorporates and exacerbates all the ambiguities and contradictions of the equally problematic notion of 'modernism' it claims to supersede, without in any way resolving them. On the other hand, the term is more easily dismissed than the configuration of assumptions, reflexes and strategies it seeks to approximate as the contours of our own cultural moment. In what follows I hope to demonstrate that, treated as a heuristic fiction rather than as a definitive descriptive category, the concept of postmodernism – to whose literary historical claims and terminological antinomies I shall return at the end of this paper – can enlighten more than it misleads and produce more understanding than it precludes.

The aspect of postmodernism I should like to explore in this paper concerns a complex of new attitudes to the experience and representation of history which has exercised considerable influence over both the production and reception of literary works since the 1950s. For at the heart of the concept of postmodernism lies the perception of a wholesale 'loss of history'; the past as no longer the ultimate referent, but merely an unprivileged effect of representation. What is represented in historical discourse is no longer the event itself, but the *simulacrum*: the image of an image for which no 'original' exists.[1] If the past is itself already, and necessarily, representation, history may be read as 'just another text' – and not even any longer a particularly meaningful text at that; certainly not a coherent, linear, teleological narrative of development and progress. While the grand narratives of human development – from the theological to the rationalistic – had already become problematic for the moment of modernism, in the alienated anguish of its break with the past, modernist art inevitably affirms the very object from which it is alienated. Postmodernism, on the other hand, inherits the modern break with the past as a *fait accompli.* The tone of postmodern art is more typically euphoric and playful than traumatised and anguished. If modernism had believed it was witnessing *'Die letzten Tage der Menschheit'* (Karl Kraus), postmodernism seems to believe it has already witnessed 'The End of History' (Fukuyama). History repeats itself, first as tragedy, then as farce.

If, as I shall attempt to demonstrate, these 'postmodern' attitudes to history are directly relevant to the context of contemporary Hungarian fiction, their emergence in that context has been informed by a set of circumstances substantially different from that which informs the homologous sense of a 'loss of history' in 'postmodernist' fiction in Western Europe and North America. While I shall return to these differences towards the end of my essay, it will be useful briefly to sketch the immediate background to recent developments in Hungarian prose, before going on to look more closely at questions of historical representation in the work of a number of major contemporary Hungarian writers.

In the mid-1960s and 1970s Hungarian fiction had been preoccupied with two major concerns: a conscientious and quasi-sociological critique of contemporary social reality, and an exposé of the repressed injustices of the recent past. For the generation of writers born either during or after the Second World War, however – for whom the experience of 1968 was more immediately informative than that of either 1945 or 1956 – both 'criticism' and 'reality' have become more problematic terms. These writers found themselves living and writing in the complex world of compromises and contradictions of the 1980s, where the strict cultural directives of the past had been displaced by the tacit and unpredictable logic of self-censorship, and where the rhetoric of reform and reconstruction had finally given way to an atmosphere of pervasive cynicism and uncertainty. 'Criticism', having grown unsure of its objects, turned inwards to recuperate in the form of a subversive but directionless *disposition*, while 'reality' for the writer, was to become that which by nature resists representation.

In this context, the representation of history as a coherent narrative would become particularly problematic. On the one hand, documentary access to certain aspects of the national past – and the recent past in particular – was categorically outlawed by the Kádár régime. On the other hand, other key events and moments in national history had been ideologically co-opted – and thus inevitably to some degree compromised or discredited – by the ruling Party in its own clumsy and transparent project of self-legitimisation. In addition to this, the blind dogmatism, ideological bankruptcy and practical failure of the grand teleological narrative of Marxism–Leninism tended to inspire a complete loss of faith in teleological conceptions of history *per se*. Nietzsche, rather than Marx, would increasingly become the spokesman for the generation of '68.

The attempt to undermine any stable notion of history as a teleological narrative and to emphasise the textual nature of historical experience is most obvious in the work of Péter Esterházy (born 1950). His first novel, *A Novel of Production* (*Termelési regény*, 1979), for example, juxtaposes a bizarre pastiche of the Stalinist 'production novel' – about a young engineer's almost surreal struggles with bureaucracy – with an account of the author's everyday life in the words of his (fictional) literary secretary – none other than Johann Peter Eckermann. The relationship between the narrative and Eckermann's reconstruction of the circumstances of its composition – itself, ironically, a novel of production in a rather different sense – is for the most part irreverently arbitrary. The life – already reconstituted as impossible fiction – and the work – whose characters include Comrade Gregory Peck and his secretary Marilyn Monroe – form two incommensurable worlds. Both sections incorporate a wide variety of historical styles, texts and ready-mades, from the implicit pastiche of socialist realism and parliamentary debates from the nineteenth century to verbatim political speeches from the 1950s and the colloquial, domestic discourse of the 1970s. The apparent ease with which these historical texts seem to merge in Esterházy's novel might be read as a suggestion of historical continuity. But Esterházy's conception of history ultimately proves more representative of the Nietzschean scepticism of his generation. Continuity is in the service of circularity, rather than teleology. In the words of the nineteenth-century novelist, Kálmán Mikszáth – with whom the 'maestro' of Eckermann's second part often converses: – 'Today's world is not the wisest of worlds; but then, good heavens, neither was yesterday's. And you can bet your boots that tomorrow's world won't be any wiser. And there's something rather comforting in that.'

Esterházy's excursions into national history are still more mis-
chievous in his *A Pocket Hungarian Pornography* (*Kis Magyar
Pornográfia*, 1984). The second section of the work consists of a series
of anecdotes, largely either from or about the 1950s. For a nation whose
history has so often been repressed, distorted and rewritten from above,
the anecdote has always provided a crucial means of self-defence as a
compensatory form of public memory. Esterházy, however, is, as usual,
quick to subvert the form he imitates. Several of his anecdotes are
actually well-known stories from the nineteenth century, where only
proper names have been 'updated'. Here is one particularly striking
example. The anecdote is entitled 'The Solution'. It involves three of
Hungary's most notorious Stalinist leaders – Mátyás Rákosi, the
General Secretary of the Communist Party, Ernő Gerő, his right hand
man, and Mihály Farkas, the Defence Minister – and the novelist Tibor
Déry, whose attempt to reconcile socialist realism with social reality
brought him into a famous conflict with the party in the early 1950s.

For some unfathomable reason, and because of the tireless efforts of
the imperialists at subversion, Rákosi found himself slipping in the
opinion polls. Mátyás was just getting ready for a great peace
convention and his officials were doing all they could to ensure that
his reception should be as glittering as possible. Comrade Gerő asked
Tibor Déry to think of a plan for the reception; something that
wouldn't cost too much, would surprise the General Secretary and
would please the people.

Déry, a formidable man in any situation, shrugged reluctantly and
said in an offhand sort of way that he couldn't think of anything.
Then, after a short pause, he began again: well maybe. . . His eyes
beaming with glee, Gerő egged him on: well, out with it!

'Our beloved Mátyás will be coming over the bridge, won't he?'

'Da.'

'Passing those two columns at the end?'

'Da, da.'

'Then why not have Mihály Farkas strung up from one of the
columns, and yourself from the other? It won't cost too much, our
beloved General Secretary will certainly be surprised, and the people
are bound to be pleased.' With that Déry took his hat and left.

Whether or not this conversation actually took place I cannot tell.
But that it was soon on everyone's lips, and that every Hungarian
heard it with pleasure – that much is gospel truth.

What reads as a very effective 1950s anecdote is actually a story from the 1850s taken from the 1957 edition of Béla Tóth's *A Treasury of Hungarian Anecdotes* (*Magyar anekdótakincs*). In Tóth's original version – if an anecdote can be said to have an 'original' – Rákosi's role is played by Franz Josef, that of Gerő by the Emperor's right-hand man in Hungary, Deputy-Governer Antal Augusz, that of Farkas by Prottman, the Budapest Chief of Police, and that of Déry by the writer, reformer and politician József Eötvös. Apart from this – and Gerő's dadaesque 'da-das' – all the details of the anecdote remain the same, right down to the closing speculation on authenticity by the narrating subject. The characteristic suggestion of historical continuity – or, viewed more cynically – circularity, deflates the exorcistic pleasure of merely naming the notorious 1950s by implicating the crisis they represented in a historical perspective which not only pre-dates and outlives them, but also seems to deny any sense of teleology.

The very form which Esterházy is subverting here is, of course, itself a specific historical product – the anecdotal representation of the national past as a kind of shorthand, compensatory substitute for any deeper interrogation of historical continuities. This is made quite clear in the next section of *A Pocket Hungarian Pornography*, entitled '?', which consists of a series of several hundred questions which continually challenge national preconceptions. Here is just one example:

First impressions can be decisive? Dates? 49, 67, 19, 45, 48, 56, 68? Is his little Lordship playing the lottery? There's always a number, *rational*, *positive*, indeed *whole*, encircling silence or noise? Instead of speech, thought, deliberation, morality? That kind of thing?

Historical continuities are also questioned in the work of Péter Nádas (born 1942). Nádas's first novel, *The End of a Family Novel* (*Egy családregény vége*, 1977), sets out to question the significance of tradition and family history in the life of a young Jew growing up in the second half of the twentieth century and closes with a profound crisis of personal and historical identity. Again the 1950s are crucially implicated in this crisis. Of the three generations represented, the second constitutes a crucial moral break. The narrator can no longer identify with his father who has made compromises with the authorities in the Stalinist era, but he is also forced to realise that the traditions which informed his grandfather's generation belong to a world which no longer exists and with which there can be no retrievable continuity. It is as if we are reading not only the 'end of *a* family novel', but the end of *the* family novel – conventionally used to sustain or interrogate historical continuities over three generations – as a genre which no longer represents a serious option for the writer.

In Nádas's next novel, *A Book of Memoirs* (*Emlékiratok könyve*, 1986), problems of historical continuity are already incorporated formally into the text. The memoirs we read appear to be three separate histories, written in different periods and narrated by different narrators: a young Hungarian living in East Berlin in the 1970s, an adolescent boy growing up in Budapest in the 1950s, and a German novelist living and writing at the turn of the century. These three narratives alternate throughout the text, their sequence indicated by colour-coded chapter headings on the front cover of the novel. The first narrator can in many ways be read as the reincarnation of the narrating protagonist of *The End of a Family Novel*. Having lost any sense of personal and historical identity within his own community, he seeks both refuge and self discovery in an alien city. Much of his story focuses on the bizarre political and psychological landscape of a divided city and on the narrator's homosexual relationship with Melchior, a young German who experiences a similar crisis of identity and finally escapes from his personal and local past to the West. Now, three years on, the narrator is trying to make sense of these events in his past, but, both because of the fallibility of memory and because of an inability to think beyond the obsessive fascination with those details to which his memory always returns him, he becomes increasingly entangled in the intricate web of his own historical text.

The story of the adolescent boy centres on his uncertainty as to the real identity of his father, and thus also his own origins and position in relation to the past. The man who acts as his father is imprisoned for an unnamed political crime by a former comrade in the underground communist movement, who now occupies a position of considerable power in the Stalinist regime. The boy suspects, but is never able to prove, that this latter figure, whom he knows to have been his mother's lover, is also his and his retarded sister's real father.

The third narrator is Thomas Thoenissen, a young German *fin-de-siècle* writer who seems to have been based, at least in part, on Thomas Mann. His narrative is also concerned with memory and self-discovery; writing both memoirs and a novel he finds that the two merge, and neither can constitute an adequate or meaningful reconstruction of the past.

Only at the end of *A Book of Memoirs* do we learn that Thoenissen is in fact the fictional creation of the first narrator, based on Melchior's German grandfather, and that the first narrator and the adolescent boy are one and the same character. The closing chapters are written after his somewhat meaningless death – he is intentionally run over and killed by boys on motorcycles on the banks of the Danube. This information is narrated by one of the character's childhood friends, Krisztián, with whom – as we know from the narrative of the adolescent – he had once had a latent homosexual relationship. Krisztián now acts as the legatee and publisher of the triple memoir. While Krisztián is able, in his own words, 'to establish beyond doubt the sequence of the chapters' in his friend's novel, even he cannot restore to the texts the absent teleology the memoirist had sought in his own memories and is forced to confess: 'even after a most thorough-going examination of the notes I could not decide what course he would have made the plot take.' Thus the reader is finally left with no privileged historical vantage point outside of the text. The history is the text, and – in Jacques Derrida's famous phrase, which has had considerable bearing on postmodern theory – '*il n'y a pas d'hors texte*'.

I should now like to turn to a writer whose attitude to history is more obviously the product of his own political experience. This is Lajos Grendel (born 1948) who lives and works in Bratislava (Pozsony). The central preoccupation of Grendel's novels is the experience and history of the Hungarian minority in Slovakia. How, Grendel asks, are the Hungarians to preserve their national and cultural identity in an essentially hostile environment of prejudice, social marginalisation and disillusion? Can this identity, indeed, be preserved at all, and if so, is it really still worth preserving? Grendel's answer to these questions is, on the whole, a cynical one. His characters live in a kind of moral and historical vacuum, seeking their true selves by trying to understand a past which consists of no more than incoherent fragments. This is perhaps best illustrated by Grendel's first novel, *Live Ammunition* (*Éleslövészet*, 1981).

The narrator of *Live Ammunition* discovers a collection of manuscripts relating to the history of the small Hungarian–Slovak town in which he lives. Many of these manuscripts date back to the period of Turkish occupation, but some also contain descriptions of life under Habsburg rule in the eighteenth century. Each new text contradicts the last in its interpretation of events and in its evaluation of the relative crimes and merits of the town's rulers. The narrator is forced to come to the conclusion that historiography is nothing more than a form of fiction, that history itself incorporates no immanent logic of progress or teleology, and that the only factor which connects one era to another is the constant suffering of man.

All this takes place in the novel's first section entitled 'First Reckoning (Historical)'. This is followed by a second section, entitled 'Second Reckoning (Literary)', in which we learn more about the character, circumstances and anxieties of the narrator, and about the present day life of the town. We also learn of the sequence of events which drove the narrator to search for his own historical and personal identity through a study of the local past. Fragments of Turkish gold had been discovered in the town, which Slovak scholars had come to excavate and analyse. Excited by these developments, the narrator's grandfather – an amateur expert on local history – had attempted to assist the scholars in their work by providing them with crucial details about the town's past. Upon realising that the scholars were not in the least interested in what he had to say, the narrator's grandfather had become totally disillusioned, and – together with the narrator's father – decided to destroy all the remnants and relics of his Hungarian past. 'We are the last Hungarians in this rotten town,' says the narrator's father, 'let us be sure to leave no trace whatsoever behind'.

In the third section of the novel, 'Final Reckoning (Final)', the narrator attempts to come to terms with, or simply to resign himself to, his own hopeless situation as a man without history or identity. The tone is both elegaic and ironic. The novel ends with a short confession by the narrator's father: 'It was all horribly grotesque. Even so, it was then I understood that this was really the end. And that whatever might follow would be nothing more than a kind of encore.' This is followed by a single, closing sentence in the unidentified first person singular voice with which the novel had opened: 'It is almost as if this confession is what we had been looking for all along and which will now suffice as a point of departure.' History may indeed be circular, rather than linear, but the figure of the local historian, archaeologist or archivist, who plays a crucial role in so much of Grendel's work, still retains an important moral function, even if only as a living product, or effect, of the history he tries in vain to recover. The fragmented archive remains a powerful symbol of a history of oppression.

This is certainly the case in Grendel's third novel, *Transpositions* (*Attételek*, 1985). Written in the second person singular, the novel 'addresses' a publisher's reader whose character, background and predicament are very similar to that of the narrator in *Live Ammunition*.

The first part of *Transpositions* is again essentially historical. After briefly suggesting the emptiness of the protagonist's present and his lack of any meaningful sense of the past, the text focuses on his recollection of a sequence of events narrated to him by his grandmother.

Her experience, however, only seems to corroborate his lack of faith in history and its meaningful articulation:

> You have no past; nor do you wish to have a past. You grit your teeth, you clench your fists, you remain silent, even when you know full well that you should speak. And at such times you think of your grandmother, of her dignified silence.

In recreating the world of his grandmother, the narrator/addressee takes us back to the last days of the Austro–Hungarian Empire, when the small town in which the family lives had still belonged to Hungary. The climax of the grandmother's story comes in her account of a sequence of events in 1914 in which her mother dies and she meets her future husband. On the latter occasion, bells are heard ringing from every corner of the town to signify the outbreak of war. The moral life of the town goes to pieces, with its inhabitants vacillating between mindless hedonism and suicidal despair, and the grandmother knows that she is witnessing the end of an era. After living through another war she falls completely silent. The period between 1914 and the present – which saw the collapse of the Austro–Hungarian Empire, the loss of Upper Hungary to the newly formed state of Czechoslovakia, Nazi occupation, and the aberrations of Stalinism – is represented as a complete and final decimation of historical continuity. Similarly, the silence of the grandmother, herself the last symbol of that continuity, signifies the irretrievable loss of the past. This loss produces a sense of direc-tionlessness, uncertainty and cynicism in the experience of the present:

> During your short life you have heard too many prophecies to believe any one of them. Your grandmother drew all the necessary conclu-sions from the suffering of two world wars and fell silent.

Interestingly, the same symbol of the baffled amateur historian or archivist confronted with the puzzle of incomplete historical fragments plays an equally important role in the fiction of Miklós Mészöly (born 1921). In Mészöly's work, however, it is employed to evoke a funda-mentally *existential* condition, rather than a historical product. This is made particularly clear in the major retrospective collection of Mé-szöly's shorter fiction published last year under the title *Once Upon a Time there was a Central Europe* (*Volt egyszer egy Közép-Európa*).

The ultimate object of Mészöly's stories is – as the title of this new collection suggests – the eternally evasive and shifting Central European past. Or rather, a collage of competing pasts; for Mészöly's narratives rarely sustain a single point of view as they shift, with the detachment of the camera, from the historical still-life to another within the frame of a single text. It is as if old photographs are being set in one frame without any immediately apparent hierarchy. The location of the stories is almost invariably the small town, surviving against the odds on the borderline of history. Mészöly's Central Europe is provincial and peripheral; pieced together through a series of often only loosely related, yet highly evocative, images, in which the past is preserved by virtue of its very dislocation from the continuum of time. The arbitrariness of the image is its own historical statement. As Mészöly comments on an old photograph in one of the stories: 'Above the group assembled for the camera the sky is empty. Maybe the pigeons of the marketplace had just flown out of the field of vision, or maybe they were just preparing to swoop back in. Either way, the void was rendered permanent.'

These lines are from *Forgiveness* (*Megbocsátás*), written in 1983. The story begins and ends with a single band of smoke – left suspended above a country town by a passing train – which refuses to disappear into the air. In the meantime we learn of the town's past and present through the eyes of a local clerk and his family as they come to terms with the ambiguous relationships and recurring motifs of their fragmented world. Detached and laconic as the presentation is, its underlying concern remains one of resignation and reconciliation. It ends with the clerk dreaming of a grandiloquent sentence with which to beg his wife's forgiveness for an act of cruel infidelity. In the dream he is unable to utter the sentence, but now at least the idea of forgiveness has entered the narrow universe of the text as a possibility and joins the other fragments of the story on an equal existential footing. Existence is the only form of possibility Mészöly's stories entertain. As the author comments on the subject of Central Europe elsewhere in the collection: 'Here all that can happen is what does happen.'

Mészöly's attitude to history as essentially arbitrary, fragmentary and discontinuous also informs his approach to story-telling, the narration of that history. For in Mészöly, fragmentation is not only the intrinsic condition of the experience narrated, but also of the process of narration itself. Mészöly's stories seem to suggest a complete lack of faith in the integrity and continuity of narrative. *Forgiveness*, for example, fuses a number of discrete histories – the reproduction of the layout of the town in an underground labyrinth of graves after a plague in the seventeenth century, the trial of the town's former mayor in 1922, the discovery of a naked corpse in a cornfield sometime before the narrated present of the story, and four months in the life of the local clerk-cum-archivist and his family – into a single, inextricable text which seems to confound any sense of meaningfully recordable time. Meanwhile, the band of smoke which hovers in suspension above the town at the beginning of the text, refuses to disperse and is still there at the end.

This undermining of the conventional continuities of narrative – continuities, indeed, upon which the very integrity of narrative depends – is, of course no less characteristic of the prose of Esterházy and Nádas. None of the texts in Esterházy's composite *An Introduction to Literature* (*Bevezetés a szépirodalomba*),[2] for example, can sustain a continuous narrative for long without the narration of a story becoming the story of a narration. Indeed, in the opening section of the final collected volume of his *An Introduction to Literature*, Esterházy advances the following semi-frivolous hybrid of paradox and tautology: 'THE NOVEL ... is the awkward fusion of the writing of a novel (which would be the novel itself) and the novel itself (which, so to speak, would contain its own writing)'. Less obviously, perhaps, Nádas's *A Book of Memoirs* sets out from a related mistrust of the significance of story-telling: 'all I can write is what is mine to write, let us say, I can write the story of my loves, or maybe not even that, for I do not have sufficient faith in myself to be able to hope to name anything more significant than the mere connections between personal stories, and I do not even believe that there can be anything more significant than these, in themselves, insignificant and worthless personal connections. . .' Where there is no faith in history as a continuous development of meaningful connections, there can be no faith in *histoire*, in the form of the story itself.

The convergences I have been trying to identify between recent initiatives in Hungarian prose fiction and 'postmodern' attitudes to historical experience and representation articulated by theorists of culture in the very different historical context of North America and Western Europe should alert us to the inevitable complexities involved in any attempt to interpret the phenomenon of postmodernism itself in comprehensively historical terms. By way of conclusion, I should like to foreground a number of these complexities and to do no more than gesture towards one way in which we might possibly move beyond them.

While much postmodernist theory, in seeing history as just another text, declines to historicise the new cultural moment it champions, a serious attempt to restore the 'end of history' to a less privileged place in a broader historical narrative had been offered by a number of Marxist critics in the West. Thus Frederic Jameson has tried to argue that postmodernism represents the 'cultural logic of late capitalism' in which art is totally dissolved into the prevailing forms of commodity production.[3] 'Late capitalism' is an odd term here; it seems to conceal a double-edged suggestion of wish-fulfilment – 'late' meaning both the last phase and already deceased. (It is interesting that Jameson's latest book bears the title *Late Marxism*.) In fact, the Marxist historicisation of postmodernism testifies more to the triumph of capitalism than to any anticipation of its imminent demise. This is quite apparent from Terry Eagleton's highly eloquent characterisation of postmodernism, which is worth quoting at some length:

> The depthless, styleless, dehistoricised, decathected surfaces of postmodernist culture are not meant to signify an alienation, for the very concept of alienation must secretly posit a dream of authenticity which postmodernism finds quite unintelligible . . . Reification, once it has extended its empire across the whole of social reality, effaces the very criteria by which it can be recognised for what it is and so triumphantly abolishes itself, returning everything to normality . . . As postmodernist culture attests, the contemporary subject may be less the strenuous, monadic agent of an earlier phase of capitalist ideology, than . . . a shibboleth or straw target, a hangover from an earlier liberal epoch . . . before technology and consumerism scattered our bodies to the winds as so many bits and pieces of reified technique, appetite, mechanical operation or reflex of desire.[4]

Whatever one makes of this as a statement of the relationship between postmodernism and consumer society, it hardly explains the emergence of postmodernist culture in a society not informed above all by the unfettered extension of capitalist reification. For, as I have attempted to demonstrate in the limited context of attitudes to history, postmodernism is not the exclusive product or property of 'late' capitalism, but can represent an equally historical response to a very different history. In order to move towards a more coherent and comprehensive characterisation of the contemporary cultural moment, it will clearly be necessary to find a very different common genealogy. Perhaps a first step might be to stand the implicit chronology of postmodernism on its head. For what has become clear over the last few years is that rather than experiencing the death throes of 'late' capitalism, we are seeing capitalism – together with its attendant liberal democratic ideology –

enter a new, vigorous and revolutionary phase. Far from being on its last legs, it has finally smashed the totalitarian regimes of Eastern Europe. Postmodernism may not prove to be a 'post' aesthetic ideology at all, but, on the contrary, a *prelude* to a new chapter in the grand historical narrative. One day, cultural historians may look back and see that what was once called *postmodernism* was in fact the moment that *prefigured* a new experience of modernity in both East and West.

This projection – or, to return to my earlier phrase, heuristic fiction – is not offered *entirely* frivolously. For there is a rat in postmodernism that stinks to high heaven. I look at the depthlessness of Andy Warhol, and can't help seeing the depthlessness and two-dimensionality of Gustav Klimt in which expression is displaced by decoration. I read Derrida and Lacan on the sliding or slippage of the signifier, and can't help thinking of Hofmannsthal's notion of *das Gleitende* as a symbol of an age where everything is, in the poet's words, 'multiplicity and indeterminacy'. I ponder Eagleton's notion of the commodity as artefact and the artefact as commodity, and can't help being reminded yet again of that other *fin-de-siècle*, of the Wiener Werkstätte, of the Gödöllő arts and crafts movement, of the secession's aestheticisation of everyday life. I think of Klimt's opening address to the Wiener Kunstschau in 1908: 'It is only upon the continuing penetration of life by art that the progress of the artist is able to be grounded.' And then I am reminded of Klimt's inordinate reputation today and how his images now decorate the kitschy posters and postcards of fashionable London canned-art shops, like Athena. And I think of the two-dimensionality of Otto Wagner's façades on the Linke Wienerzeile, the eclecticism of Ödön Lechner, the fusion of kitsch and innovation in the Palais Stoclet, or in the buildings of Károly Kós. And then I have another look at the new Mercury telephone boxes and at the 'post-modern' buildings sprouting up around me on the Isle of Dogs.

Depthlessness, the loss of referentiality, eclectic historicism, the aestheticisation of the commodity – the signs, perhaps, of a culture which perceives itself to have run out of ideas. And yet what followed all this at the turn of the last century was not the end of art, but a new beginning – just to stick with the example of the Austro–Hungarian Empire – the modernism of Loos and Schoenberg, Ady and Bartók. Could postmodernism itself finally turn out to be a kind of *pre*-modernism, a secession, a *fin-de-siècle* decadence before the discovery of a new modernity in the twenty-first century?

Notes

1. See Frederic Jameson, 'Postmodernism, or the Cultural Logic of Late Capitalism' in *New Left Review*, 146, July–August 1984, p. 66.
2. In the first half of the 1980s all of Esterházy's novels and most of his shorter fictions were published under the same umbrella title *An Introduction to Literature (Bevezetés a szépirodalomba)*. These works were brought together in one volume under the same title in 1986.
3. Jameson, 'Postmodernism'.
4. Terry Eagleton, 'Capitalism, Modernism and Post-Modernism', in *New Left Review*, 152, July–August 1985, pp. 61–71.

7 Recent Prose of Hana Ponická and Ol'ga Feldeková: Dissident Autobiography and Aesopian Fiction
Norma L. Rudinsky

Events in Czechoslovakia since 17 November 1989 have broken down ideological rules that formerly condemned or distanced literature lying outside the narrow category of socialist realism. As a result new comparative studies can provide a more complete picture of Slovak literature than we have had in the past. Literature is no longer divided into the four streams of officially praised works, of 'Aesopian' works that were published but treated with suspicion, of dissident *samizdat* and *tamizdat* works, and finally of exile or ethnic literature that was ignored by home-based critics. Literary historians will modify the current Marxist periodisation of literary epochs and presumably reintroduce categories such as naturalism that were almost subsumed under the political heading of critical realism. One may also expect that genuine gains in developing literary history, for which Marxist analysis was in certain ways more useful for the Slovaks than the positivist historical methods used in pre-war Czechoslovakia, will not be thrown out with the bathwater.[1]

Literary criticism may change more drastically than literary history, in part because it too has sometimes employed Aesopian language. In addition to the likely import of Western-style psychological or Freudian criticism and archetypal Jungian criticism, one can expect expanded use of Mikhail Bakhtin's literary concepts (which were already fostered because of Soviet acceptance) and accelerated and widespread return to the structuralism and semiotics of the Prague Circle within a general return to pre-Marxist culture.

A slower, more problematic import from the West will probably be feminist criticism and re-examination of genre categories to enlarge the literary canon by including, for example, more early female writers, who typically wrote letters and memoirs rather than fiction or poetry. The lack of genuine women's movements in Eastern Europe means that literature by women has seldom been considered from a feminist viewpoint, whether by critics or women authors themselves. An obvious exception is Christa Wolf of East Germany, especially in *Cassandra* (1983), but no comparable figure appears in the literature of Czechoslovakia. Yet sisterhood, resistance to patriarchal customs, refusal of female passivity, and similar feminist concerns can doubtless be found by internal textual analysis. To a small extent my essay is intended as a contribution to the necessary effort to integrate the former separate streams of Slovak literature, to re-examine genres and enlarge the canon to include particular kinds of female writing.

The two works I am comparing here are dissimilar in genre, since Hana Ponická's *Lukavica Notes* (*Lukavické zápisky*) is an auto-biographical work and Ol'ga Feldeková's *Red Squirrel* (*Veverica*) is a short novel. However, autobiography is not simply narration of a person's life and times in a single sincere voice. Such ostensible simplicity dissolves as soon as one recognises in autobiography many of the same literary techniques of narrative, characterisation, tone, voice and symbol that construct fiction. Part of the special pleasure and interest of reading autobiography comes from perceiving the author's view of herself. The difference between the author's self presented in autobiography and a main character presented in fiction, or the difference between 'truth' in fiction and 'truth' in autobiography, may thus be considered quantitative, not qualitative.

The long tradition of autobiography and memoir (from Augustine's penance addressed to God through to Jean-Jacques Rousseau's self-examination and the contemporary public self-justification underlying the historical and political memoirs of world figures) also includes numerous women's writings.[2] A new variety of personal narrative, however, arose within the dissident movement. In so-called desk-drawer literature the autobiographical element of writing for oneself was reinforced by dissidents who could not reach their natural public, and it was magnified by the existential moment of risk in which the dissident was faced at least with metaphorical death in authorship without audience, if not actual imprisonment or death. Some of these works fit the tradition of political and historical memoir, while others are closer to autobiography where construction of the self is the primary project. It is this latter aspect, the self constructed in the dissident's existential moment, that gives *samizdat* autobiography its special poignancy and immediacy.

Pre-November 1989 literature cannot be simply divided into dissident
samizdat and officially published works, however, because it must
include the category of Aesopian literature which masked its dissidence
to gain official tolerance or at least to avoid suppression. Aesopian
literature was written in the same circumstances as dissident works
(even if with less courage), and it gained a corollary (even if lesser)
intensity and force. This existential corollary also underlies my
comparison of a dissident autobiography and an Aesopian novella.

Hana Ponická's *Lukavica Notes* was written in the late 1970s and
early 1980s, circulated as *samizdat* and printed only in July 1989 in
Toronto.[3] It narrates Ponická's refusal to sign the official condemnation
of Charter 77, then her decision to protest at the Union of Writers'
ostracism of forty writers expelled in 1972 during the 'normalisation'
period, then the resultant persecution she experienced. Moving from
New Year's Eve 1976 to New Year's Day 1978, the three-part structure
follows both the calendar year 1977 and the events that transformed
Ponická into a dissident. Her personal transformation makes *Lukavica
Notes* an autobiography more than a memoir. The political context
remains, but her essential project is the construction and revelation of
herself: the modest, naïve, untested woman who expects to ignore
totalitarian power and live her own life unobtrusively, and who
discovers that she cannot. The titles of the three parts concentrate this
story: 'Return from Escapism' (*Návrat z úniku*)' 'Summer in
Lukavica' (*Leto v Lukavici*) and 'The Stone Guest' (*Kamenný host*').
Titles of chapters name four political events: '*Le Monde*' (that is, the
French newspaper article on Poniká on 4 May 1977), 'Appeal against
her own expulsion from the Writers' Union' (*Odvolanie*), 'Trial'
(*Proces*) and, 'Without a Warrant' (*Bez príkazu prokurátora*). Other
chapters have symbolic titles that will be taken up later.

An English-language summary and evaluation of Ponická's work by
Mary Hrabik Samal and Zdenka Brodska has been published in *Cross
Currents*. Samal and Brodska consider more closely than I am doing the
historical context of Ponická's work and its relation to the Czech
dissident movement that doubtless encouraged her to persist in her
protest.[4] They cite the reference to Božena Němcová's *Babička* in the
name Viktorka that Ponická gives to a village woman and in the rural
atmosphere that is broken, however, by the Kafkaesque quality of the
political events she narrates.[5] Such echoes from Czech or Bohemian
literature are indisputable, but also present are unnoticed elements
relating Ponická's work to her own earlier lyrical prose that is
distinctively Slovak and to other Slovak writers.

Ponická's first-person narrative juxtaposes her desire to escape into the village and her compulsion to protest at the simple facts of injustice and intellectual waste. This straightforward account of political events becomes self-deprecating as she recognises the naïveté of her initial expectation that her dissent would go unpunished. Self-deprecation, however, does not bridge the distance between her still too-modest view of this breach and the totalitarian demand for total conformity. That distance is great enough to create dramatic irony. Martin Šimečka in an afterword to the Toronto edition says the effect of Ponická's 'pure *naïveté* is extraordinarily strong' because she reveals herself as an optimist who 'understands nothing of the nature of power, doesn't want to break with the powers-that-be, and does all she does from the sheer and, in the right sense, naïve need to say what she thinks.'[6] Ponická is not interested in political analysis and shows no particular grasp of the post-totalitarian dictatorship she is up against, as she makes passing reference to pre-war democracy, fascists and Stalinists. This single persistent female figure, however, provokes such hysterical opposition from the male official writers and the Slovak Communist Party Central Committee that their own disproportionate actions, not hers, expose their fearfully shaky foundations. Ponická's modest proposal to the Writer's Union turns out to be Swiftean indeed in this powerful irony.

The feminist content of Ponická's image remains implicit, since she presents herself as an underdog against the establishment rather than as a gender victim. But as she describes her female colleagues at the Writers' Congress, we feel her scorn and regret at how they are co-opted into celebrating the Congress with elaborate clothing, even ball gowns, and coiffures of extravagantly coloured hair while she herself wears serviceable boots and a pullover (pp. 66–67). She expected to find at least partial understanding and support from women writers who had themselves previously been censored, but she was disappointed.

Along with political events, we are given flashbacks to Ponická's childhood, told of visits to her children and grandchildren, and especially treated to the easy rhythms of life in the old village mill where she lives with her third husband and their frequent guests. It is this extra-political picture that turns the work from historical memoir to autobiography, though the focus on dissidence is never lost. For example, while waiting in a rural railway station, Ponická recalls travelling as a child to market with her grandmother, who kept a small shop, and she compares unfavourably the tight, withdrawn faces of her present fellow travellers to the lively, unrestrained, varied expressions of her grandmother's customers, the 'exploited' women who crowded the dark small shop at the end of their shift in the local textile mill (pp. 49–52). As she recalls her childhood sleep beside her grandmother in their feather bed, she suddenly forms the sought-for sentence to begin her planned protest at the Writers' Union Congress: 'We have been living for almost nine years in a state of extraordinary social tension' (p. 52).

Within this narrative, however, we see fictional techniques of characterisation throughout the book. They reveal Ponická's sense of mission developing in response to the hysterical official condemnation of her small breach of normalisation. Dreams reveal her turmoil and unconscious fears. She remembers the old advice of her colleague Dr Jozef Felix, who persuaded her to translate Simone de Beauvoir's *Les Mandarins* so that she could incorporate what she had learned of social values into her own work (pp. 140–141). She is now beginning to understand those social values. preparing a biographical study of the early poet Andrej Sládkovič, she applies his exhortation 'Appeal to your own times' (*Na svoj čas sa odvolaj*) to her own return from her former escapism, and is satisfied that she is now fulfilling the mission which fate has set for her (pp. 172–173). This modest woman, who had earlier been the inspirational wife-muse (that is, the object and means) of two major Slovak poets (the surrealist Štefan Žáry and Ján Kostra), is now seen as acting on her own. Her act of writing this account becomes her discovery and assertion of herself as subject.[7]

Techniques of fiction to characterise Ponická's transformation are not the only nor even the most singular, literary feature. Striking symbols appear throughout the work, some of which are so sustained and developed that they become allegorical.

These symbols begin with the title of the first chapter, 'The Green Butterfly' (*Zelený motýl'*), in which a dormant butterfly lying in a champagne glass turns into a simile of Ponická's dormant conscience and her effort to stir to life the consciences of other official Slovak writers. This is foreshadowed in her dream of puppets dancing in the Writers' Union castle at Budmerice where only the butterfly is alive (pp. 11–12).

In the second chapter, 'The Spring Damned Up' (*Zastavený prameň*), a new symbol of life and moral growth begins upon Ponická's return to Lukavica from the Writers' Congress where she was not allowed to read her protest. The millstream is swelling with water from a new mineral spring opened accidentally by geologists' drilling, and rumours circulate of a new spa (pp. 98–99) because this new spring is stronger than those of the nearby resorts of Sliač and Kováčová. But to preserve these established spas the new spring is cemented up. The first massive loads of concrete only spread the water into many tiny streams (pp. 102–103), and when the whole current is finally closed off, the nearby age-old sulphur waters used by the villagers are enriched from an underground passage of the dammed-up spring (pp. 293–294). These events relate explicitly to political events: the first damming up of the spring occurs just before orders from the Central Committee stop all Ponická's publications and royalties (p. 103), and the second occurs after her expulsion from the Writers' Union when she can see in the new spring a sign that 'no power once erupting from the earth was ever lost, but only changed in form'. The essay she writes on this belief becomes her first desk-drawer work (p. 204).

The sixth chapter has a briefly developed metaphor of an old but sound crab apple tree whose bitter fruit has helped cure Ponická's ulcer (p. 303). Trees feed into the veins of life, and their leaves show the 'map of local events' (p. 305). Ponická's interrogation and strip search in Bratislava are prefigured by the death of a small mink in the paws of a tom cat (p. 371), which repeatedly evokes her own fate (pp. 379–380, p. 421). The invasive police power (pp. 406–407) is also represented by the final major metaphor, the 'stone guest' in Alexander Pushkin's short tragedy *The Stone Guest* (*Kamennyi gost'*) about Don Juan overcome by the stone commandant, who is evoked for Ponická in a new statue of a Soviet soldier in Bratislava. The remodelled 200-year-old mill that she and her husband retire to, while it remains their actual refuge, also easily symbolises escape from the political powers in Bratislava and Prague. The welcome distraction of the mill's need for repairs, the care of fruit trees, the organic vegetable garden, and the uncorrupted village life in Lukavica all have this same status as potential symbols which, though real events, are resonant and evocative.

Many incidental images appear, such as migrating wild geese, fledgling birds in nests, or frogs croaking in the night. Ponická's omnipresent use of physical nature appears as sacramental. This life she describes as lived close to nature becomes an essential part of the dissident's 'life in the truth'. Or to reverse the sacramental view, her dissident protest becomes a part of the unspoiled truth of green nature. Such emphasis upon physical nature is probably Ponická's chief novelty among dissident writers in Czechoslovakia, by which her work differs for example from the depiction of uncorrupted social nature one finds in the 'chaste' character of Ferdinand Vaněk created by Václav Havel and the other Czech playwrights who picked up the Vaněk character.[8] Among the relatively few Slovak dissidents Ponická's work differs from the rediscovered political idealism in the essays of such socialists (or former socialists) as Milan Šimečka and Miroslav Kusý.[9] Her emphasis upon betrayal of physical nature differs from the central metaphor of betrayal of the most intimate human relation, the sexual relation, that becomes so prominent in Dominik Tatarka's *Scribblings* (*Písačky*) and *Conversations* (*Navrávačky*).[10]

It is this sacramental view of nature in *Lukavica Notes* that provides the closest relation to Ol'ga Feldeková's *Red Squirrel* (*Veverica*), despite the differences in style, tone and genre of the two works. In both, a natural time period acquires thematic and formal functions and serves as calendar and climax of each narrator's new insight. Ponická's work covers exactly one year and Feldeková's one day. This use of cyclic periods may also be read as characteristic of 'women's time', in the phrase and meaning of Julia Kristeva.[11]

Feldeková's *Red Squirrel* (1985) is a short but powerful novella of under 100 pages.[12] Set in an Orava village during the critical period of collectivisation in the late 1940s and early 1950s, the work is a mixture of allegory, parable, realistic fiction and history. Its intense compression, terse intellectuality and disparate, discontinuous symbols relate it to the magic realism of Latin American authors with their grotesque, violent, fantastic events dressed in realistic detail and held together more by the reader's questions than authorial direction. Though Feldeková has said that she was influenced by Gabriel García Márquez, she also had purely Slovak and Czech antecedents in surrealist poetry as well as in the lyrical prose tradition from J. C. Hronský through Vincent Šikula.[13]

This mythic, fantastic element of Feldeková gives a mythic symbol for the Orava district (and by extension all of Slovakia) in a 'red squirrel', which is also the nickname of the main female character, a young red-haired village girl Žofia. This symbol is suggested at once by the dedication of the book to a Finnish poet who told Feldeková that 'orava' in Finnish means 'squirrel', but the symbolic relation becomes certain only at the end after Žofiá Veverica's baby has been kidnapped and she herself has disappeared into Budapest and forgotten how to speak Slovak. Then the narrator, after a night of writing, opens the door to the dawn, and a beautiful red squirrel appears. In the context this tiny female animal acquires an abstract significance which informs and empowers the preceding mysterious details of the plot. The unhappy world Feldeková has shown becomes at last a natural and hopeful world as we are reminded that nature itself is mysterious and unknowable, yet fecund and optimistic. As an image for Slovakia the tiny, cosy, provident but untamed squirrel is strikingly original even while evoking the earlier nature symbolism of the school of lyrical prose. The mythic element of this squirrel is more radical than Ponická's sacramental symbols of nature, but the images are consonant.

The complex treatment of Žofia is strikingly effective. Paradoxically she seems heroic in not revealing the father of her illegitimate child (apparently the young neighbour Jožko who is just entering the seminary to become a priest) and also in falsely naming the son of a rich former capitalist to satisfy her mother and the gossipy neighbours (pp. 20–23). This moral mix-up in her actions that are both sacrificial and self-serving is followed by her sudden marriage to a Pole from Krakow who has fallen in love with her baby and who soon kidnaps it and disappears. Left alone, she writes four prose poems with haunting themes of loneliness (pp. 51–55), but when Jožko abandons the seminary and returns she accepts from him a bird that has her baby's voice, and she refuses the marriage proposal of the man she had falsely named as the father. She is finally ready for happiness with Jožko just before he is killed in a mysterious accident. After three days of grief-stricken silence, Žofia and her bird-child disappear. Despite such a wildly erratic plot, the self-contained, autonomous Žofia is invested with a solemn dignity that makes her later happy marriage in Budapest appear as a suitable personal reward, while her old symbolic position is filled by the new squirrel that appears on the narrator's doorstep.

Feldeková's other female characters are several village mothers and a caricatured faith healer. As with Ponická's work, the feminist content remains implicit, yet one can easily see in the female nature symbol a version of the Mother Earth and Mother Sláva traditions that are so prominent in Slavic and especially Slovak literature. Ján Kollár's *Daughter of Mother Sláva (Slávy dcera 1824)* and Andrej Sládkovič's *Marína* (1846) are obvious examples. This connection is probably unconscious on Feldeková's part, and the critical difference is that now the female nature figure is seen acting on her own, not as a muse or support for the male figures.[14]

Another major point of comparison (and contrast) lies in the kind of irony allowed by the two works. Though sometimes self-deprecating, Ponická is not an ironist, and the dramatic irony we recognise comes from our own knowledge of the totalitarian power she sets herself against as she (like Kafka's K) almost offhandedly prepares her speech, then her appeals, without recognising their certain failure and severe penalties. The deepest, most powerful irony (in the disproportion between Ponická's slight female protest and the male hysteria it provokes) is unintended, like the ironies of history or natural catastrophes: it is so-called situational irony.[15] The sardonic irony in *Red Squirrel*, on the other hand, involves the whole society, not one single event. An example of D. C. Muecke's general irony, it is unstable, covert and infinite in the categories of Wayne Booth, as is the irony of absurdist literature as well as of magic realism.[16]

This pervasive irony makes any reading of Feldeková's work less than secure, but clearly sardonic political satire flashes when silver airplanes drop thousands of leaflets printed with the single word 'Happiness' during the worst cultural shock experienced by peasants being forced into simultaneous modernisation, industrialisation and collectivisation (pp. 58, 90). This shock occurred at the same time as extreme changes in the position of the Christian church in Slovak life, which are also indicated in the novella. On one level Christianity is reduced to superstition in a post-Christian world where the old institutions seem as outdated as the old farming methods. Yet on another level only the corruption of the Christian institutions is condemned, not their essence. For example, when the former seminarian Jožko is suddenly killed in a mysterious accident, the beautiful black horse seems to signify corruptible nature and death as well as Jožko's priestly vocation, and it is the atheist father who experiences a premonition of Jožko's death and sees 'miraculous' signs following it. Such unstable images were obviously useful Aesopian instruments in the period before November 1989, because they covered and obscured sensitive subjects such as the satire on collectivisation and the ambiguous attitude toward Christianity found in Feldeková's book.

A further comparison appears in the first-person narrators of the two works. Feldeková's dual narrator differs from Ponická's straightforward narrator in that it carries the (Šikula-like) point of view of both a child experiencing events and an adult remembering and commenting upon them. We see hints that this dual narrator also is autobiographical, however, and certainly both narrators focus their personal growth in an exact social scene. The authorial persona constructed behind the unstable, mystifying symbols and satire of Feldeková's novella, on the one hand, and the person behind the localised symbols and straightforward narrative of Ponická's work, on the other, are similar commentators on the two worst periods of Slovak socialism: the post-February Stalinism and the normalisation of the 1970s and 1980s.

Red Squirrel enjoyed official publication by the Slovak Writers' Union, yet it went almost unreviewed with only three newspaper commentaries and nothing in the official literary magazines. Feldeková's slippery, unstable irony helped her avoid outright condemnation, but it gained her no approbation. The only extended newspaper report condemned Feldeková's self-destructive 'playing' with the plot and the 'onslaught of poetic fantasy' to which the plot falls victim.[17] Alexander Halvoník's basic criticism was that 'a more demanding aesthetic principle [presumably he meant 'socialist realism'] requires more explicit social content and more serious meaning' than he saw in *Red Squirrel*. Yet what could carry greater significance than the satiric symbol of Slovakia with its ultimately hopeful outcome?

Ol'ga Feldeková's novella may now be analysed without the distorting prism of socialist realist criteria, and Hana Ponická's autobiography now belongs officially to the mainstream of Slovak literature. For the first time we may look forward to a cross-fertilisation of formerly dissident and formerly Aesopian works that bodes well for the analysis, and ultimately for the creation, of a richer Slovak literature as a whole.

Furthermore, when an explicitly named and consciously accepted women's movement begins to form, we can expect it to broaden the reference and range of female writers as well as to inaugurate feminist criticism. The theoretical equality of the sexes advocated (though not implemented) by Marxism–Leninism and their actual equality under oppression, as well as women's real experience of education and almost universal employment outside the home, have certainly brought a new consciousness that can easily turn feminist. The potential already exists in the widespread recognition that women's burden has been doubled while many men have not taken on a new share of responsibility.

Without the taboos of Marxism–Leninism this consciousness will appear in historical and critical studies and in literature. The new line may well continue and develop the cyclic nature themes and the autonomous women characters found here in Hana Ponická and Ol'ga Feldeková.[18]

Notes

1. For a very brief treatment of this analysis, see my 'The Context of the Marxist–Leninist View of Slovak Literature 1945–1969,' *Carl Beck Papers in Russian and East European Studies*, No. 505, Pittsburgh, University of Pittsburgh Press, 1986.
2. See, for example, the essays in Estelle C. Jelinek, ed., *Women's*

Autobiography (Bloomington: Indiana University Press, 1980). On general autobiography see also Elizabeth W. Bruss, *Autobiographical Acts*, (Baltimore: Johns Hopkins University Press, 1976), pp. 1–32, and Huntington Williams, *Rousseau and Romantic Autobiography* (Oxford: Oxford University Press, 1983).

3. Hana Ponická, *Lukavické zápisky* (Toronto: 68 Publishers, 1989). Ponická was born in 1922 in Halič in south-eastern Slovakia; her other works include occasional pieces in several genres, collected stories in *Boughs Halúzky* (1955), major translations from French, Italian, and Hungarian literature, and especially children's books featuring her most popular character Štoplík. All translations from Slovak texts are mine, and page references are given in the text.

4. Ponická's relation to Czech dissidents apparently grew close, but she left the relevant chapter 'Prague Meetings' out (*Praha stretaní*) of her published manuscript. See her statement in 'Stretnutie Hany Ponickej s Martinom Kvetkom,' *Naše snahy*, 26, 2, March–April 1990, pp. 5–6.

5. Mary Hrabik Samal and Zdenka Brodska, 'The Lukavica Notebooks,' *Cross Currents*, 9, 1990, pp. 241–256. I am grateful to Mary Samal for sending a pre-publication copy of their manuscript.

6. Martin Šimečka, '*Príbeh o jednom čine*', in Hana Ponická *Lukavické zápisky* (Toronto: 68 Publishers, 1989) p. 465 and p. 467 respectively.

7. Domna C. Stanton says that autobiography became for women 'an act of self-assertion that denied and reversed woman's status,' in her 'Auto-gynography,' in *The Female Autograph: Theory and Practice of Autobiography from the Tenth to the Twentieth Century* (Chicago: University of Chicago Press, 1984), p. 14. Feminist use of the term 'autograph' instead of 'autobiography' emphasises the writer's self more than her life and times.

8. Václav Havel's three one-acts and five plays by three other playwrights are collected in *The Vaněk Plays: Four Authors, One Character*, ed. Marketa Goetz-Stankiewicz (Vancouver: University of British Columbia Press, 1987).

9. For English texts of their works, see Milan Šimečka, *The Restoration of Order: The Normalisation of Czechoslovakia 1969–1976* (London: Verso Editions, 1984), and Miroslav Kusý and Milan Šimečka, 'Dialogues with the Young Generation: A First Dialogue,' *Cross Currents: A Yearbook of Central European Culture*, 6, 1987, pp. 249–274.

10. Dominik Tatarka, *Písačky* (Toronto: 68 Publishers, 1984) and *Navrávačky* (Toronto: 68 Publishers, 1988).

11. Julia Kristeva's article 'Women's Time' is considered seminal because she analyses Frederick Nietzsche's belief that female subjectivity is linked to repetition in *cyclical* time as well as to *monumental* eternal time. Both notions conceptualise time from the perspective of mother-hood and reproduction. This link does not exclude the *linear* time of history and politics (as well as language), however, and the new generation of feminists will have to reconcile the place of women's cyclical time in linear activities. See the new translation of Kristeva's 'Women's Time' by Alice Jardine and Harry Blake in *Feminist Theory: A*

Critique of Ideology, ed. Nannerl O. Keohane, Michelle Z. Rosaldo, and Barbara C. Gelpi (Chicago: University of Chicago Press, 1982) pp. 31–53.

12.   Ol'ga Feldeková, *Veverica* (Bratislava: Slovenský Spisovatel', 1985). Feldeková was born in 1943 in Martin; her earlier works consist of children's books, several television plays, and two collections of short stories, *St'ahovanie na mieste* (1976) and *Dievča a št'astie* (1979).

13.   For a brief exegesis of Feldeková's novella and this tradition, see my 'National Antiheroes: Symbolism and Narrative Voice as Coded National Identity in Ol'ga Feldeková's *Veverica*', in *Modern Slovak Prose Fiction since 1954*, ed. R. B. Pynsent (London: Macmillan, 1990), pp. 205–14. This is a revised version of a paper given in a conference at the University of London in September, 1987, which was translated into Slovak as 'Národní antihrdinova: ohlas Urbana a Hronského v dielach Šikulu, Jaroša a Feldekovej, *Romboid*, 8, August 1988, pp. 67–73.

14.   A long treatment of this tradition in Slovak nationalist literature with its sequence from male poets' apotheosis of woman as national muse to women writers' appropriation and transformation of this muse into an autonomous nationalist writer on her own, appears in my *Incipient Feminists: Women Writers in the Slovak National Movement* (Columbus: Slavica, 1991 (in press)) especially Chapters 1, 2 and 4.

15.   D. C. Muecke, *Irony* (London: Methuen, 1970) pp. 28–29 and passim.

16.   These categories are in Wayne C. Booth, *A Rhetoric of Irony* (Chicago; University of Chicago Press, 1974), Part III. See also Muecke on general irony pp. 66–81.

17.   Alexander Halvoník, 'Hra s príbehom (osudná)', *Pravda*, Bratislava, 1 August 1986.

18.   Research for part of this paper was supported by a grant from the International Research and Exchanges Board (IREX) in Bratislava in 1986–1987 with funds of the National Endowment for the Humanities and the United States Information Agency. None of these organisations is responsible for the views expressed.

8 Milan Kundera's Wisdom of Uncertainty and Other Categorical Imperatives: The Experience of the Contemporary Romanian Novel
Michael H. Impey

In an article published in 1984 in the *New York Review of Books*, Milan Kundera claimed that the hundreds and thousands of novels printed in the Soviet Union and East Europe add nothing to 'the conquest of being... They uncover no new segment of existence; they only confirm what has already been said.'[1] In this essay I will take as a point of departure a number of positions espoused by Kundera on the aesthetics of the novel and explore their validity for an appraisal of contemporary Romanian fiction. Why Kundera? Because he is a rare example of a writer who has transcended a dissident past to establish himself in the West not only as one of the world's foremost novelists but also as a critic of remarkable analytical powers. But more than that, because his voice is among the most authentic in recording the benumbed, stultified anguish of a whole generation of people in East and Central Europe in the years that followed the end of the Second World War.

Early in *The Art of the Novel* Kundera argues that the value of a literary work can only be fully seen and understood in a supra-national context. And literary value he defines as the import of its discovery in the sequence of discoveries that constitute the history of the European novel.[2] Such a position poses a severe dilemma for the specialist of Romanian literature. If we exclude universal spirits such as Eugen Ionescu and Emil Cioran (whose culture is largely transnational), Romanian writers have failed to gain a receptive audience in the West. Nor have the works of dissident Romanian writers such as Paul Goma or Dumitru Tepeneag attracted the kind of attention that might have been expected given their exile status. Those novelists widely regarded as most representative of the Romanian spirit fare poorly in translation and often pass without comment in the international literary press. A recent example would be the cool reception given to a fine translation of D. R. Popescu's *The Royal Hunt* (*Vînătoarea regală*), where one reviewer rejected the parallel with Gabriel García Márquez's *One Hundred years of Solitude* and failed to understand that the incidence of rabies in the village where a series of extraordinary events take place is a political allegory for a far more widespread rabidity in Romanian life, a spiralling element of self-destruction brought on by forces that seem beyond the ken or control of local, state or party authorities.[3] A similar fate also befell earlier translations of novels by Mihai Sadoveanu and Liviu Rebreanu, although in these cases the quality of the translations may have been partially responsible. It is possible that works by authors I propose to discuss in this essay, Marin Preda, Augustin Buzura, and Nicolae Breban, would experience the same neglect were they available in translation. If we discount the possibility of a cultural imperialism in letters that excludes outright all literary works that fail to measure up to some nebulous system of Western-imposed values, existentialist philosophy and abstract modes of discourse, an area for debate that necessarily lies beyond the scope of the present discussion, then it might be useful to consider whether they are held to be deficient because they appear to follow history too closely or whether they are to be ridiculed simply because they happen to have been written and published in what was an Eastern bloc country. In order to shed some light on the impossible relationship between the freedom of art/literature and totalitarian truth that 'excludes relativity, doubt, questioning', and which can never accommodate what Kundera calls 'the spirit of the novel',[4] I have chosen to examine their contribution to Romanian literature in particular and European literature in general.

For Kundera the novel's essence is both 'the spirit of complexity' and 'the spirit of continuity', where 'each work is an answer to preceding ones, each work contains all the previous experience of the novel.'[5] In the early 1970s Petru Popescu, then a young novelist enjoying success and critical acclaim, advocated a direct, socially-committed approach to literature, and especially an urban literature that addressed everyday problems rather than a rural literature that lacked a natural audience.[6] The novels he himself wrote often offered a moral lesson for a youthful protagonist educated in doctrinaire egalitarian beliefs and the myth of human perfectibility.[7] Indirectly, largely through his desire to revalidate the careers and experiences of former officers of the Romanian Royal Army, Popescu brought attention to one of the thorniest issues of Romanian culture in the post-war Stalinist years, the survival of bourgeois thought and morality. To apply the term bourgeois to contemporary Romanian literature introduces a paradox. On the one hand, most if not all Romanian writers followed Marxist–Leninist ideology during the 1950s in representing the bourgeoisie as the principal class enemy and created heroic working-class models that had little basis in reality. On the other hand, more recent fiction (including some of the works we are to consider here) seems to relate the term to principles of conformism and servility that are deeply embedded in the socialist ethos.

The first Romanian writers to exercise their independence from party dogma included a number of poets who adopted the Labişian formula of 'struggle against inertia' and openly expressed their contempt for the debasement of language brought about by the practice of ideological reportage during the Stalinist period.[8] And yet, over the last ten or fifteen years, many of the leading novelists have appeared to be writing, in the guise of fiction, works that bear at least a surface resemblance to ideological reportage in their obsession with historical truth and political necessity – the so-called political novels. They undertook such a task not because they were subservient to the interests of state or party or because they felt impelled to practise indirection or *ketman* (to use the phrase that Czesław Miłosz gave in *The Captive Mind*, New York, 1953, pp. 54–81, to a private belief system that conflicts with a public avowal of doctrinaire or alien principles, a belief system that must be protected at all costs by mask or subterfuge from the scrutiny of those in positions of power), but because they opposed the obliteration by a party dynasty of the country's past, in particular of a vibrant bourgeois culture between the two World Wars. We should, however, be careful not to condemn works simply because they appear to exercise an ideological function. As Alberto Moravia pointed out, while ideology, as the superimposition on character and action of a deadening essence, may be characteristic of the propaganda novel, with the metaphorical novel it may be the living essence of the action, an invitation to combat simplistic reductionism and the quick easy answer.[9]

Until quite recently in Romania, literature in general, and the novel in particular, remained one of the few forms of continuity and resistance for those who still possessed the power of memory, and constituted the only forum for relatively free and open criticism of the path to social and cultural genocide. Not by design but by necessity the novel greatly expanded its area of influence and took over the role which in other countries, especially in the West, would be considered more properly the domain of journalism, history, and other forms of expository prose writing. That it did so by creating works of remarkable vision and complexity, and it is to be hoped of enduring value, is a measure of the seemingly limitless resources of the human creative spirit that has survived – at least in Romania – times of great adversity, regimented thinking, and political turmoil.

Faced with the oppressive reality of a progressively dehumanised existence, it is hardly surprising that some writers sought escape by taking refuge in a world of fantasy, in the myths of the past, or more simply in worlds that offer their readers the warmth, nourishment, security, and sense of wellbeing that they lack in their daily life. Such themes – we might call them techniques of survival – are present in all of Buzura's five novels, and indeed in much of the best fiction written by Romanian writers since the end of the Second World War. Thus we find in a novel by Nicolae Breban, *Road up to the Wall* (*Drumul la zid*), published in 1984, the creation of parallel existences that allow the protagonist, Castor Ionescu, to retire each night to an attic room under the stars and there ponder the mysteries of the universe and advance his study of the New Testament, thereby effectively separating himself from the immediate demands of family and society.[10] In a concluding passage of his seminal study of the Romanian national psyche, *Zalmoxis: The Vanishing God*, Mircea Eliade explains *Miorița*, a folk ballad that celebrates misfortune and death in a cosmic wedding ceremony, as the awakening to consciousness of 'the terror of history.'[11] Castor too seems to be reacting at a quasi-religious level to the realisation that an ideal world is irrevocably lost (indeed his own name suggests a permanent division of self) and that Romania, given its geographical position and a record of historical submission, has little hope of recovering its political independence. It would not do, however, to accuse Breban of defeatism since, in the end, Castor proves a weakling and it is his much abused wife, with her sturdier virtues and commonsense values, who survives and triumphs.

In other works of the same period we find a longing to return to an Edenic, atemporal, mythic setting, to a country of youth and primordial existence, to a country house which is remote, isolated, self-contained, not subject to arbitrary intervention by the state, a place of refuge, a sanctuary. Such a sanctuary may be sought in the external world or in internal psychic space and time. Prison itself may offer men and women the chance to rediscover their inner freedom, while a psychiatric clinic, as with Buzura's most recent work, *Refugees* (*Refugii*, also published in 1984),[12] may ultimately be a place where the non-conforming, the enfeebled, the persecuted, seek shelter from the harsh and perplexing exigencies of outside existence, a place whose walls may be there as much to keep those outside from getting in as to keep those inside from getting out, a place where Pirandellian riddles about the nature of form and reality, sanity and madness, seem wholly appropriate.

Withdrawal into the self, into an indeterminate psychic centre, has always been the special province of literature. Thus other forms of evasion might include retreat into the private world of the intellect, of creative faculties, into religion (Zen Buddhism was briefly in vogue among some writers and artists before its practice was stamped out by the Ceauşescu regime), into self-perverting *ketman*, with its abject acceptance of the inevitable and the immutable, into hedonism, sexual gratification, petty abuse of power, or finally into despair, psychosis and suicide. One of the dangers of such tactics of evasion is psychic splitting, the fragmentation of consciousness, not being able to establish a permanent identity of sense of self (as with Castor Ionescu or with Ioana Olaru in *Refugii*). In other circumstances it may be the challenge of maintaining one's integrity, keeping one's *conştiinţa* (both conscience and consciousness) whole, uncorrupted, in the face of tyranny and the atrophy of thought. Such was the situation faced by Victor Petrini, the protagonist of Marin Preda's valedictory novel *Most Beloved of Native Sons* (*Cel mai iubit dintre pămînteni*, 1980): twice convicted on trumped-up charges, Petrini's real guilt lay in having preserved *intact* and *unalienated* his ability to think and feel freely.[13] In an epoch marked by compromise, of '*conştiinţe scindate*' (equally 'divided loyalties' and 'split personalities') Petrini maintains his integrity ('*conştiiţa nescindată*,' I, pp. 315; my italics); he refuses to adopt 'the forms of deceit and dissembling open to thought', in short he remains true to himself.[14]

Any society tends to be a Procrustean bed, to which the individual is forced to adjust by assuming an unnatural position. Those who prove incapable of accommodation may suffer the fate of the victim in the Greek legend and have their feet cut off. In a totalitarian society, such as that established by the dictatorship of the proletariat, which in Romania followed the abdication of King Michael in 1947, heads are shortened instead of legs, that is to say, strenuous efforts are made to truncate free thought and reduce everyone to mindless equality (III, p. 264). Going back to those terrible years, Preda views matters in a somewhat different light. His premise, the premise on which the validity of the novel rests, is that not all heads are willingly proffered. Thus the new society controlled by the Communists and their adherents may prevent Victor Petrini from teaching philosophy and from publishing his research, but it can find no way, short of putting him to death, of forbidding him to think. The prison guards and the secret police torture his body, but they fail to cripple his mind. Similarly, on an emotional level – since the structure of the work is based on an extended analogy of hearts and minds – the defeats Petrini meets in his love affairs with Nineta, Căprioara, Matilda (who becomes his first wife) and finally with Suzy are incapable of dulling his feelings. Like Terence, Victor Petrini might proudly claim: '*homo sum, et nihil humani a me alieno puto.*'

In what sense is Victor Petrini, the subtlest of intellectuals, a native son (*un pămîntean*)? In the sense that he is one of the few characters among a multitude in Preda's vast novel, who refuse, come what may, to relinquish their ties with the past. In the midst of widespread disaffection, if not total alienation, Petrini remains himself, kindred in spirit to the free peasants (*răzeşii*) of Transylvania who never failed to return to their homesteads and to rebuild their humble wooden churches once the tide of ravaging Tartars or Poles had receded. The mission Victor Petrini undertakes, unwittingly or not, is to oppose the incidence of *estrangement* among his countrymen, and it is precisely this opposition (that of the *pămîntean*, the *ab origine* dweller, to the *venetici* (foreigners), whether they be outsiders or merely those who introduce ideas and practices *alien* to the autochthonous spirit of the people) that makes him *cel mai iubit*, most loved, of native sons. Despite appearances, Preda's novel is not about love, or at least only about love – as the narrator himself pretends – but about alienation. Love is a pretext, a subterfuge, whereby the author presents the vast and profound alienation that followed the seizure of power by Popular Front forces in 1946–47. Through his presence in the process of estrangement and by registering its echoes in the conversations of those who surround him – Matilda, Suzy, family, friends, fellow detainees or workers – Victor is able to reconstruct it in all its amplitude and profundity. Victor is a modern Dante who traverses the widest reaches of this world, a modern hell in which man is not only estranged from his Maker but from all primordial impulses to good. It is a hell with no exit. Since no mentor as wise and detached as Virgil appears, Victor's only guides are the damned themselves, who accompany him from one hellish pit or *bolgia* of alienation to another. Their sole culpability is a grotesque parody of original sin: inappropriate social origin, religious or political belief, and independence of spirit.

Where heroic models of Promethean revolt or Christian martyrdom pose too daunting a challenge (for not everyone possesses Petrini's mettle) how should the ordinary, average, law-abiding citizen preserve some measure of psychic equilibrium in a chaotic, hostile, alien world, where the values and accomplishments of the past are derided and belittled? Two other avenues remain open: for the élite, the workplace, for everyone else, the family. In *Pride (Orgolii)*, Buzura's third novel, published in 1977,[15] the protagonist, Ion Cristian, is a professor of medicine and a renowned cancer specialist. He is a man of unquestioned authority, revered by students and colleagues alike. He is proud of having been able to rise above the petty squabbles that plague every academic community, of having turned his back on the radical political transformation that had built a 'new' society on the bones of the old (the time and location of this novel, I should add, is Cluj in the late 1960s and early 1970s), and of having succeeded in immersing himself in his work, in developing new surgical procedures and diagnostic skills, in his teaching and publications. As a man nearing the end of a remarkable career, it might be supposed that Buzura has selected a protagonist as invulnerable as most to the destructive forces of class hatred, ideological opportunism, greed and envy.

But this is far from being the case with Cris who, at the opening of the novel, in a typically Buzurean moment of *ruptură* (psychic rupture), faces a crisis of conscience and consciousness. At a time when he is already showing signs of physical and moral collapse, with premonitions of impending death, when he is assailed by memories, the tyrannies of the past that take possession of the present and interrupt his normal professional activities, he has to deal with the reappearance of Redman, a man who was once a close friend but who had betrayed him and participated in his torture and degradation. And the telling symbolism of the names (Cristian/Redman) of these antagonists hardly needs to be underlined. What is more surprising is that their significance should have escaped the eyes of state censorship, the watchdogs of party and leader! Buzura's approach is tantamount to shock therapy; he sets off a psychological time-bomb in order to trigger long-suppressed emotional trauma. What Cris finds when he attempts to probe the labyrinthine edifice of his consciousness, with its many barred doors and windows, is that such an explanation is not amenable to rational thinking and scientific determination. But then, as Kundera points out, the paradoxical nature of human action is one of the novel's great discoveries: 'Between the act and himself, a chasm opens.'[16] Once more Cris must climb the barricades and face down his accusers. He must abandon the moral reclusion in which he has lived since his wife's death, the secure world of professional accomplishment and clinical detachment, and come to terms with his feelings of inadequacy, with self-doubt, above all with the broken promises and lost opportunities of his relationship with Stela, his wife, and Andrei, his son.

In his exploration of the past, Cris' imperfect memory is at times aided, at times thwarted or misdirected, by Redman's own recollections and insinuations. The peculiar challenge of *Pride* is that Buzura fragments the narrative voice, introducing not only monologues addressed by Redman to Andrei, but also the demented contributions of an anonymous informer whose self-appointed role it is to spy on Cris and report suspicious activities to higher authorities. With Redman, history repeats itself, once again Cris finds himself in a triangular situation where Stendhal's three triangular desires ('envy, hatred, and jealousy') or *ressentiment* in the erotic sphere might be applied to the peculiar, perverted relationship between Cris, Redman, and Stela in an anterior life, and between Cris, Redman, and Andrei in this one.[17] Bent on psychological domination and personal revenge, Redman exploits the many fissures and cracks in a father's relationship with his son in order to destroy the man who in earlier years was his rival for the hand of Stela.

In fact, Cris faces the dilemma that confronts any man whose private loyalties or whose personal and professional principles conflict with the laws and demands of society at a given time and place. Marin Preda in his novel *The Intruder* (*Intrusul*),[18] published as early as 1970, used a similar incident to crystallise the challenge posed by the conflict of irreconcilable principles. Just as Cris had risked all by insisting on treating a wounded anti-Communist partisan, so there too the protagonist, in an act of apparent heroism, placed in jeopardy his career, his position in society, and ultimately the affection of his wife in order to save a man who was deemed not worth saving. Henceforth the world was to be divided, a strange new hierarchy in a socialist society, between those predestined for salvation and those not.

In this series of revelations by Redman, a certain ambiguity prevails, for even if we are unable to accept at face value all of Redman's protestations, in some measure the actions and thoughts of Cris, let alone those of the other participants in the drama, are cloaked in silence and mystery and may have a meaning that is not totally clear even to those most intimately involved. A typical situation in Buzura's work is to have the guilty and the innocent, the interrogator and his victim, the torturer and the tortured, share their mutual experiences, confess to each other their most intimate thoughts and feelings so that they themselves may have a better understanding of what they were and what they did. They are the sort of conversations heretics must have had with their inquisitors before being consigned to the flames. At times, as we have seen with the anguished attempts of holocaust survivors to understand their destiny, the process may be cathartic, at other times, it leads to suicide or insanity, but an ultimate, definitive explanation always escapes the interlocutors. It is the nightmarish world of Kafka in which the faceless bureaucrats in the Castle are empowered to voice their own doubts and misery. The tragic-comic effects of self-incrimination, what Kundera calls 'the horror of the comic', yields to a melancholic awareness of human failure, but not of human limitation.[19]

The experience of arrest, interrogation, and detention gave Cris a profound understanding of the human condition: this awesome increase in knowledge is suggested metaphorically by the comparison Redman draws between Cris' eyes *before* arrest (his pupils were mere pinpricks because of the effort of peering through a microscope) and *after* arrest (his eyes grew enormous and a strange light shone in them, as though from another world); in effect his eyes now took on the function of the same microscope, which is to reveal to other human minds that which would otherwise remain invisible or misunderstood. Despite the demiurgic impulse and the moment of hubris that may afflict any privileged creator, this too is the function of literature. We should not forget that Buzura prefaces *Pride* with a citation from Camus: 'When detail is the life of a man, it represents for me the whole world and all history.'

A chance remark by Varlaam, the security agent most directly responsible for Cris' mistreatment, underlines the microstructural and macrostructural elements in this complex interweaving of family and ethics, individual exigency and collective imperative – what Kundera refers to as 'the appeal of time'[20] : 'We have both in larger outlines approximately the same goal. You seek the health of man, I do the same for society' – thereby drawing a glib but fascinating parallel between the aims and techniques of a physician and those of an interrogator-torturer.[21] But it is Cris himself who draws the clearer distinction: 'There exists a sort of transmissible cancer . . . the most dangerous sort, whose etiology has been known for thousands of years, and another unknown cancer, which merely destroys a single organism, and with this one, as with the first, we are perhaps fighting in vain, for the moment in vain.'[22] Kundera describes this eruption of history into the personal in this way: 'The period of *terminal paradoxes* incites the novelist to broaden the time issue beyond the Proustian problem of personal memory to the enigma of collective time, the time of Europe, Europe looking back on its past, weighing up its history like an old man seeing his whole life in a single moment.'[23] Cris is both a character with a clearly delineated personal (his) story, but also the embodiment of a Transylvanian ethos that has its roots in the ethnic and religious pride of the *The Transylvanian School* (*Şcoala ardeleană*), an educational reform movement going back two centuries or more and which was instrumental in preparing the way for independence after the First World War. Cris fails to save his wife. She dies from cancer. Perhaps on a metaphorical level the cancer that ultimately destroys her is the social disease of class enmity and dissension and the attempted desacralisation of family bonds. And it is an awareness of this condition, with its tentacles spread beyond the limits of any one mind or of any one epoch, that Cris voices in the name of humanity.

Redman's basic accusation, it would seem, is that Cris is not *un om politic* (a political being), that he did not swim with the tide, bending his head before the uplifted sword, adapting his ideological position to changing conditions, but that he struck out on his own, undertaking the task, with obsessive pride, of combating cancer and, at the same time, failing to see what consequences his indifference to politics might have on the lives of his wife and son.[24] It gradually emerges, however, that while Cris may be justly accused of turning a blind eye on the jockeying for power at the local level he does not stand condemned of indifference or complacency in the terms Redman advances. Cris' failure, a moral rather than a professional failure, is that he refused to acknowledge that one totalitarian system was replacing another, and that ultimately the cancer he was working to overcome in the bodies of individual men and women was merely a symptom of a far more dangerous and far more widespread system, a cancer that has affected man's spiritual condition and destroyed all hope of a normal life wherever it has made its presence felt.

In leaving his secure professional world and venturing once again into the political arena – to renew the battle against the menace of spiritual cancer that he, and only he in the view of his son, has a chance of eradicating – Professor Cristian accepts his past and becomes a more complete human being, free to bare his soul and reach out to his son and friends for understanding and compassion.

Eugen Simion has written that in his first novel, *The Absent Ones* (*Absenţii*), Buzura 'has assimilated intelligently *the confusion of planes of reality*, analysis within analysis, direct discourse and free indirect discourse, the automatism of thought, the juxtaposition of dialogues, in order to suggest the intermittent, capricious flow of rapid, penetrating and disorganised thought.'[25] Thus Buzura continues and builds on the Central European and American tradition of Modernism. What is true of *The Absent Ones* is no less true of *The Refugees*.

The Refugees too starts on a similar moment of crisis – only that here there is no immediate illumination and lucidity, following the fragmentation of consciousness. Instead, we observe Ioana Olaru, the protagonist, in her fumbling, confused attempts to come to terms with reality. We discover, as she does, that she was brought to a psychiatric hospital late at night, by persons unknown, in a state of virtual collapse. The point of departure in the novel is her partial recovery of consciousness, though she is still under sedation and suffering from temporary amnesia.

Buzura has chosen a woman of intelligence and education as his first 'heroine'. But Ioana is also naïve, trusting, easily deceived, quite unable to come to terms with life as it really is. She lives her life on two separate planes: 'In fact, which is my real life, the one from within, the one of illusions, nostalgias, fulfilments of thoughts, or the one that I live outside, mechanically.'[26] The impression is left that Ioana has never really been in control of her own destiny; she allows others to dictate the terms under which she should live and all too often she places herself in situations from which there is literally no escape.

Yet Ioana's sense of loneliness and despair, her inability to resist the demands society makes upon her, her sense of inadequacy, purposelessness and mortification may go beyond the personal. It may stand for a wider malaise, that same social cancer we saw affecting society in *Pride*, and which pervades in one form or another every novel written by Preda, Buzura and Breban. It is instructive that Buzura chose to employ a female protagonist only when his vision embraced contemporary society. We have seen how male protagonists are closely linked to philosophical, historical and socio-political issues. In writing about conditions immediately prior to the December 1989 revolution, perhaps Buzura felt himself on safer ground with a female character such as Ioana who has no past of social or political commitment with which to confront the present. Even so, this novel, the last he published before the overthrow of the Ceauşescu regime, was not withdrawn by the authorities without good reason. One consideration certainly was the savagely brutal and harshly ironic figure of Socoliuc, the mayor and party potentate of Măgura, whose portrayal may have struck too close to home for some among the party leadership. But the figure of Ioana, forced to seek shelter in a mental asylum, also represents the lot of women in

Romania until a few months ago, forced to do double duty as wife/ mother and fellow worker, hounded by officialdom for their reluctance to bear children when the very necessities of life were lacking. We shall have to wait until the appearance of further volumes in this projected cycle of novels to see whether Ioana will be given the chance to fulfil her independent destiny.[27] The implication of Ioana, free at last from therapy, humiliation and social constraint, as a prefigurement of Romania's rebirth is hardly one that will escape many readers.

In a passage from *The Art of the Novel*, Kundera defines Broch's use of the word 'polyhistorical' as 'marshalling all intellectual means and all poetic forms to illuminate "what the novel alone can discover": man's being.'[28] Such a view may go a long way to explain the peculiar position of the Romanian novel over the last fifteen years or so, as beacon, rallying-point, votive lamp, and implacable opponent of the totalitarian spirit. But we should do well to remember, with Kundera, that 'the importance of this [so-called dissident] art does not lie in the fact that it accuses this or that political regime, but in the fact that, on the strength of social and human experience of a kind people . . . here [in the West] cannot even imagine, *it offers new testimony about the human condition.*'[29]

Potentially there seem to be two limiting factors. The first is the role of state censorship and Party control in restricting avenues of exploration because 'totalitarian truth excludes relativity, doubt, questioning.' The second is the apparent failure of Romanian culture, in its backward, Little-World, antediluvian state, to keep abreast of developments in Western art and culture. Marin Preda, as we have seen, describes the various stages of estrangement (of man with his philosophical under-pinnings, with his literature and history, the very lifeblood of a nation, with his commerce and industry, buildings and architecture, law and justice), an estrangement which, if followed through to its logical conclusion – and we perhaps see its results today in the 85 per cent of the Romanian population that voted for *no change* in the status quo – leads to a state of almost total dehumanisation. The point, however, is that Preda, perhaps because of his immense prestige, perhaps because there were sympathisers working behind the scenes, was able to describe this process and give his fellow countrymen (those at least able and willing to read what he had written in his final *témoignage*) the chance to examine their own conscience. His vast novel, like those of Buzura and Breban, embodies 'the spirit of complexity', which is one of Kundera's essential criteria for the novel as a living force.[30] In its layers of ambiguity, confusion of planes of reality, fragmented narrative voice, in the intrusion of historical events and personages (so characteristic of the postmodernist novel in the West), in the ironical juxtapositions of history and individual stories, in its relentless pursuit of concrete detail, it struggles to free itself from ideological contamination, sometimes with great clarity and eloquence, always with honesty, at other times by parodying the twisted, tormented language of official double-speak.

Preda, no less than Buzura, living in a world in which every thought, word or deed might be interpreted as a lie, as deception or prevarication, as betrayal, had the courage to express that *wisdom of uncertainty* that Kundera imperiously demands of literature if it is to be a living force.[31] And yet, paradoxically, still battling with man's 'innate and irrepressible desire to judge before he understands', his 'inability to tolerate the essential relativity of things human',[32] Preda continues his search for meaning, for the restitution of cherished but long-lost precepts, and his voice claiming on the last page of *Most Beloved of Native Sons* that '*dacă dragostea nu-e, nimic nu-e*' (if love doesn't exist, nothing exists) echoes the 'why' on the lips of countless innocent victims, above all in Christ's temporary wavering before submission to death on the cross.

If participation in 'the sequence of discoveries that constitute the history of the European novel' is a necessary precondition for validation, then we must admit to a few reservations. The contemporary Romanian novel only intersects on occasions with the European novel in its Central European (Kafka-based) format; mostly, it evolves independently. There are parallels and points of intersection, as one might expect, but the Romanian novel primarily maintains its own sequence of discoveries and draws on its own experiences and its own deep reservoir of myth and symbol.

The Romanian novel, however, does meet another of Kundera's criteria, 'the spirit of continuity'.[33] It is here that Romanian writers such as Preda, Buzura and Breban have left their deepest imprint. I would argue that one of the saving features of the contemporary Romanian novel, perhaps of Romanian art and culture at large, is that it stubbornly resists, to cite Kundera once more, any 'eschatological belief . . . that one History ends and another (better) one begins, founded on an entirely new basis.'[34] Victor Petrini, Ion Cristian, and to a lesser extent Ioana Olaru, are created characters of great persuasion, yet they also seem to embody those millennial virtues (and defects) that have served the Romanian people so well in their fight for survival. In the atmosphere of social and cultural genocide that existed in Romania until December 1989, literature alone seemed to offer a way out of the ontological labyrinth in which men and women were (and perhaps still are) trapped. In their examination of hearts and minds, these three novelists point the way to a society free of ideological constraints, capable of passing beyond the limitations of bourgeois (and perhaps socialist) experience without trampling on its memory.

Notes

1. 'The Novel and Europe,' *New York Review of Books*, XXXI, 12, 19 July 1984, pp. 15–19
2. *The Art of the Novel*, translated from the French by Linda Asher (New York: Grove Press, 1988) p. 6. All subsequent citations are from this edition, henceforth referred to as *Art*.
3. *The Royal Hunt*, translated by J.E. Cotrell and M. Bogdan (Columbus: The Ohio State University, 1985). The review in question by Raymond Rosenthal appeared in *The New York Times Book Review* on 3 November 1985.
4. *Art*, p.14.
5. *Art*, p.18.
6. An issue discussed from various viewpoints in the first ten chapters of *Between Socrates and Xanthippe* (*Intre Socrate şi Xantipa*) (Bucharest: Editura Eminescu, 1973).
7. See in particular his *The Bacchic End* (*Sfîrşitul bahic*) (Bucharest: Cartea Românească, 1973).
8. Although Nicolae Labiş died in 1956 at the youthful age of 21, he was a powerful inspiration for many of his generation. The phrase is taken from his third voloume of poems, *Struggle with Inertia* (*Lupta cu inerţia*), published posthumously in Bucharest in 1958.
9. *Man as an End; A Defence of Humanism. Literary, Social and Political Essays*, translated from the Italian by Bernard Wall (New York: The Noonday Press, 1966) p.17.
10. *Drumul la zid* (Bucharest: Cartea Românească, 1984).
11. *Zalmoxis: The Vanishing God. Comparative Studies in the Religions and Folklore of Dacia and Eastern Europe*, translated by Willard R. Trask (Chicago and London: University of Chicago Press, 1972) pp. 253–56.
12. *Refugii* (Bucharest: Cartea Românească 1984).
13. *Cel mai iubit dintre pamînteni*, vols 1–3 (Bucharest: Cartea Românească, 1980). All subsequent citations are from this edition.
14. The exact context of this quote is as follows: 'No, I had no taste for learning the forms of deceit and dissembling open to thought so as to create for myself the illusion of remaining free when I made the decision to publish a text whose stupidity I was fully aware of'), my italics, *Cel mai iubit*, II, p. 199.

15. *Orgolii* (Cluj: Editura Dacia, 1974). The translation of the titles of Buzura's novels presents special, often insurmountable problems, since by using the plural forms of words normally used only in the singular he is trying to suggest the ambiguity and relativity of certain concepts. Thus the title *Orgolii*, with its implicit meaning of levels and categories of pride, not only distinguishes between Old and New Testament readings, but demonstrates that what is tenacity, resolution and stubborness in one person may seem arrogance or hubris to others.

16. *Art*, p.24

17. René Girard, *Deceit, Desire, and the Novel; Self and Other in Literary Structure*, translated by Yvonne Freecer, (Baltimore: Johns Hopkins Press, 1965) pp. 11–14.

18. *Intrusul*, 2nd ed. (Bucharest: Editura Eminescu, 1970).

19. *Art*, p.104.

20. *Art*, p. 16.

21. *Orgolii*, p. 254.

22. *Orgolii*, p. 182.

23. *Art*, p. 16.

24. According to some people, the necessity to compromise and temporise, is an attitude firmly set in the Romanian mind and in historical precedent; the proverb '*capul ce se pleacă, sabia nu-l taie*' (the sword does not cut off the head bowed before it) gives a more succinct and pithy form to the advice Ştefan cel Mare, on his deathbed, gave to his successor, his son Bogdan, that it was better to yield to the Turks than enflame their passions, much as a wise sailor would not set sail in the teeth of a gale – see Dimitrie Cantemir's *History of the Ottoman Empire* (in the antiquated translation of Ios Hodosiu, Bucharest, 1876, p. 272).

25. *Scriitori români de azi*, I, 2nd edition revised and expanded (Bucharest: Cartea Românească, 1978) p. 489.

26. *Refugii*, p. 50.

27. Buzura has named this cycle *The Wall of Death* (*Zidul morţii*). *Refugii* (1984) was the first volume published. A second volume *The Road of Ashes* (*Drumul cenuşii*) appeared at the end of 1989 but was not available at the time this study was prepared. At least one section of the third volume has already appeared in the literary press in Romania: *The Way of the Blind* (*Calea orbilor*), *România literară*, XXIII, 16, 19 April 1990, pp. 14–15.

28. *Art*, p. 64.

29. 'Comedy is everywhere,' *Index on Censorship*, VI, 6, Nov–Dec 1977, p. 6.

30. *Art*, p. 18.

31. *Art*, p.7.

32. *Art*, p.7.

33. *Art*, p. 18.

34. *Art*, p. 67.

9 The Dilemmas of the Modern Bulgarian Woman in Blaga Dimitrova's novel *Litze*

Elka Agoston-Nikolova

In this essay an attempt is made at sketching a few governing principles in Blaga Dimitrova's work. We shall look particularly at those elements which can be defined as *feminine* in Blaga Dimitrova's novel *Litze*.[1]

In the last decades an extensive range of studies has been conducted on the subject of women's writing in Western Europe and the United States: the study of '*écriture féminine [feminine écriture] écriture du corps*';[2] the question of gender of the artistic text;[3] postmodernist theories on intertextuality.[4] All of these studies stress the ideological nature of meaning and knowledge and see the feminine element as *marginal* as opposed to *central*. Julia Kristeva[5] defines totalitarian systems in terms of the opposition:[5]

male	–	linear, dogmatic
female	–	circular, subconscious

However, very little of these theories has ever been discussed in literary criticism in Eastern Europe. The cultural and political situation clearly imposes a different assessment of male/female relationships. When on a recent visit to the University of California at Berkeley, Elena Bonner was asked what role women have played in the struggle for freedom, she answered:

> You know our country is on such a low socio-economic level that at the moment we cannot afford to divide ourselves into 'us women' and 'us men'. We share a common struggle for democracy, a struggle to feed the country.[6]

This problem is expressed in women's writing in Bulgaria as well and it seems that where the stress lies on the struggle of the individual against

74

the totalitarian system, sex differences play a minor role. On the other hand, outside the political struggle women writers have raised their voices for recognition of women's plight within the still very strong patriarchal family tradition. The official theory is that women in Eastern Europe are emancipated, equal to men, making their careers in the public life of their country. But the truth is that women have been saddled with a double role – on the one hand the economic necessity for a second income in the family, on the other the patriarchal tradition which expects a woman to be a good mother, excellent cook and fervent housewife.

In Bulgaria there is also a struggle going on for the freedom of the individual (male or female) from the suffocating dogma of the totalitarian system and a struggle for a new meaningful language in literature. For a long time much of the literature produced was stilted and dull, because of a lack of personal involvement by many authors and a general vagueness of literary types. Refuge was sought in 'safe' historical, criminal, or fantastic themes.

Blaga Dimitrova's novel *Litze* was written in 1977 and published in 1981 in a period of relative liberalisation in Bulgarian culture. Very soon afterwards the book disappeared from the bookshops and Blaga Dimitrova saw herself isolated, banned from public life. She continued to think and work as a courageous and honest person and nowadays in post-November 1989 Bulgaria she is an active advocate of democracy.

The title page of the novel shows a woman's head, but there is no face, just a blank space where thunderstorms rage. The double meaning of the word *'litze' – person* and *face* – symbolises a woman searching for her face, her identity. It is in a way a rite of passage, which is a painful and difficult transition: from blindness and withdrawal, to a new identity – open-minded and brave.

The main character, Bora Najdenova, is a woman of considerable social and personal integrity. In the past she has been a resistance fighter against fascism. After the death of her beloved, she maintained the Communist ideals of her youth for a new and just society. She has become a lecturer in Marxist theory at the University of Sofia and slowly and unobtrusively has turned into a dogmatist, separated, divorced from reality. Every evening she retreats to her tiny apartment, which is described as a 'monk's cell', where she relives the past.

An extraordinary and stormy meeting one evening with a student whose expulsion from the university she voted for, changes her life. On learning that he is also left without anywhere to live, she invites him to share her apartment until he finds something else. She is thus forced to listen to someone who represents the extreme opposite of her own status – that of the politically unreliable, those to whom all roads are closed. His bitter criticism makes her listen and try to find out whether there is any truth in his allegations.

Gradually Bora realises that she has seen only what she wanted to see and her eyes begin to open to a society in which young people are bitter, sarcastic and materialistic. There are no ideals, no moral principles and there is no honesty. When she begins a sociological inquiry among her students and asks them what is of greatest value in their lives, she is confronted with an impenetrable wall of sarcasm and indifference:

'The greatest value? We have had no instructions about this!'
'Can't you answer without instructions?'
'We may make a mistake.' (p. 167)

Bora feels defeated, 'I have no common language with them.' (p. 168) Blaga Dimitrova's characters are constantly faced with an inability to make themselves understood. Communication is difficult. Many words are devoid of any meaning. One does not hear them. 'Words, words, words. They don't get through to you. You don't even hear them.' (p. 169) Bora makes a brave attempt to break through the language barrier, which she calls a 'curtain of words' (p. 169). Between her and her students, between her and the man she is trying to help, there is a wall, because for a long time words have been misused and have lost their meaning.

This failure to communicate has been noted in studies on women's literature.[7] Texts written by women often express this failure while at the same time ways are sought to create new means of expression. Julia Kristeva in '*La femme, ce n'est jamais ça*' sees the feminine behind the words created by ideologies, as that which cannot be expressed by such words:

J'entends donc par 'femme' ce qui ne se représente pas, ce qui ne se dit pas, ce qui reste en dehors des nominations et des idéologies.[8]

Blaga Dimitrova's attempt to go beyond the words introduces a third presence into the narrative, an intuitive one, beyond time and space, a *rubber plant*, present from the start in Bora's apartment. This structural device allows the author to introduce an inner language, a current of emotions which marks with precision the emotional charges in the atmosphere. It is the missing link with nature, the biological rhythm which affects the characters, induces certain thoughts or feelings and in its turn is profoundly affected by them. The man and the woman are part of a greater reality, in touch with a cosmic force. A new poetic language is introduced by means of the rubber plant. Maybe it will succeed in inducing the characters 'to plunge into the well of the soul' (p. 70), to reach 'inner illumination by the light of the cosmos' (p. 232), 'to learn by means of touch, feeling, meditation, silence, bliss. Maybe it will save the individual or will be destroyed by him' (p. 589).

Bora Najdenova and Kiril Argirov, her uncomfortable room-mate, share a common obsession with the past. Their present is dominated by a powerful drama in the past. Time as an artistic category is circular – the past invades the present and memory plays a subversive role. In Bora's case, it reverts back consciously or unconsciously (most often in her sleep) to an idealised past; her memories prevent her from living in the present and prevent her from properly assessing it. For Kiril, the past carries a double weight. First as a traumatic experience of the individual's failure to change the course of events and the guilt that follows afterwards, and secondly as the weight society places on the individual's participation or non-participation in the past. Both Kiril and Bora are burdened by the past. Both rediscover the present and experience love as a painful road, as the revelation that there is no escape from the individual responsibility or guilt. For Kiril, it is his feeling of guilt that, as a nineteen-year old cadet, he took part in an execution, while for Bora it is the revelation that she carries guilt also for her long years of blindness, conscious or unconscious.

> We are all guilty. Every one of us bears a burden of guilt. And each one of us participates personally in the common guilt. (p. 586)

At the end of the narrative, time has made a complete circle. Again it is evening, dark outside, again Bora feels tired as on that first evening of their meeting. Has everything been a dream? (p. 586)

For the heroine there exists no line between the present and the past. One moment she is typing a report on her typewriter, the next moment she is sitting in an attic room, she is young and she feels cold (pp. 57–60).

Time as a category in Blaga Dimitrova's work is always the all-embracing time where past and present intermingle. Even a simple object like a watch is not just an object, but as the watch of her beloved, although it belongs to the past, it is carried into the present. And each time Bora and Kiril look at it, the past invades their thoughts and emotions.

Time is not a linear denomination of movement and growth, but an emotional experience. Julia Kristeva speaks of this emotional time as a woman's unique way of experiencing time:

> *Le temps des femmes est un temps purement affectif, qui déforme sans cesse les structures et les découpages pré-établis.*[9]

But it is also because of the 'living' past that Bora begins a search for the truth, which in its turn will transform her into a new person. This new attitude to life and society affects her social position. In a degrading public meeting of the faculty, she is criticised and expelled from the Party. This will inevitably lead to the loss of her teaching position.

> And now – the living death . . . Sentenced by one's own kind to be buried alive in non-existence . . . not to be oneself, to take off one's face and to exchange it for a blank.
> Better so, than to have a tarnished face. (p. 463)

This 'death' in her present situation is the next step in the rite of passage, which Bora is going through.

The totalitarian system with its systematic refusal to respect the privacy of the individual, has created its own rites. Integration and acceptance are prerequisites for a 'normal' existence. Blaga Dimitrova's struggle to go beyond the limits set by society has created in the fictional plight of Bora Najdenova a possibility for the individual to be born again with a new face. The process she is going through can be called a *separation rite*.

Arnold van Gennep designated the periods of abrupt change in the life cycle of the individual, the life-crises, as *rites of passage*, consisting of three major phases: separation, transition and incorporation.[10] Modern societies may have reduced the ritual element in the rites, or may have changed the ceremonies, but they have created new rituals for the integration of the individual into the social life of the community. These rituals impress upon the individual the need, after an approved period of apprenticeship, to become 'worthy' of membership. One can mention in this connection the Pioneer's entrance ritual, the entrance into the Komsomol organisation and the much less accessible membership of the Communist Party – the gateway to privileged life.

The aversion of many individuals to this collective form of existence, the usurpation of their private thoughts, has created under totalitarian systems a new 'rite of passage' – the conscious desire to disintegrate in order to become free. Bora Najdenova goes through three stages of passage:

1. *separation* – From doubt and disbelief to horror at the truth about the system she has supported. She feels separated from her students whose masked indifference, tough jargon and materialistic attitudes shock her. She leaves Sofia and goes on a *journey*, to check on some facts. (pp. 187–234)

2. *transition* – For days on end she lives in a delirium of fever, dreams of the past and nightmares of the present follow each other, while she is oblivious of the passage of time.

3. *separation from the collective (rebirth)* – When she recovers from her illness, Bora is a new person. The spring air fills the room with freshness. Everything seems to have assumed a new form. The man and woman feel this renewal with every cell in their bodies. The rubber plant assimilates and translates all these impulses:

> Against all diseases of the age, against murder, violence, indifference, suspicion, estrangement, against all recklessness and destruction – love rebels. (p. 487)

But Bora and Kiril's love is burdened with an emotional trauma from the past. Ostracised by their colleagues and acquaintances because of their critical and unorthodox behaviour, how long can they stand the isolation? They experience a short period of great tenderness and closeness and then part – each to go their own way. Between them is the past, between them is the system. Who is responsible, who is to be blamed? It is Bora Najdenova who voices the final theme of the novel:

> Everybody carries responsibility for everything. With participation or without participation. Until this is understood, we will not be human beings. And society will be just a collection of beasts, not a human community. (p. 579)

They part, each one to go their own way, each one determined to look at the truth 'without a blindfold' (p. 587). Although the lovers part, the end of the novel is not tragic, because Bora and Kiril will continue to live as human beings, will carry bravely their individual guilt, looking *at* the truth and looking *for* the truth.

Bora Najdenova is not the only female character in the novel. In her search for the truth, she comes in contact with many other women: colleagues, friends, students. Blaga Dimitrova offers in *Litze* a realistic, critical picture of the everyday life of the Bulgarian woman. As a student she is sarcastic, quick to see where her interests lie, 'emancipated young women with the mask of whores on their faces' (p. 164). In sharp contrast to these women, is the young student Kapka Rasheva – who is expelled from the university only because she didn't want to be the girlfriend of the Komsomol secretary of her group. This event nearly ruins her whole life. Quite a different type is the journalist Emma – elegant, cruel, calculating Emma, choosing her men only if they are rich and influential. Emma, who hastens to destroy Bora's happiness by supplying the missing facts about Kiril's past. In the background, in the course of Bora's wanderings, there are many images of women – tired, defeated, de-feminised from long standing in queues after a day's work.

> But most women trudge along with knitted brow, deadbeat from the long round of shopping after the working day. She stares at their shapeless figures. These women are indifferent to their own appearance. At this moment they have forgotten that besides being beasts of burden, they are also women. (p. 426)

Bora Najdenova herself is different – idealistic, critical, a career woman dedicated to her teaching. In her love relationship with Kiril, there is a curious mixture of traditional behaviour and a reversal of roles:

> He is the supplicant, not humble, but bitter, ironic.
> She stands socially higher. She has the connections.
> When she falls ill, he is the nurse.
> She takes him to her apartment.
> But when they fall in love:
> He takes initiatives, protects her from the curiosity of her colleagues, brings her flowers.
> He is strong, muscular, tanned.
> She is the 'lonely woman' who finds 'refuge' in his arms. (p. 354)

Both are weak, both are strong. The traditional role patterns are disturbed. Both are in a state of transition.

Litze is not a comfortable book to be read by the fireplace. It is a shout, a protest. It ends by posing the question: *'Will they allow us to be ourselves?'* (p. 587)

Blaga Dimitrova as a person, writer and poet represents the new Bulgarian woman – critical, just, romantic, intuitive, with a strong sense of personal responsibility.

She raises her voice for the 'cruel silences' of so many generations of women, 'unsung, misunderstood' and together with 'the poets among the women' in her land intends to 'rend the air with a moan and a shout'.[11]

In conclusion: what is the *feminine* element in Blaga Dimitrova's work? This essay is just a preliminary study of what in the course of future research may grow as a systematic approach to Eastern European women's studies. Even at this early stage certain *feminine aspects*, as already defined in current women's studies, underline Blaga Dimitrova's critical preoccupation with women's lives:

1. The difficulty of communicating within the language of the system and the search for *new means of communication*, where intuition plays an important role.
2. A *different approach to the category of time: emotional time* seen as an ever revolving axis with no strict demarcation of past and present.
3. A 'rite of passage' involving separation from existing norms and restrictions in the search for a *new identity*.

But parallel to these elements, there is the interest in the individual's fate under a totalitarian regime. Blaga Dimitrova raises her voice for the individual's right for self-knowledge and personal integrity.

Notes

1. The quotations in this paper are from the 1981 edition of *Litze*, B'lgarski pisatel, Sofia. The Bulgarian word *'litze'* is not easy to translate within the context of this novel. It means both 'face' and 'person'. Translations of the fragments quoted are by the author of the present essay.
2. Mainly in the work of Hélène Cixous, *Writing Differences. Readings from the Seminar of Hélène Cixous*, ed. Susan Sellers (New York: Open University Press, 1988)
3. DeLauretis, T., *Technologies of Gender: Essays on Theory, Film and*

      Fiction (Bloomington: Indiana University Press, 1987).

4.   Hutcheon, L., *A Poetics of Postmodernism: History. Theory. Fiction* (London: Routledge, 1988).

5.   Kristeva, J., *Polylogue* (Paris: Editions du Seuil, 1977).

6.   Quoted from Elena Bonner's speech in Berkeley, 'On Gorbachev', in *The New York Review of Books*, May 17, 1990, pp. 14–17.

7.   Garcia, I., *Promenade Femmilière. Recherches sur l'écriture féminine* (Paris: Editions des Femmes, 1981).

8.   Kristeva, J., 'La femme ce n'est jamais ça', *Polylogue*, p. 519.

9.   Kristeva, *Des Chinoises* (Paris: Editions des Femmes, 1974) p. 40.

10.   Van Gennep, A., *Rites of Passage* (Chicago: University of Chicago Press, 1960).

11.   Quoted from 'The Women Who Are Poets in My Land', in Blaga Dimitrova, *Because the Sea is Black*, selected and translated by Nico Boris and Heather McHugh (Middletown: Wesleyan University Press, 1989) pp. 15–16.

10 Silk, Scissors, Garden, Ashes: The Autobiographical Writings of Irena Vrkljan and Danilo Kiš
Celia Hawkesworth

INTRODUCTION

In this essay I propose to examine points of similarity and difference between two volumes of autobiographical prose written in Serbo-Croat. *Garden, Ashes (Bašta, pepeo)* by the Serbian writer Danilo Kiš (1935–1990) first appeared in 1969, while *Silk, Scissors (Svila, škare)* by the Croatian writer Irena Vrkljan (b. 1930) was published in 1984. This twenty-year gap between the appearance of the two volumes is sufficient to account for much of the difference in tone. It may therefore appear that the basis for a comparison between the two works, stimulated by the similarity of their titles, is arbitrary. Nevertheless, the earlier work may be seen as throwing certain characteristic aspects of the later one into relief. It is the contention of this essay that some of the fundamental differences between the two works are conditioned as much by gender as by the date of publication, although to an extent the two are inseparable: Irena Vrkljan's work belongs to a body of work written by women in Europe in the 1970s and 80s from an explicitly personal, and consequently female, starting point.

I

It is the similarity between the titles that offers the initial stimulus for the comparison between these two works. Similarly constructed, the two-noun titles are equally suggestive and point to the essentially lyric quality of each work. From the notion of beauty and richness contained in the first word to the destruction in the second both convey a fundamental sense of loss which in each case underlies the whole work.

The 'garden' of Kiš's title may be seen as the archetypal garden of childhood, with all its associations of freshness, innocence and magic. The 'ash' expresses loss, but not the violence that would have been conveyed by 'flame'. It creates rather a soft, wistful atmosphere, and there is a sense in which, even in this lifeless form, ash endures. All of this is conveyed without reference to the specific content of the work, so that its general direction may be anticipated in advance.

Vrkljan's title conveys a similar contrast, but it does not stand on its own in the same way: the words can be fully understood only in relation to the incident to which they refer. In the work the bale of silk acquires a particular significance in that it seems to be one of the very few memories of the author's childhood that she seeks to preserve. It is a moment when the child seems to step into that magical, privileged world of Kiš's garden, where colours are brighter and textures richer than in adult life and where the subsequent sense of loss is the more poignant. The 'scissors' suggest an irrevocable, violent interruption, even without reference to the text. In the incident described, however, they represent not only destruction, but the constant presence of fear: of scissors poised forever over the magical sea-horse's severed head.

Nevertheless it would be inappropriate to lay too much emphasis on the two titles: Irena Vrkljan's was chosen for the Croatian edition by the editor. Characteristically, she had first published the work in Germany (where she lives for half of each year) with a factual title, devoid of mystification – *Tochter zwischen Süd und West*, 1982.

II

The titles simply provide a starting point; the works share several areas of common ground in their subject matter. These include: the rough chronology of each, where the war features as a mysterious dark background, impinging only indirectly and understood only in retrospect; the way other characters dominate the narrative at certain points; and the fact that each work may be broadly described as an account of awakening, including sexual awakening.

If the comparison has a more profound validity, however, it is in the notion of loss conveyed by the titles. For the works share an essential quality which may be defined as the underlying pain which gives each work its particular resonance.

In *Garden, Ashes* the sense of loss entailed in passing out of childhood cannot be disentangled from the child's loss of his father. To the child, the circumstances of his father's disappearance are mysterious. Too young to understand the events of the war and his Jewish father's arrest and imprisonment, the child is not psychologically convinced of his father's death. His sense of loss is not therefore acute as it might have been in the case of sudden death, but diluted by the constant possibility of return, particularly as his childhood was in any case punctuated by his father's unexplained temporary absences. Because of these circumstances, the figure of his father continues to haunt the narrator's adult life. The account of the child's experience is therefore shaped by an adult's more measured sense of loss, so that the text becomes increasingly coloured by an impulse to preserve not only the private childhood garden, but also an association with a remarkable individual.

This experience leaves the reader of *Garden, Ashes* with a sense of questions left unanswered, an open-endedness. The same quality also characterises *Silk, Scissors*, although in this case the unanswered questions are more generalised, not associated with any one figure or incident. The central pain of this work is similarly general, but with the crucial difference that it may be expressed more as an awakening into the reality of childhood as a nightmare rather than awakening out of its dream.

III

It is the nature of the differences between the two works, however, that is the focal point of this investigation.

Irena Vrkljan's account of her life is not confined to her childhood but continues on into adulthood, revealing the essential nature of the author's prose writing to date as a quest. Her purpose is fully to understand the nature of her experience of the world, past and present – for the present contains the past and cannot be separated from it. By contrast, Danilo Kiš looks back to childhood as to a finite, privileged land, now irrevocably lost.

Garden, Ashes may thus be seen as a more conventional work, belonging to a widespread genre of autobiographical evocations of the bright innocence of childhood. From the first scene, describing in minute detail the sensations of the child's being woken by his mother entering the room with the familiar tray clinking with the luxurious promise of refreshment in the warm comfort of his bed, the reader is drawn into the rich atmosphere of a child's ability to revel in individual moments for their own sake. One of the most compellingly attractive features of this work is the potent lyricism of its language:

> Without opening my eyes, I knew from the crystal tinkling of teaspoons against glasses that my mother had set down the tray for a moment and was moving toward the window, the picture of determination, to push the dark curtain aside. Then the room would come aglow in the dazzling light of the morning, and I would shut my eyes tightly as the spectrum alternated from yellow to blue to red. On her tray, with her jar of honey and her bottle of cod-liver oil, my mother carried to us the amber hues of sunny days, thick concentrates full of intoxicating aromas. The little jars and glasses were just samples, specimens of the new lands at which the foolish barge of our days would be putting ashore on those summer mornings. (pp. 3–4)[1]

Irena Vrkljan's work belongs to a different and less common strand of autobiographical writing: one that may be termed the account of a 'quest'. In this case the author looks back, not at all to conjure up scenes of the past for their own sake, but in an effort, which may be painful, to understand the present and how it was reached. Vrkljan's starting point and enduring impulse is a sense of dissatisfaction with existing categories and ready-made models. Her work may be seen as a study of the roots of this dissatisfaction, and consequently as focused on the sources of discomfort and constraint.

As in the case of Kiš, the essential nature of Vrkljan's earliest fragmented memories is emotional. But, unlike the associations of warmth and security conveyed by his account, the moments Vrkljan chooses to highlight are coloured by a sense of resentment. What are described are moments when the child begins to be aware of herself as an independent being. Gradually the fragments come to form the façade of a bourgeois childhood which is never accepted because it is associated always with notions of deceit and constraint. And this growing consciousness is inextricably connected with a growing awareness of powerlessness.

Looking back on her childhood, the author comments:

> What I see, I recognise, is not a haven. A child's body is a target full of holes through which pass rain, upbringing and rivalry.
>
> (Vrkljan, p. 74)[2]

Increasingly alert, she is anxious to avoid any of the comfort that may come from images: 'Pictures are also a flight from content. And they satiate in a terrible way.' (p. 74). This impulse may be seen as diametrically opposed to that of Kiš, whose prose brings individual moments alive in order the cherish the memory of a scene for its own sake.

An example of Vrkljan's rigorous refusal to be beguiled by pictures is her memory of the little yellow stick she had as a child. At Christmas – that time of archetypal magic in childhood – her father would attach a candle to it and use it to light the highest candles on the Christmas tree. But Vrkljan does not dwell on the potential charm of this moment of anticipation, light and joy: in the same breath, she tells us that for the rest of the year her father used this stick to beat her with. Another incident described involves a boisterous game with her father in which an accident left her with a scar. Later he would maintain that a servant had dropped her. And the adult looking back observes: 'Reality aroused anger in him.' (p. 76) In other words, the child's growing awareness of herself is bound up with an awareness of deceit. In turn this conscious-ness is inseparable from a sense of revolt, of refusal to accept the adults' terms, to go along with the elaborate construct of a bourgeois childhood and the role she is expected to play in it. One passage is a lengthy indictment of this role-playing:

I looked for Christmas presents in the cupboards, but I pretended that I still believed in Jesus coming to our house. That pleased my parents, I didn't want to be without that pleasure. I hated flowers in vases because they soon fade and smell bad, but I picked them and offered them sweetly to Mother. I didn't like going to the zoo, but I begged to be taken, it was all wrong somehow, I was unable to be what I really was, they didn't allow it. Perhaps childhood is often nothing but this game, the game of playing a child for your parents, your teachers, all grown-ups. . .

My parents, burdened by their day-to-day cares, never saw through those rituals. They couldn't have, I took painstaking care over everything, I knew clearly that I had to keep deceiving them, sitting on the floor, crying with a stupid teddy bear in my arms. I would pinch the cat in passing, I fell over, tore my dresses, I lied, stole biscuits, read love stories in secret, broke the teapot and never confessed, all of that corresponded to the image of a child, and they were all misdemeanours we commit because we are sitting in a prison, in the field of play of an old-fashioned family we are deceiving, which is deceiving us... (pp. 32–33)

Both works acknowledge the fragmented and selective nature of childhood memory, but in the case of Kiš all through the work we are more conscious of the shaping mind and conscious art of the adult. This difference in approach is conveyed in the authors' whole procedure as well as in detail. It may be illustrated by the account in each work of the narrator's first sexual awakening.

Vrkljan's description comes in a chapter entitled 'The Microscope'. The bewilderment and potential for heady charm of this experience is thus typically given concrete and ironic solidity in the mundane objects associated with the older boy as he works at his university assignments in the communal courtyard.

The account of sexual awakening in *Garden, Ashes* is far more elaborate, more of a 'set-piece' in the work. The girl in question attracts the adolescent narrator's attention because she is always just quicker than he is in answering questions in class. This arouses a latent 'hunter's' instinct in him and he resolves on 'conquest' as the only way to beat her. He may thus be seen to step easily into an established pattern of male pursuit and dominance. 'My every gesture, my every word becomes *cagey*, (p. 59) ['Calculated' would seem to be a more accurate translation-ed.] Once this ritual conquest is completed, the children face each other frankly and share in the process of physical exploration and discovery. While the episode is recounted with characteristic freshness, displaying something of the extravagant imagination which the narrator attributes elsewhere to his father, it draws readily on wide literary associations:

Relying on recent developments in aerostatics and aerodynamics and on the latest achievements in aircraft design [. . .], and counting on originality and shock effect, I built several airplanes, very original ones, with stabilisers on the tail and wings, with weaponry and all the rest. But I left the big surprise for the end – although the design itself, by its boldness and originality, was sufficient to astonish. My airplane, thanks to a little stabiliser skilfully camouflaged under the wing, was capable of landing on my shoulder. [. . .] I tossed the airplane up in the air. I had carefully installed all the instruments in advance, of course. The craft took off like a sea-gull, heading toward the light. And then, just as all the students were holding their breath, it changed direction in an abrupt and unexpected spasm, made a spectacular loop, almost grazed the window with its wing, made a turn around Julia's head like an amorous pigeon, and returned obediently to my shoulder. Before coming to a full stop after this dangerous and exciting flight, it shook its tail like a magpie and then stiffened, devoid of all its sublime traits, transformed by a magic wand into a bird without a sky, a swan without a lake. I stole a glance at Julia: at that instant, she was ready to give in, to submit to me. (pp. 59–60)

IV

In considering effect of the language and style of each volume, it may be said that the convention of giving the narrator of *Garden, Ashes* a fictionalised persona establishes the 'rules' for both author and reader. The work becomes a generalised statement about childhood as a finite landscape, within which the author is free to mix reality and fantasy, allowing scope for intense lyricism in the language. The evocative vigour of its language is the most striking feature of this work. It gives the impression of working 'outwards', of conjuring up, bubbling, effervescent, building on the outline of experience a rich, colourful landscape of emotion. Such a use of language is not an arbitrary indulgence, but legitimised by the author's intention to evoke the magic landscape of childhood:

The branches of the wild chestnut trees on our street reached out to touch each other. Vaults overgrown with ivy-like leafage thrust in between these tall arcades. On ordinary windless days, this whole architectural structure would stand motionless, solid in its daring. From time to time the sun would hurtle its futile rays through the dense leafage, these rays would quiver for a while before melting and dripping onto the Turkish cobblestones like liquid silver. We pass underneath these solemn arches, grave and deserted, and hurry down the arteries of the city. Silence is everywhere, the dignified solemnity of a holiday morning. (p. 4)

By contrast, the impression created by the equally carefully chosen language of *Silk, Scissors* is of paring down, stripping back to the essential, so that the central idea of the quest is expressed at every level of the text. Characteristically, the work begins with a thirteen-line synopsis, a bare summary of the content of the work and its impetus. There is no attempt to fictionalise: quite the contrary, as may be seen in the precise location of the author's father's grave. In this brief summary, as in the whole volume, only the key facts are given – those which contain meaning for the author. It is worth considering this passage in more detail as it is typical of the style of the whole work.

> My mother sits in a room on the fourth floor in Zagreb and cannot
> express her melancholy. My sisters live far from one another in their
> kitchens. Around them children shout, soups bubble on stoves. In
> Homburg, in Palmotić Street. The Partisan V. is dead, the Bosnian
> mountains abandoned. My father lies in Mirogoj cemetery, section
> nineteen, grave number four. A painter, a friend from the provinces,
> did not find his redemption.
>   Thirteen years of living in West Berlin. My friends in Charlotten-
> burg, in Steglitz. Claudio encouraged me, Benno made space on his
> desk. (p. 9)

For Vrkljan, the essential fact about her mother is that she cannot, and
could never, articulate what Vrkljan sees as the oppressive nature of her
role in bourgeois family life. What is most important about her sisters'
adult life is that they are far from one another, the remaining details
listed here characterise most women's lives, a pattern of life which
Vrkljan herself has rejected. The only facts mentioned about her father
contain the implicit regret that this is all that can be said of a whole
lifetime. The painter friend follows thoughts of her father because of
the important role he played in guiding her, father-like, out of
childhood into a world of new values. These concentrated statements
contain far more than they say and as such are typical of Vrkljan's
evocative but bare prose style.

The introduction of a change in style resulting from the inclusion of
letters from the author's two sisters giving their own version of important
events from their shared childhood does not interrupt the reading. It is
quite in keeping with the author's intention of discovery. On the one hand
this conforms with all Vrkljan's prose works which give an account of a
life inseparable from others, while on the other hand her sisters' versions
of their shared childhood may reveal aspects of which the author herself
was unaware. This is perhaps the opposite of the private world evoked by
Kiš and indeed by most conventional accounts of childhood, where the
main focus is the individual, unique, perception.

V

The evocative account of the luxurious warmth and protectiveness of
the childhood described in *Garden, Ashes* is bound up with the

nostalgic sense of its inevitable loss. Any potential sentimentality in the work is avoided in the way the narrative comes to be increasingly dominated by the figure of the child's father, whose extravagant nature and anarchic inventiveness are adequately conveyed in Kiš's language. These two closely related focal points of the narrative ensure its essential nature as a celebration. The memories are to be cherished as the rational, grey world of adulthood encroaches. But there is no conflict between the two phases of the narrator's life: the only questions raised concern the unsolved mystery of his lost father's whereabouts.

In the case of *Silk, Scissors*, however, the world of the child is seen as a deceptive construct of bourgeois convention. Her growing consciousness of her artificial role in this world cannot be separated from a sense of revolt, rejection and a desire to escape. What is both new in Vrkljan's work in the context of Serbian and Croatian literature and at the same time typical of much women's writing of her time is the fact that these emotions are crystallised in anger. On the one hand this toughness of tone is not conventionally associated with women, who are expected, like the portrayal of the mother in Kiš's work, to be tolerant, understanding and submissive. On the other, for all the specific, factual detail about Vrkljan's life her tone of voice speaks for all women.

The essential difference between these two works, conveyed at every level, from the events described to the language, is that, for all its freshness of style, Kiš's work traces a well-trodden path. The narrator cherishes the security of his childhood, certainly, and the mystery surrounding his father will drive Kiš to continue searching for this attractive figure through his writing in later works as well. Nevertheless, the work conveys a strong sense of the confidence with which it will be possible for the young man to emerge from the protection of childhood into an adult world in which he will have a role. The question of the narrator's gender is not highlighted because it is not an issue. There is an implicit assumption that the experience described traces a pattern generally applicable to all children, regardless of gender. In other words, the work reflects the familiar assumption that the experience of the male is the norm. By contrast, Vrkljan's work is explicitly the account of the experience of a female child. Once she has seen through the construct of childhood that convention seeks to impose on her, nothing is certain: she must fight to forge her own path and establish a pattern of behaviour for herself, which will correspond to her personal perception. This explains the tautness of the writing, the positive value attached to the notion of 'anger' and the conscious identification of the author with other women who have struggled to throw off the constraints of conventional expectations.

The dedication to *Silk, Scissors,* which follows immediately on from the synopsis quoted above and therefore implicitly includes the references to her mother and sisters' situation, illustrates the inclusive nature of Vrkljan's quest:

Virginia Woolf. Charlotte Salomon. Women who wish to escape from childhood. Against false submissiveness. For anger. And for remembrance.

Notes

1. The references are to *Garden, Ashes* translated by William J. Hannaher (London and Boston: Faber & Faber, 1985).
2. The references are to *O biografiji: Svila, škare, Marina* (Zagreb: Grafički zavod Hrvatske, 1987). The translations are my own. (C. H.)

11 Kazimiera Iłłakowiczówna: The Poet as a Witness of History, and of Double National Allegiance

Danuta Zamojska-Hutchins

Śpiewaj dales, słowiku, śpiewaj tylko dla mnie:
ja twą pieśń opowiem, ani slowa nie sklamię
przepiszę ją świeżą na czysto
pytająco, zapłakaną, perlistą
K. I. 'Slowik Litewski'

Sing on, oh nightingale, sing for me only:
I will tell your song, not a word shall I lie,
I will re-write it fresh, copy-clean
questioningly, in tears, pearly.
K. I. 'Lithuanian Nightingale'[1]

INTRODUCTION: THE POET AS WITNESS

In his programmatic work *The Witness of Poetry*[2] Czesław Miłosz reminds us that the poet is charged with the mission to bear witness to the events of history. Miłosz insists that even when nobody else is, the poet must be the conscience of a nation.

Long before Miłosz's observation Kazimiera Iłłakowiczówna carried this poetic mission through her life's work. Despite her ideological indebtedness to Piłsudski she has led us on a compassionate poetic odyssey through the occasionally grandiose, tragic, and pathetic events of Polish history. The ardour and lively lyrical detail of her imagery are typical of a native Pole. Her poetry, however, unlike her life, clearly divides her allegiance between Lithuania – the country of her birth, and

93

Poland – the country that nurtured her through her early years as an orphan. Her poetry is most fully alive when she whips up our conscience (even if the whips are made out of sand, like the familiar whip of Mr Twardowski in Mickiewicz's poem). In 'Sand' (*'Piach'*, 1928, p. 82) she suggests that whipping up our national conscience is also one of the poet's duties. In 'Look through clear eyes' (*'Spójrz czystymi oczyma'*, 1928, p. 72) she calls us to join her in fulfilling her duty and to witness 'the truth that was sold and crucified'. If we fail to hold onto our memories of our native land we perish, she warns in 'A warning', (*'Przestroga'*, 1928, p. 90). She realises that only when the words of the compelling poetic duty have become effective will she be able to 'depart into the background'.

Witnessing the recent history of Poland and Lithuania through her personal engagement in the government, described in her memoirs,[3] Iłłakowiczówna's life spanned two World Wars and three successive political systems. Born in 1892 in Vilnius, and raised in the *'kresy'*, or 'the outback' according to the manners and sensitivities of the two countries, she has paid homage to both of them in her poetry and prose. Her prose relates her personal account of the events of Piłsudski's rule. Her short stories instruct and inspire. Her poetry distils her perception of human nature, and of the fate of the people. Many of her poems and short stories address the young, including children. However, their message is intended for all the people, regardless of age. She dwells on the poetic detail of everyday life in the Polish and Lithuanian countryside, yet even her light, frivolous verses contain a lesson in the cultural and aesthetic values of their peoples. Her apparent focus on everyday life, and her frequent, almost formulaic, address to the young might explain the rather mystifying silence about her work in Czesław Miłosz' *The History of Polish Literature.*[4] It is unusual for Miłosz, who in birthright and spirit is her twin, to have passed her up in silence. One might wonder whether his disdain of patriotic sentiment, obvious in his recent memoirs, did not influence some of the choices and omissions in the critical assessment of the Polish literary heritage. The following excerpt from a 1987 entry in his 'Year of the Hunter' may serve as a justification of his silence:

Country, native land, nation: *les choses vagues*, things misty, as Paul Valéry used to call them; that means things which escape definition, too overloaded with emotional meanings. It is better, therefore, not to press the lid down on this realm. Suffice to note that things are not quite good, when belonging to a given nation is one's dominant characteristic. Valéry did not have to be preoccupied with France, nor did he have to even ponder what it means to be a Frenchman. Frenchness was the air he breathed. However, a Pole is above all a Pole, a Lithuanian is a Lithuanian, a Ukrainian is a Ukrainian. It is also curious that, when he wants to serve his nation with his intellect, with his pen, with his art, what he does is touched by a blemish, proportionate to his national zealousness.[5]

A BARD WITH A WILLOW REED IN THE SHADOW OF THE MARSHAL

The most frequent topics of Iłłakowiczówna's poetry reflect her concern with the fate of her nation. Universal, human concerns are second to these and appear chiefly in her later poems. Her poetic focus rests on her personal views, but her ideological dedication owes its impetus to her life-long friend and mentor, Marshal Joseph Piłsudski. Having grown up as 'a girl from a good home', in that old Polish tradition which valued a girl's poise and appearance more than her intellect and self-determination, Iłłakowiczówna could aspire to no more than a Cabinet post at the side of her beloved Marshal. She was eager to give up her life for his cause, but, when she offered to serve him as a soldier, she was politely told that her mind enhanced by her Oxford education was too precious to waste on a battlefield. Her social and political ideology owes as much to his guidance as it does to her undeniable eagerness to be guided by him. That aspect of her work and life was obviously disregarded by post-war Poland, and shrouded in silence by critics and friends alike, despite the opposing reasons which might have conditioned their silence.

A poem in the volume entitled 'Out of the House of Slavery' (*Z Domu Niewoli*) was dedicated to Piłsudski as a sign of the hope for freedom that she and the entire nation had attached to the rising new leader. It was he who was to lead them out of the house of slavery. The poem was written in 1914, but has not been reprinted in any of her post-war anthologies. Embittered by the Communist hatred of Piłsudski's memories the poet remembers her mentor in an intensely lyrical symbolic poem smuggled by Pawel Hertz into her 1977 volume of retrospective self-evaluations. The poem, entitled, 'A trace sprayed over by wormwood' ('*Zasypany piołunem ślad*', 1977, p. 268), pays homage to her 'mighty friend' through the folklore symbolism of the scenery she depicts in it. The path of this poet's memories softens the sound of her footsteps for it is covered, ash-like, by the tiny petals of the grey bitter herb used as an absinthe tonic and as a rare brandy in Polish folk remedies. The 'laurel leaves' due to the Marshal are thus symbolically fragmented and scattered over the fields, but instead of obliterating his memories, they shield his burial ground from intruders.

The eloquence of wormwood as a folkloric symbol is enhanced by other poems. In 'The Drought' (*'Susza'*, 1976, p. 64) from her volume 'Departure into the Background' she makes wormwood the only survivor in an enchanted, stark and lifeless world. In the same volume she is the sorceress announced in the title of another poem and enumerates herbs, animals, birds, dragon, snake, talking water, and tears amongst the insignia of her shamanic power. Empowered here as 'A witch' (*'Czarownica'*, 1976, p. 30), she resurrects the Marshal, and through her memories of his power, she promises in this poem's conclusion:

Your dream the first in the world in my place has its native land
and with me dwells the joy you have banished into alienation,
but if you come to me, having beguiled the armed guard,
then your own sleeping heart shall I in a small box show you.

Iłłakowiczówna's attempted poetic witchcraft demonstrates her subconscious response to the overwhelming power by which Piłsudski directed her ideas in inter-war Poland. In a poem from her 1928 volume, entitled 'In the shadow of greatness' (*'W cieniu wielkości'* p. 30), she has finally admitted that 'as if in a shadow of a great sycamore. . .I am growing in the shadow of a giant'. She feels then both stifled and empowered as she herself becomes the Marshal:

When I try on his armour,
a tide of miraculous power flows into me,
by another's is my arm victorious,
My eyes become a flash of the spirit,
in my heartbeat beats a might star!

Bewitched, she resolves to put on her leader's attire and, as she gazes into the vastness of his immense horizon, she asks for union with 'God's mighty, engulfing Breath'. Iłłakowiczówna is not alone in her frequent use of metempsychosis as a tool of poetic narrative. The same device had been used by her Polish contemporary, a woman poet and dramatist, Maria Pawlikowska-Jasnorzewska, and by another famous Slavic female bard Anna Akhmatova.[6]

The title poem in her cycle 'Three Strings' (*'Trzy Struny'*, 1971, p.

45) shows a bardic Homeric figure whose harp has only three strings
intact as a result of thunder, evocative of the wrath of Zeus. One is for
mourning, another for swearing vengeance, and the third one blows
across the fields in a gallop of ire. The third string, attired in a blood-
stained uniform, calls to arms. The synecdochic representation of the
bard in this poem is deliberate. It serves as an incentive to Polish and
Lithuanian youths to join Piłsudski's army and liberate the country. In
addition to inspiring patriotic feelings among her young countrymen
the bard is Iłłakowiczówna's poetic *alter ego*. Using a substitute self as
a bard, she has symbolically accomplished a self-offering for the
Marshal. Transformed, through metempsychosis, into a volatile steed,
she defies Piłsudski and ultimately wins by pen the battle denied to her
sword. Yet this symbolic defiance does not culminate in freeing herself
from his shadow. A vivid folkloric version of the harp in 'And this
Little Reed is of Green Willow' ('*A Ta Dudka z Zielonej Wierzbiny*',
1971, p. 48) reiterates the offer of self-sacrifice. The stark lyricism of
the amassed images of her plundered, outraged countryside evokes
feelings of anger, pain and shame. Each image culminates in a refrain,
formally appropriate for the folk reed. The green willow reed 'has one
tone only . . .'. It asks who shall be the avenger. The unstated
conclusion 'if not I' clearly addresses Piłsudski in this poem. However,
at that point her target shifts to the Russians. The title of this cycle
explains the juxtaposition of the two bardic figures in those two poems.
It echoes Felicjan Faleński's cycle 'Songs from the House of Enslavement' ('*Piosenki z Domu Niewoli*'), in which, as I have pointed out
elsewhere, this nineteenth century poet warns the Russian occupants:
'These people may forgive their own shame, but they will rise up to
avenge the wrongs done to their fathers'.[7] Iłłakowiczówna's poem, like
Faleński's, is directed against the Russians. They are identified as her
target also in her diary, as she recalls the circumstances surrounding her
work on these poems: 'With my collar-bone bruised by the gun's butt-
end I was writing an anthem for Joseph Piłsudski's army.'[8]

She continues sketching her poetic 'background' to national
memories in her cycle 'All the Souls Bells' ('*Dzwony Zaduszne*', 1971,
pp. 257–58). Written in 1917, and published in the same volume (pp.
257–58), it suggests the prayers which would be consonant with the
sounds of All Souls church bells. The prayers are offered for all the
glorious moments of Polish history: from the exploits of Władysław
Warneńczyk through the Polish participation in the Spring of the
Nations at the side of Garibaldi, to the campaign for Santo Domingo.
Iłłakowiczówna asks for our prayers:

For all who have fallen into ashes,
stamped out at the prime of their youth,
for our childhood in chains,
for our youth – in the tomb;

for the prisoners, who for years
as moles were blinded in the dungeons,
for the uprisers, bayonetted in the woods
lost on the gallows;

for the terrible right of enslavement
etched by shame on our souls.
for the wings broken in flight,
for the hearts shut up in our breast

for the song, that crawled in the dust
and had no power to rise.

While she also recalls Poland's past glory in her volumes, such as *Death of the Phoenix* ('*Śmierć Feniksa*, 1922), *The Fishcatch* (*Połów*, 1926) and in *Heroic Ballads* (*Ballady Bohaterskie*), the fourth poem of this cycle expresses hope for Poland's recovery. Iłłakowiczówna promises: 'and ours will be the Native land, and ours the will and the rule' (p. 56). These hopeful words stand out as rare inspiration, for few other poets dared to inspire Poles of that epoch. Iłłakowiczówna's poems are empowered by her eventual breaking away from the Marshal's political tutelage. She accomplishes it as she witnesses the split among his supporters. He dares to criticise all those who engage in personal vendettas that endanger the fate of her nation. Poem 'X' in this cycle issues a clear warning against domestic squabbles as Iłłakowiczówna reminds those who used to work for Piłsudski and turned against him that it is not proper to 'sink in our own bosom the knives forged for the knave.' The pupil becomes the sage in poem 'XI', as she continues her admonitions: instead of poisoning hearts with suspicions, we must carry the flame ignited by the holy blood of our martyrs, she concludes in poem 'XI'.

THE POET AS A FIGURE OF NIOBE: UNIVERSAL SENTIMENTS IN NATIONAL LAMENT

'The Vigil of Return', from 1917, invokes a deity. In this cycle the poet becomes a holy channel of supplication for her orphaned, homeless people. Eight poems of various metric length constitute the cycle. Iłłakowiczówna's supplications are humble and proud at the same time. She will go, her knees bleeding, to ask God's love and protection for her country, which, some tell her, is dead. She believes against all odds that through those who cherish the image of Poland, her country will be reborn:

> We have seen Thee aglow in the smoke of fires,
> the abandoning birds have cried out Thy name,
> and you were – like a giant vision in the clouds.
> Then turned into a silent mist, spreading far far away
> you went on as the essence of our souls, our blood, our flesh
> yes, you lived on as young Phoenix midst the ashes.
>
> (poem III, p. 171)

Should the poet be ever found guilty of treason, poem 'IV' is a plea for return, even if to judgement and scorn, nonetheless a return to her motherland. The poetic persona throughout the poem is masculine in gender. Promising to be 'the servant of Thy serfs', she becomes a male peasant: 'I am Thy peasant' (*jam Twym chłopem*). Poland's name appears in this poem only attributively: 'on Polish soil' (*na polskiej ziemi*). These structural devices broaden the referent. What might have sounded sentimentally chauvinistic gains a universal human perspective. Her refrain sounds a wailing note, not unlike the voices of Hebraic or Greek mourners, with the cadenzas reminiscent of Aida's aria '*O patria mia*':

> If I am guilty – those centuries-old
> voices of my kinsfolk may judge me,
> on Polish soil may the red hangman
> lift up my head by its hair!
> If I am guilty, may the plough furrow me,
> as my soul turns – a scar,
> may I be scorned – ash at Thy feet,
> Oh my Native land, my Native land!   (poem IV, pp. 172–173)

Figuratively the poet becomes an offering for her native land, her head is 'lifted off her body by a blood-stained hangman', then she is cremated, 'ash' at her country's feet. Note the power in the meaning of polysemous Polish '*proch*'; equivalent to three words in English: 'dust', 'ash', and 'gunpowder'.

A much longer poem, 'VI' (pp. 175–176), specifies Poland as the object of a prayer. In its form and context this poem is vaguely suggestive of Mickiewicz's invocation to Lithuania from his epic poem 'Pan Tadeusz'. Probably thanks to this resemblance, it, too, escapes the stigma of sentiment. Iłłakowiczówna's poem, like Mickiewicz's, is in thirteen-syllable rhymed verse. Her imagery echoes his rural pictures. Yet her landscape, unlike his, conveys sombre scenes of decay and desolation:

To the hamlets, where the thatch is crooked, the gates are broken,
to the homes, where rain pours in through the cracks
to the settlements and the mines, where wrong reigns. . .
oh, Poland. . .
Midst snow-drifts drowning on our way, by the last bit of strength
    propelled,
abandoned to the mercy of fate, ruled by chance,
we go – to share Thy white Vigil Wafer
oh, Poland!   (poem VI, p. 175)

The unusual delay of both the subject and the verbal component in this section of her poem amplifies its semantic possibilities. At first it seems to be a toast to the Polish countryside. However, the sombre scenery evoked in it would disqualify it as a toast-celebration, or as a joyous toast. The stanza that follows disambiguates the message: the Polish exiles appear in it as those who have always tried to return to their native land. Despite its decay and desolation they long to return there, just to be once again among their family and friends, and to gather at the Christmas Vigil table, to share with each other the traditional Polish Christmas Wafer.

Iłłakowiczówna strengthens the image of Poland as the country of one's desire in the next poem. Here she presents an image of details of the *Wigilja*, the most Polish of all the Christian customs. As the elaborate Christmas Vigil preparations are detailed, including the Blessed Wafer ceremony, one can perceive Iłłakowiczówna's double national allegiance in the mingling of the dishes, some of which are customarily from central Poland, while some are from the 'outback'.

She asks whether the hay will be placed under the table-cloth for the Vigil Supper, and whether there will be ground poppy seed. Both of these customs are typical of central Poland. She also asks, however, about the *kisiel*, which is a type of sour pudding, and she insists on the *kutja*. Both of these are from Lithuania.

In the final poem (p. 178) her poetic cadenzas again hark back to Mickiewicz, specifically to his 'Ode to Youth'. Again she invokes Poland, and hopes to be worthy of returning to her. In this poem the invoking persona is in the plural: 'we'. The plural, and lack of specific reference to Poland in the refrain, contribute to the breadth of referent. In it she embraces all the Polish people. Her imitation of Mickiewicz is deliberate. She corroborates our intuitive discovery of her poetic source in her diaries in which she admits to her fondness for the imitative mode.

The preceding four poems create a continuum: from the universally human loving embrace of one's native land Iłłakowiczówna turns to the specific love of Poland. In this manner, and through the inclusion of the detail from a Polish Christian ritual she places her contemporaries within the universal human context. She suggest, without openly stating it, that the specifically Polish national allegiance is a constituent of a general human allegiance to the concept of a nation. Through this unstated suggestion she achieves her poetic aim, expressed later in her poetic theory. Her theory reveals the aim: 'To express oneself so as to betray nothing of oneself, that is the aim of many beautiful and complex metaphors. (Sometimes, however, while carefully avoiding a specific topic, one may be able to outline it as clearly as does the Sun which does not shine through an object, but creates its shadow.')[9] Connecting her longing to return to her personal Poland of dual allegiance with the universal love of any native land one has lost, Iłłakowiczówna has realised her aim, her Platonic 'shadow effect', the art of understatement, which she learned from the British in her studies at Oxford.

THE COLOURS OF A NATION

Iłłakowiczówna's attachment to her native land continues to the end of her life. In her poems from the volume *Leafless poems* (*Wiersze bezlistne*) she resumes the topic in the December 1939 'Native land' ('*Ojczyzna*', 5, p. 268). The courage and power she wills her countrymen through that poem is because and in spite of the Nazi occupation of

Poland. The white lilac that springs out of the tears shed over the graves
of those who gave their lives for Poland mingles with 'their martyrs'
blood' and rises as a powerful image of the white and red, the Polish
national colours. (It is noteworthy to remember that not so long ago
Amy Lowell used the lilac to symbolise the national colours of the
United States).

Iłłakowiczówna raises the Polish banner again for courage in 'The
red and white' ('Czerwone i białe', 1977, p. 271). She promises in it:

> When the warm days will come
> after the first spring storm,
> I shall walk outside after the torrent
> magnified and triumphant,
> turned into a red and white rose.

In 'The March of General Bem' ('*Marsz Bema*', 1977, p. 276) she
points out again that history is our conscience and we must keep it
alive. 'The Grave of a Polish Soldier' ('*Grób polskiego żołnierza*',
1977, p. 278), one of her poems written between 1949–1951, is the most
likely inspiration for the monument to the Second World War heroes of
Warsaw, the famous 'Nike of Warsaw', placed in front of the Grand
Theatre and Opera Building on Warsaw's Victory Square. The mood
and the conclusive image of this poem more than coincidentally
prompt the image of the flight-captured Nike of the monument. In the
poem, describing the desecration of a Polish soldier's grave abroad,
Iłłakowiczówna consoles her people, presenting to them her vision of
Nike who comes to the grave and mournfully pierces the heart of the
dead soldier (a merciful act, according to eschatological elements of
Polish folklore, as the staking of the corpse prevents vampirism).

The image of the Polish national flag is also present in the title poem
of Iłłakowiczówna's volume *The Irresponsible Heart* (*Lekkomyślne
Serce*, 1959). Doubting the self-image, to gain poetic distance,
Iłłakowiczówna asks her 'daring heart' whether it is red, or white? The
ensuing dialogue is a formal device offering her an introspective look at
her own allegiance. The 'red' and 'white' acquire another symbolic
referent, and besides the Polish flag colours they signify the Russian
split into Bolsheviks and Mensheviks whose soldiers wore, respectively,
red and white bands on their caps. Her questions in this poem, such as
'nobody will hold it against you, but tell us, pray what do you uphold
nowadays?' (1959, p. 7) disclose the secondary symbolic element of the

two colours. They become a symbol of political, in addition to national, allegiance.

The poet concedes that her sad memories are 'red and white' as little flowers on an English dress, in these colours is her native country: 'the flow to which someone mighty had strung me'. Therefore, she will not confess to anything else during this questioning. The ending of this poem suggests the atmosphere of a secret police interrogation, rather than a dialogue of self-examination. That is why the questioner becomes silent, she is afraid to betray her inner thoughts. The 'someone mighty' who has influenced Iłłakowiczówna's political leanings is, of course, Marshal Piłsudski.

PERSONAL INTEGRITY AND POETIC INDEPENDENCE UNDER THE MURKY SHADOWS OF POLITICAL OPPRESSION

Iłłakowiczówna's political leanings are by no means straightforward. While in 'Nostalgia', a poem among her occasional verses, she asserts: 'what was Polish cannot be changed'; she contradicts herself in another poem as she admires the 'great wind of changes' sweeping through post-war Poland (1959, pp. 24–5). In principle, the poet is not opposed to the Communist reshaping of Polish society. She has always felt compassion for her less fortunate compatriots (1971, p. 268). The images juxtaposing the pre-war, unequal social order and the promised sweeping Communist changes express Iłłakowiczówna's socialist and Christian tendencies. Yet, not fooled by Communist promises, she clearly perceived the shortcomings of the Polish post-war reality, marking her perception with irony, as in the conclusion of 'The symbolism of shop-windows' (*Symbolizm witryn*, 1971, p. 108):

> Learn, oh, my nation,
> our list of symbols, it'll do you no harm,
> you will stop being simpletons, you will achieve true culture.
> No shopkeeper will need to look at you with superiority
> should you – forgetting the symbols of the shop-windows,
> seeing a lemon in the window – demand a lemon.

The lemon in this poem is a very real object, craved by most people in Poland, a symbol of the painful shortages of consumer goods there. Iłłakowiczówna's irony targets another frustrating element of living conditions in her contemporary Poland. In a poem satirising the two most frequent reasons for the inefficiency of the Polish retail trade, she lists them as its title: 'Repairs and Inventory' (*'Remont i Remanent'*, 1959, p. 109) while she satirises the inept, disorganised life under Communist rule in the true-to-life images she develops.

In 'There is no place for me' (*'Nie ma dla mnie miejsca'*, 1971, p. 12) of 1948, she finally concedes that, because of her ambivalent stance on the 'offerings' of Communism, she feels equally unfit for the Polish reality at home and for the coteries of the Polish émigrés in exile. This poem conveys a moment of regret over her decision to return to Poland in 1947 from her exile in Romania (1958, pp. 197–214).

Iłłakowiczówna had plenty of reasons for unhappiness on account of her return. One of them was the issue of free speech. In her volume *Three Strings* (*Trzy Struny*), the poem 'The Death of a Singer' (*'Śmierć Śpiewaka'*, 1971, p. 72) condemns the censorship of art. The poet identifies herself in it as both the silenced singer whose lips have been forcibly shut, and a powerless prisoner whose hands have been bound in chains:

> They have closed up my lips by force,
> both hands they have bound in chains:
> so today I see the leaves turn gold,
> and glimmer in every breath of the wind,
> I see a living soul in every tree,
> yet I do no know how to say it in a song.

Iłłakowiczówna, who died in 1983, was a poet of irrepressible national allegiance. She has borne witness to the history of her two nations. She felt that her work might have been inadequate to the task of the poet as the conscience of her nation. Nevertheless, she pressed for the return of her compatriots to the moral values of the free. She did it with deep emotional engagement and intellectual dedication. She deserves a place among the literary élite of contemporary Poland, and her works need translation and critical attention. She has left a testimony and an apology in the final stanzas of her invocation to her two mothers:

> What I have not fulfilled and what has torn my heart,
> when under a mask of victory I have carried defeat,
> shall rest a ripe harvest in the hands of these dead,
> and what was always heavy, will be lightened.
> Take off all my yokes, all my armour,

the fear, that has stunned me, the sin that has killed me. . .
So we shall rest in peace together, in paradise, or in the grave
– oh, my mothers, mothers, my mothers.
'Lithuanian Nightingale' (1971, pp. 626–7)

Notes

1. Kazimiera Iłłakowiczówna: The title poem from a 1936 volume. In *wiersze Zebrane* (Warsaw: PIW, 1971) p. 559. All the translations of Iłłakowiczówna's poetry included here are my own. References to poems will be given by year and page number to the following volumes: *Z Głębi Serca* (Warsaw: Gebethner & Wolf, 1928): *Niewczesne Wynurzenia* (Warsaw: PIW, 1958): *Lekkomyślne Serce* (Czytelnik, 1959); *Wiersze Zebrane* (Warsaw: PIW, 1971); *Odejście w tło* (Poznan: Wydawnictwo Poznańskie, 1976); and *Poezje Wybrane przez Pawla Hertza* (Warsaw: PIW, 1977).
2. Miłosz, Czesław, *The Witness of Poetry* (Cambridge, Massachusetts and London, 1983).
3. Iłłakowiczówna, *Ścieżka obok Drogi* (Warsaw: Towarzystwo Wydawnicze 'Rój', 1939).
4. Miłosz, *The History of Polish Literature* (Berkeley, Los Angeles, London: University of California Press, 1983).
5. Miłosz, *Rok Myśliwego* (Paris: Instytut Literacki, 1990) pp. 144–5. All the translations of Miłosz' writings included here are my own.
6. Ketchian, Sonia, *The Poetry of Anna Akhmatova: A Conquest of Time and Space* (München Slavistische Beiträge: Verlag, Otto Sagner, 1986). Especially consider Part Two.
7. Zamojska-Hutchins, Danuta, 'Felicjan Faleński's Faceja – A New Interpretation in the Light of His Poetry and of Other Poetic Echoes of Jan III Sobieski's Vienna Victory' in: *Znaczeni Odsieczy Wiedeńskiej i Jej Odbicie w Kulturze Polskiej. Materiały z Konferencji*, 1983, Wladyslaw Miodunka (ed.) (Warsaw: Wydawnictwo Polonia, 1984) pp. 34–40, p. 36.
8. *Ścieżka obrok Drogi*, p. 39
9. Iłłakowiczówna, 'Coś Niecoś o Pisaniu Wierszy', a talk given in 1957 in Poznań and London. In *Niewczesne Wynurzenia* (Warsaw: PIW, 1958) pp. 220–9.

12 Ukrainian Avant-Garde Prose in the 1920s

Myroslav Shkandrij

Current Soviet literary reassessments have done much to revise our picture of the 1920s. Experimental or avant-garde writing – a prominent feature of the decade's latter years – has, as yet, hardly been touched by this process. The virtual elimination of this current from all histories published after the 1930s, and the refusal to grant it serious scholarly attention, distort our understanding of the dynamics that operated in Ukrainian literature during these years. Far from being peripheral, as is often suggested, this current was, in fact, quite central both to literary politics and formal-aesthetic developments. Indeed, in the literary wars of the day it had ambitions of hegemony.

Avant-garde writers, as broadly defined here, saw themselves as harbingers of the new revolutionary culture, actively involved in demolishing the old and erecting the new. The issues raised were both formal and ideational (questions of politics, ideology). In both cases, writers were endeavouring to work against given conventions. Until the collapse of all counter-conventional trends and the enforced conformity of the 1930s, most prominent 'revolutionary' writers tested the waters of experimentation. This was especially marked in prose works from 1928–30. The assimilation of formalist theories (especially of Eikhenbaum, Shklovsky and Tynianov) and the drive to produce a modern literature for the new Ukrainian market, led to a stream of experimental novels in these years.

The conventional and the innovative are, of course, relative concepts. In the post-revolutionary period proponents of the new culture initially directed their attack against the populist traditions that still held sway in a predominantly peasant and illiterate nation. Tensions soon became apparent, however, among the self-styled avant-gardists themselves. These exploded in the great literary discussion of 1925–1928 and played a role in the internecine struggles of the 1930s.

Three related issues concerned the avant-garde in these debates: the permissible and desirable degree of formal experimentation in literature, of radicalism in politics, and of national concern in culture. 'Revolutionary' positions on all these issues were initially claimed by all currents, although commitment was defined variously – particularly to nationalism, where a distancing from supporters of the defeated Ukrainian People's Republic (Ukrainska Narodna Respublika – UNR) was required. In the early 1920s the avant-garde attitude had united many young, revolutionary writers, who saw themselves as the vanguard in all three fields. By the early 1930s, however, any camaraderie between groups had dissipated. Why this happened is a complex story that cannot be analysed here, but it could be pointed out that two issues caused fundamental disagreements.

The first was a clash between 'aesthetics' and 'politics'. One group defined art as 'cognition' and used the term 'contemplating reality' to stress art's purpose and role in furthering self-awareness. The second defined art as 'construction' and counterposed the term 'changing reality' to emphasise its more immediate political function. Although many writers were disturbed by the implications of entirely subordinating aesthetics (cognition) to politics (construction), they were compelled by the beginning of the 1930s to refuse the Romantic notion of art's 'higher purpose', of its disinterestedness, and to accept its service role. Art was not to be the sister of philosophy, but the handmaid of politics.

The concept of literature as autotelic (something that found its justification and end in itself) became less and less compatible with its definition as heterotelic (finding its justification outside itself, an intervention into politico-cultural life). The first concept impelled writers toward questions of craftsmanship: a concern with landscaping, background, full psychological portrayal, rhythmic organisation – which drew charges of ornamentalism, psychologism and lyricism. The second increasingly isolated literature's political function, favouring only clear dramatic conflicts, transparent construction and a convincing didacticism. This tendency was, in turn, accused of näiveté, simplification and dogmatism.

Often the debate was framed as a contest between psychological portrayal and the depiction of socio-political conflict; sometimes as a duel between intuition and logic. The first current, of which many writers in VAPLITE (Vilna Akademiia Proletarskoi Literatury – Free Academy of Proletarian Literature) were typical, often sought the lyrical invocation of moods, indicated the dangers of an excessive faith in rational speculation; the second (notably the futurists) aimed at a completely intellectual, rational prose. To the latter the music of Alexsander Scriabin and the work of the young Pavlo Tychyna were, at best, harmful mystification, at worst, counter- revolutionary mysticism.[1]

The functionalist quest for clarity tended toward an avoidance of reverberation, subtext and undertone. Sensuous perception was sacrificed to the intellectual apprehension of social processes and political dramas.

A second major split occurred over attitudes toward Russian literature and culture. Pastiche and the parody of stereotypes, of outdated forms and attitudes (particularly the image of Ukraine in Russian writing) recur in Ukrainian literature of the 1920s. Some writers, however, found such a literary trend and cultural attitude offensive. The ensuing debate led to some interesting theorising. Mykola Khvylovy published three pamphlet cycles and wrote an article entitled 'Ukraine or Little Russia?' which was confiscated in 1926 and only became available in 1990.[2] In the latter piece he argued that the relationship of Ukrainian to Russian literature should be one of antithesis. Russian literature, in his opinion, was marked by reactionary traditions (chauvinism and mysticism in particular) which act as a brake on progress, whereas the young vigorous cultural renaissance taking place in Ukraine rendered it more able to create a new culture.

Until very recently Soviet critics have lauded the victory of politics over aesthetics and centralism over nationalism – precisely the process lamented by emigré criticism, and by recent writing in Ukraine. The theoretical problems raised by this debate are, however, little illuminated by a simple reversal of preferences. The current tendency to substitute one political content for another (*natsrealism* for *sotsrealism*, a now politically popular 'national' line for the once mandatory socialist line), obscures the deeper issues involved. A new generation of critics in both the Ukraine and the West is only now beginning to tackle the complexity of problems caused by the interaction of politics and form. The canonisation and decanonisation of certain works, the prioritisation of genres and of formal devices, caused by the imposition of a Stalinist political culture in the early 1930s, require further study. The following comments are meant to raise some questions that have yet to be elucidated and to remind readers that much of the corpus of literature produced in the 1920s (now designated by the cliché 'the sunken Atlantis') still remains unavailable and unanalysed after more than sixty years of censorship. The more experimental writing, which constitutes a significant part of this missing chapter in literary history, has perhaps received the severest treatment at the hands of censors and is still summarily dismissed by many critics.

If we view the three sets of issues mentioned (formal experimentation, political radicalism, national self-awareness) as autonomous, but mutually connected dynamics, the avant-garde can be seen as arguing for change and decanonisation of the classics, the accepted authorities and dominant images within each. Throughout this period there were, however, powerful counter-currents beneath the surface which dictated an overall drift toward consensus and which compelled each avant-gardist to compromise in some degree with the conventional in form, in political and national culture. One can, of course, never be absolutely free of convention – every opposition is itself a form of dependency – but the uniqueness of the Ukrainian situation is to be found in the steadily increasing pull of the national movement. In politics the Ukrainian left had from the beginning seen the social revolution as inseparable from national liberation.[3] In literature, this was linked to a vision of a reborn, joyous, liberated society; a counterweight to the 'barrack-room' socialism envisioned by disciplinarians.[4] This overall consensus was destroyed by intervention from the centre, which first cut short the literary discussion in 1928 and then, in a dramatic volte-face in 1933, declared Ukrainian nationalism the main enemy, effectively halting the Ukrainisation drive declared ten years earlier.

The revolutionary and immediate post-revolutionary years had produced several experiments in prose. Ihnat Mykhailychenko's *Azure Novel* (*Blakytnyi roman*, 1918–19) was a work whose symbolic system was so cryptic that one critic described it as 'probably the most confused and incomprehensible work in the history of Ukrainian literature'.[5] Mykola Khvylovy's *Blue Etudes* (*Syni etiudy*, 1923) and *Autumn* (*Osin*, 1924) had set new standards for revolutionary prose. His psycho-political thriller, *Woodsnipes* (*Valdshnepy*, 1927) was considered so explosive that its second part was confiscated and has never been published.[6] Valeriian Polishchuk's *A Basket of Berries. Stories, Aphorisms, Flashes of Thought and Creativity, Paths of Thought and Allegories of One Stung by Life* (*Kozub iahid. Opovidannia, aforyzmy, bryzky mysli i tvorchosty, stezhky dumok i alehorii liudyny, iaku zhyttia pryperchylo*, 1927) was iconoclastic not merely in formal and political terms; his outspoken treatment of sexuality led to the charge of pornography – one that stayed with him throughout his career and was used to curtail the publication of his journal *Avant-garde* (*Avangard*) in the early 1930s.

A conscious attempt was made by the futurists to produce a 'leftist' prose in the last two years of the decade. Their chief theorist Oleksa Poltoratsky cited Geo Shkurupii, Oleksa Vlyzko and Oleksa Slisarenko as exemplary exponents.[7] Shkurupii displays a technical mastery of longer prose in his *Doors to the Day* (*Dveri v den*, 1929) and *Jeanne the*

Batallionaire (*Zhanna batalionerka*,1930), which celebrate the victory of technology over superstition, rationality over emotion, revolutionary consciousness over national romanticism. His demystificatory practice also includes challenges to conventional sexual mores – particularly in the chapter 'Eros Train' (*'Poizd eros'*) from the latter novel. Iconoclasm was always a strong suit with the futurists. It provides a thread to this work. Poltoratsky makes it clear in his articles that the formalist concept of *ostranenie* or 'making strange' was being deliberately extended to the political and cultural spheres; it was viewed as a tool in the re-education of society. He called for more attention to the 'ideological function of artistic devices.'[8] The iconoclasm was selective, however, aimed primarily at Ukrainian populism and nationalism, and as such it found support in Stalin's new line of 'class war'.

Dmytro Buzko's *Holland* (*Hollandia*, 1930), a work unavailable today, created a stir when it first appeared and represents this author's most extreme experimentation. It is crowded with devices of defamiliarisation, authorial intervention and extended digressions on topical issues.

Oleksa Vlyzko's *Sphinx* (*Sfinks*, 1928), a precursor of the literature of the absurd, is notable for its extravagant similes and extended metaphors.

Leonid Skrypnyk's *The Intellectual* (*Inteligent*, 1929), written in the form of a film-script, represents perhaps the most outspoken attack on the quicksands of *pobut*, routine, and the dead hand of middle-class conformism. It deals with recalcitrant material: the deadening and ugly, the average and instructive. Nevertheless, a dry chronicle of a typical city-dweller's life is enlivened by the ironic acceptance of the involuntary act and the author's contempt for ornamentalism and emotionalism. The book is a rationalist's protest against the emotional pull of received notions, of art, and even of biological drives. In his determination to banish everything superfluous and confusing from life, Skrypnyk was even prepared to suggest eliminating metaphor from language.[9] Believing that the architectonics of a novel demand typical administrative and engineering skills, he favoured a deliberately transparent, purposeful construction.

The constructivist Valeriian Polishchuk produced the now unavailable and practically unknown *Hryhorii Skovoroda* (1929), a personal interpretation of the 'Ukrainian Socrates' which mixes poetry, prose and blank verse. Polishchuk, whose avowed aim is to disturb the reader, portrays the philosopher as an escapist from political reality. In contrast to Pavlo Tychyna's portrayal of Skovoroda from this period,[10] Polishchuk's hero turns from political action to mystical contemplation:

> Yes, I shall go. . .I shall go.
> I see vain desires
> Have conquered your souls.
> You are choking in the temporal and material,
> And have buried your souls in tombs.

> Так, я піду . . . Піду.
> Я бачу, суєтні бажання
> Опанували ваші душі.
> Ви захлинулися в сьогоднішнім і матеріяльнім
> А душі заховали в гроб.[11]

This attitude is condemned by the author.

As the above notes attest, the avant-garde achieved its shock effect not only through an assault on traditional beliefs. Formal experiments such as the mixing of genres and the introduction of new ones, such as the film-script, were part of the pursuit of novelty. Two of the most sophisticated writers of the 1920s, Iurii Ianovsky and Maik Iohansen, produced works so innovative in this regard that they have so far, like Mykhailychenko's and Khvylovy's, practically defied analysis.

Ianovsky's short-story collections *Mammoth Tusks* (*Mamutovi byvni*, 1925) and *Blood of the Soil* (*Krov zemli*, 1927) brought him recognition as one of the outstanding writers of the decade. His early stories were strongly influenced by film techniques and eschewed the naturalism or naïve realism favoured by the more pedestrian writers who thronged to such organisations as Pluh (Plough) and VUSPP (Vseukrainska Spilka Proletarskykh Pysmennykiv – the All-Ukrainian Union of Proletarian Writers). The story 'Mammoth Tusks', for example, is a parody of the hackneyed revolutionary plot. Soviet power in the village is represented by a gang of thugs who attempt to murder an honest peasant. He outwits and exposes them. The film-script 'directions' allow the author to comment ironically upon the devices of the popular spy-murder story. Another early experimental story, 'In November' ('*V lystopadi*'), describes Oleksander Dovzhenko at work on a painting, struggling to give form to an inner vision. It is both a study of the creative process and a critique of the cliché-ridden mind.

Ianovsky's most daring experiment in longer prose, *Master of the Ship (Maister korablia)* was published in 1928. Contemporary Soviet criticism condemned it and the official attitude has remained almost unanimously negative. It is in many ways a prototypic avant-garde work. As such it rejects conventional structure. There is no plot in any accepted sense, no conventional characterisation. The refusal to follow any beaten path is the book's guiding formal imperative. The motivation for this, however, is not so much the desire to shock, as the effort to articulate an authentic, personal view of reality. In one early scene, for example, Sev (who personifies the director Dovzhenko) describes the sea to the narrator:

> if only they wouldn't paint it blue, adorned with beautiful epithets. There have to be seagulls flying above, mewing and crying, petrels who sense the approaching storm, and ships with white patches of sail. . .
> – And a sailor, bronzed and fine-featured – I add in support. – He has to carry messages and be in love with some tawny daughter of India, pining and day-dreaming on the watch-deck. . .

Sev goes on to contradict this image:

> The sea is not blue at all, and the seagull cries because it wants to eat, not because it yearns for someone. There are dirty grey wind-blown sails on the ship, and just this detail stirs my blood. The ships hurry to make port, to avoid being caught in a storm. They fear the sea, and their proud appearance comes from their alacrity. They are desperately afraid, but travel, pitch, weave from wave to wave, or rather the waves roll their foamy sides under them. Around is the terrible sea, an abyss of water and rage. Occasionally it beckons with a friendly blue tone, sometimes it joins with the sky and begins to charm. But its nature is treacherous, appealing and severe.[12]

The first description, composed of received images, is contrasted with the second, a deliberately elaborated personal vision. Complexity in characterisation, paradoxical details ('treacherous, appealing and severe'), an avoidance of sentimentalism ('the seagull cries because it wants to eat') are emblems of Ianovsky's style. It is also noteworthy that the authentic vision is articulated gropingly, imperfectly, and is the product of more than one author. Like Khvylovy and others writers of the 1920s, Ianovsky reveals a very modern self-consciousness and epistemological uncertainty, one that echoes nineteenth-century Romantic irony and prefigures more recent postmodernist experiments.

The desire to see several sides of a picture at once, to combine opposites in order to obtain strong, memorable images has been described as a 'baroque' feature of the 1920s.[13] Like the primary device of negation, it represents an attempt to break down accepted patterns of thinking and feeling, to reconstruct a new, more 'dynamic' model of perception. When Ianovsky describes a theatre, he presents a number of classes, each with its own taste and behaviour. If love is being described, a mini-panorama is at once drawn: the love of prostitutes, of a deaf-mute couple, and his own. If he speaks of generations, we are at once presented with three different and hostile perspectives: the ageing narrator's, his children's and the reader's. Himself a representative of 'high' culture and refined tastes, Ianovsky refuses to be cut off from the world of strong emotions and colourful characters associated with popular, or 'low' genres. He links the two by combining 'romances' with mass appeal (adventure tales, sea narratives and popular yarns) with a modernist negativity, self-consciousness and complexity. This accounts for his constant shifting between narrative paradigms and cultural idioms.

If in Shkurupii's *Doors to the Day* the new Ukraine had been portrayed from a futurist perspective during a trip down the Dnipro from Kiev, Maik Iohansen's *The Journey of the Learned Doctor Leonardo and His Future Lover Alceste to the Switzerland of the Steppes (Podorozh uchenoho Doktora Leonardo i ioho maibutnoi kokhanky Alchesty u Slobozhansku Shvaitsariiu,* 1929) presents a parodic image of the country during a less uplifting voyage. The story challenges the tastes of the common reader and disappoints his/her expectations. Iohansen, a talented linguist and critic, a well-read man who found himself rather out-of-place among 'proletarian' writers with little formal education, produced a work that abounds in literary reminiscences: Viktor Shklovsky, Boris Pasternak, Laurence Sterne, Valeriian Polishchuk and Cervantes among them. The hero's picaresque adventures combine realistic detail and a prosaic setting with the fantastic and absurd. Love and the night transform the mundane into the miraculous, giving scope for apparitions and unexplained occurrences.

Critics have recently discovered in this work a forerunner of later magic realism.[14] One émigré critic, Ihor Kachurovsky, has given the book high praise, calling it Iohansen's most important contribution to the literary heritage.[15] It remains, nevertheless, unanalysed even by sympathetic critics.

Viktor Petrov (pseudonym V. Domontovych) is another erudite and sophisticated writer who is virtually unknown to Soviet readers and whose collected works are now being collected and republished in the West. His *Girl With Teddybear* (*Divchyna z vedmedykom*, 1927) and *Doctor Seraphicus* (*Doktor Serafikus*, written 1928–29 but revised and published 1947) are charming portrayals of the inefficacy and pusillanimity of academic intellectuals in the 1920s. They contain an implied polemic against the avant-garde and are critiques of the blinkered rationalism that gripped more than the futurists during this decade. Iurii Shevelov has written:

> Domontovych not only affirmed the irrational nature of man and the impossibility of establishing the kingdom of reason. He went further. He stated, that those propagating the idea of reason's domination were themselves irrational.[16]

This explains the inclusion of an episode from Machiavelli in *Girl With Teddybear*. Discussing terror in Machiavelli, Domontovych writes: 'Love is not always soft and gentle; sometimes it is cruel and severe. And often in an act that at first sight appears brutal and monstrous one can observe the lofty impulse of a spirit devoted to love.' Shevelov notes that no Soviet critic has detected the central importance of this episode. It is a key to the book's guiding idea: uncontrolled human behaviour and the conflict between intentions and acts. In this work, published in 1928, the author foresaw the terror of the 1930s carried out in the name of humanity's future happiness. He also provided a defence of aesthetic concerns at a time when these were considered frivolous or harmful: encoded in the work is a commentary on Plato's (and, by implication, Stalin's) banishment of some artists from the ideal state.

Domontovych's subtle irony is directed at the decade's construction novels. The hero of *Girl With Teddybear*, Semen Kuzmenko, is a collective parody of the heroes in construction novels like F. Gladkov's *Cement* (*Tsement*, 1925). The portrait of the avant-garde poet is similarly a parodic montage of several contemporaries, among them Velemir Khlebnikov, Todos Osmachka and Mikhail Semenko.

The above listing hardly exhausts the category of experimental prose writing. While some idiosyncratic products will remain curiosities, such as the 'concrete prose' of Andrii Chuzhy (recommended by his editors because he 'imitates no one')[17] of the fashionable jointly-written novels, other experiments in the final two years of the decade (by Geo Koliada, Iurii Smolych, Oleksa Slisarenko, Dmytro Hordienko and others) deserve attention.

Tensions and contradictions were inevitable in a movement aiming at such ambitious and radical change in both literary tastes and political consciousness; it produced a range of theoretical positions and practical examples which defied all efforts at synthesis: the intuitive clashed with the rational, the inner life with political engagement, the sophisticated with the prosaic. Although any real consensus was destroyed by the imposition of a pseudo-unity from above in the early 1930s, it is important to remember that these writers nevertheless retained many shared concerns. It is clear that they thought of themselves as a movement (even in his suicide note Khvylovy mentions his nemesis Semenko), that they responded to one another's works implicitly and explicitly, and were moved by a similar inspiration. Khvylovy, for example, found the movement's spirit analogous to the German *Sturm und Drang* period. His slogan 'Carthage must be destroyed!' echoes those of Poltoratsky ('doing things in a new way') and L. Skrypnyk ('going one step further'). The threads that bind these writers, as well as the choices that divided them, have still to be elucidated.

Only today can some of these works be mentioned as a prelude to their re-publication. Their recognition as part of a current with a coherent and dominant interest in literary experimentation and the psychology of aesthetic response has yet to be recognised.

Notes

The author wishes to thank the Research Grants Committee (University of Manitoba/Social Sciences and Humanities Research Council) for assistance in the preparation of this essay.

1. For comments on the Russian composer and pianist Aleksandr Scriabin (1871–1915) see: Oleksii Poltoratsky, *Nova generatsiia*, 1, 1928, p.50 and Leonid Skrypnyk *Inteligent*, 1929, p.139. Tychyna was a favourite target of the futurists; he was dubbed 'deeply reactionary', *Nova generatsiia*, 4, 1928, p.302, and Ukraine's 'worst poet', *Nova generatsiia*, 10, 1928, p.236.
2. Mykola Khvylovy, 'Ukraina chy malorossiia?' *Vitchyzna*, 1,1990, pp. 181–8 and 2, 1990, pp. 168–78; and also *Slovo i chas*, 1, 1990, pp. 7–31.
3. This is evident in leading anti-Bolsheviks like Volodymyr Vynnychenko, and in writers from the indigenous Ukrainian Communist movement (the Borotbists) like Hnat Mykhailychenko, Andrii Zalyvchy, Vasyl Chumak and Vasyl Elansky who are today considered the originators of Soviet Ukrainian literature.
4. See, for example, Maik Iohansen's 'Komuna' which appeared in the first

por-Bolshevik Ukrainian literary publication, *Zhovten*, 1, 1921, pp. 17–18. A longer version of the poem opened the first publication of Ukraine's Proletarian Writers' Union, *Hart. Almanakh pershyi*, 1924, pp. 5–10. The poem was edited in later editions to tone down the liberation rhetoric.

5.   B. Kovalenko, 'Prozaiky pershoho pryzyvu', *Molodniak* 1, 1928, p.115.
6.   Part one appeared in *Vaplite. Literaturno-khudozhniy zhurnal*, 5, 1927, pp.5–69. Part two was to appear in issue no. 6. This issue was destroyed and the journal banned.
7.   See Oleksii Poltoratsky, 'Praktyka livoho opovidannia', *Nova generatsiia*, 1, 1928, pp. 50–60.
8.   Poltoratsky, 'Sotsiolohiia zasobu "ponovlennia" (ostraneniia)', *Krytyka*, 7, 1928, pp.102–15.
9.   Leonid Skrypnyk, 'Hazeta', *Nova generatsiia*, 2, 1929, p.56.
10. Tychyna worked on his 'symphony' from 1920–1940, but quite intensively in the early 1930s. It has been re-published recently with extensive notes and alternative drafts; see Pavlo Tychyna, *Zibrannia tvoriv u dvanadtsiaty tomakh*, Kiev, 1983.
11. Valeriian Polishchuk, *Hryhorii Skovoroda. Biohrafichno-lirychnyi roman z pereminnoho bolianoho ta veseloho zhyttia ukrainskoho mandrivnoho filosofa*, Kharkiv, 1929, p.98.
12. Iurii Ianovsky, *Tvory v piaty tomakh*, vol. 2, Kiev, 1958, pp. 40–41.
13. Iurii Lavrinenko, *Rozstriliane vidrodzhennia: Antolohiia 1917–1933. Poeziia, proza, drama, esei*, Paris, Instytut literacki, 1959, p.367.
14. Iurii Koval, 'Na shliakhu do "romantyky budniv"', *Vitchyzna*, 4, 1987, p.170.
15. Ihor Kachurovsky, 'Pro tvorchist Maika Iohansena', *Ukrainske slovo*, Paris, 30 October 1988.
16. Iurii Shevelov, 'Shostyi u groni. V. Domontovych v istorii ukrainskoi prozy', in V. Domontovych, *Proza. Try tomy*, vol. 3, Suchasnist, 1988, p.169.
17. *Nova generatsiia*, 2, 1928, p.158.

13 Oppressed and Enlightened: Ukrainians under Austro–Hungarian Rule in Karl Emil Franzos' Historical Novel *Kampf ums Recht*

Lydia Tarnavsky

In 1772, following the partition of Poland between Austria, Prussia and Russia, Western Ukraine, then a part of Poland, was annexed into the Austro–Hungarian Empire. Ukraine, its history, people and culture drew the attention of Austrian writers. Literary themes taken from Ukrainian folklore, the life of the peasants and the life of the bourgeoisie, appeared in the works of such Austrian writers as Leopold von Sacher-Masoch, Hans Weber Lutkow and Emil Karl Franzos.

This paper focuses on the historical novel *For the Right* (*Kampf ums Recht*) by Karl Emil Franzos (1848–1904), which was published in Breslau in 1881. The setting for this novel is Carpatho–Ukraine in the 1830s during the reign of the Emperor Ferdinand. At this time, Carpatho–Ukraine was an Austrian crownland; however, the territory, formerly a part of the Polish Kingdom, remained under Polish local jurisdiction. Because the territory was also entrenched in feudalism this created the opportunity for the Polish overlords to exploit the Ukrainian peasants, who were bound by law to render them labour, services and farm goods.

The plot of the novel centres on a conflict which arises between the Ukrainian villagers of Zulawce and Wenzel Hajek, a Czech agent hired by the wealthy absentee Polish landlord to manage his estate. Hajek cheats the villagers of their common grazing pasture, causing the villagers to rebel against the Polish landlord and to seek bloody revenge. Taras, the protagonist of the novel and the chosen leader of the village, takes it upon himself to redress the wrong. He calms the villagers and directs them to seek legal, not bloody retribution.

Convinced of the objectivity of the Empire's judicial system, he presents the villagers' case to the district counsel (*Kreisamt*) in Kolomea, then the higher courts in Lemberg (Lviv), and finally to the Emperor himself in Vienna. In each instance the ruling is in favour of the landlord. Taras loses faith in the Austrian judicial system and takes matters into his own hands. He turns against the authorities and becomes an outlaw, avenging the peasants' common wrong.

Underlying the emotions and ideas which motivate the protagonist in this movel is the author's own understanding and perception of the Ukrainian experience under Austro–Hungarian rule. It is the purpose of this essay to study the novel as a reflection of the author's view.

Critical to the understanding of the author's viewpoint is a consideration of the author's biography and ideology, which strongly influenced his perception of the world. Karl Emil Franzos was born in Czortkow (today Czortkiv), Galicia, in 1848. He was a descendant of a French Jewish family by the name of Le Vert, which settled in the Austrian crownlands during Karl Emil's great-grandfather's time. The family accepted the surname Franzos in accordance with the Austrian Emperor Joseph II's decree that Jews of Galicia and Bukowina must take on German family names.[1] This was the beginning of the Germanisation process of the Le Vert family. The Germanisation took greater root when Karl Emil's grandfather went to study German literature, philosophy and history in Lemberg (Lviv).[2] Enthralled with German culture and its spiritual leaders Schiller, Goethe and Kant, he brought up his son, Karl Emil's father, as a German, with a strong sense of national identity.[3] By the time Karl Emil Franzos was born, the Franzos home was a '*deutsche Kulturinsel*'[4] (a German cultural island), and Karl Emil was brought up to be a German patriot. From early childhood he was indoctrinated by both his father and one of his early tutors, Heinrich Wild, to revere German culture and to identify himself principally with it rather than his Jewish heritage. Reminiscing about his childhood Karl Emil writes: 'The German national feeling, of which I am full and which has long been a part of my life, was instilled into me since my childhood. I was no more than a toddler, when my father said to me: "By nationality, you are neither Pole, nor Jew – you are a German."'[6]

Karl Emil Franzos' reverence for German culture and his sense of German nationalism was reinforced during his high school and university education which took place in German schools. Educated entirely in the German tradition, Franzos embraced the political and philosophical ideas of later nineteenth century Western Europe. He became a proponent of Rationalism and a believer in Josephinian politics. Rationalism extolled the virtues of human reason as the tool of intellectual inquiry which leads to progress, innovation and human achievement in all fields. Josephinian politics, in turn, represented the policies and reforms of Emperor Joseph II, the enlightened Austrian despot. Joseph's reforms included the abolition of injustices and inequalities among his people, and the improvement and promotion of a general wellbeing through centralised administration.[7] Joseph II strove to 'convert the [ethnically] many-faceted monarchy into a "single province equal in all its institutions and responsibilities" and "a single mass of people all equally subject to impartial guidance." '[8] Joseph believed that although the Empire join hands together in good will and warm friendship a pyramid of achievement and merit would be formed at whose apex would stand the Emperor himself as the civil servant.'[9]

With Rationalism and Josephinian politics in mind Franzos championed the idea of Germanisation of the ethnic minorities within the Habsburg Empire. He focused his attention particularly on the Slavs. His rationale for this was based on his perception of the state of affairs in Eastern Europe and the character of the Slavs. It was popularly believed by Westerners that the Slavs were genetically inferior to Western Europeans; they were 'base, backward, servile, sordid, barbaric, indolent and wild';[10] their 'society was in decline . . . they exhibited no symptoms of civilisation',[11] and the regions they lived in were 'comfortless and in a backward state of cultivation.'[12] Franzos shared that view and believed that what Eastern Europe and the Slavs needed was a good dose of Westernisation/Germanisation. Franzos believed that through his literary works he would bring the light of reason and the spirit of progress, achievement and civilisation to the Slavs. Having spent his childhood in the Ukraine, where his father worked as an Austrian civil servant (district physician) Franzos had a special sentiment for Ukrainians and targeted them for re-education and cultivation. Franzos believed that the merits of Germanisation were so obvious that if the Ukrainians were only exposed to Germanisation they would not only appreciate its merits, but embrace it as he had.[13]

It was these views and political ideology that Karl Emil Franzos expressed in his literary works, of which fifty-two focused on the Ukrainians. His historical novel *For the Right* is considered his most successful work in his attempt to educate the Slavs in general, and the Ukrainians in particular.

Franzos begins his novel with a description of the region and its people to make clear to the reader that this area and its people are indeed in need of Germanisation. He invites the reader to imagine boarding a German train, a shining symbol of German industrialisation and civilisation.[14] As the train passes through the Carpathian mountains the traveller gazes through the window and sees 'grey cottages'[15] and 'poverty stricken fields',[16] and beyond them the village of Zulawce, whose 'thatched dwellings are as poor as anywhere in that part of Galicia.'[17] According to the author, the people in this village are backward and uncivilised: their dress is non-Western and ill-suited for their work; their diet is coarse and simple; the way they rear their cattle and till their fields is inefficient and unproductive; their speech is coarse and unsophisticated; their society is simplistically structured – they do not acknowledge officers of the crown and do not hesitate to take the law into their hands 'meeting injustice with a bullet or a blow of the axe.'[18]

Having thus described the region and its people Karl Emil Franzos begins to slowly phase his programme of Germanisation into the region.[19] His agent for implementing this programme is the novel's protagonist, Taras Barabola. Taras is a village outsider, blue-eyed, blonde. He is thoughtful, selfless, adaptable, productive, industrious – an embodiment of German virtues.[20] The villagers of Zulawce sense his superiority and choose him as the village judge, the highest position of leadership in the village. In this capacity he plays the role of the Teutonic mentor, personifying the German spirit of enlightenment, progress and achievement, and implementing a programme of reform. First he teaches the villagers to respect the Austrian crown and obey the dictates of the Emperor, to whom he humbly refers as the Kaiser, 'our Father', divinely empowered and incapable of any acts of injustice. As a result of Taras' influence the villagers of Zulawce accept the Austrian social order, that is, Austrian dominion and the advantageous position of the Polish noble in the Galician crown land. Second, he guides the village community (*Gemeinde*) from primitivism to enlightened behaviour, so that despite greater demands and manipulation by the overlords, the villagers learn to swallow their pride and make sacrifices in order to maintain the social order. They relinquish all forms of violence, subordinating the individual will to the authority of the village judge, the Polish overlord, and the Austrian magistrates. Lastly, Taras becomes an innovator/educator. He introduces new farming tools and methods of cattle and sheep grazing which lead the village to prosperity.

With the help of his protagonist, Karl Emil Franzos has, thus, drawn a picture of Germanisation in progress and its fruits, as seen in the formation of an ideal Galizian village founded on Austrian principles of statehood and German virtues. To this point in the novel the author has extolled only the positive attributes of Germanisation. To have stopped his novel here would have been too simplistic for a writer as astute as Karl Emil Franzos. He therefore creates a conflict in his novel which raises the question: is the German way the best? To answer that question Franzos pits Taras Barabola against the Austrian system in order to see if that system, which has thus far promoted social order and prosperity in the village, can also in times of strife protect the villagers' rights. The conflict is presented as seen through the eyes of Taras. As mentioned, it revolves around the communal grazing pasture,which is taken from the villagers by the Polish overlord. An appeal to the Austrian Emperor to intercede is rejected. The lack of resolution of the conflict causes Taras to become disillusioned with the Austrian system and see it as nothing more than a caricature of the ideal system.

In putting the Austrian system to the test, the author concedes that there are discrepancies between the programmatic intentions and the practical realisation of political ideology. For example, at the lowest level of the judicial authority, that of local magistrates, court officials, judges and lawyers in Galicia, Taras finds a multitude of cheating, immoral investigators and shrewd charlatans whose commitment to upholding justice is dubious. During an investigation and subsequent hearings of the case Taras discovers that witnesses are bought and bribes are given in order to sway the testimony in favour of the Polish overlord. At a higher level of authority, the distant Austrian courts, Taras also finds that there are long delays in due process of law. When the Zulawce villagers approach the courts they are told that they must wait several years before their pleas are heard. Turning to the highest level of authority within the Austrian system, the Emperor himself, Taras discovers that the Emperor is nothing more than a figurehead too busy to care, too narrow in his vision to see, too insular in his relationship with the ethnic minorities to react to their immediate needs. During Taras' audience with the Emperor, the Emperor appears to pay more attention to the strangeness of Taras' ethnic garb than to the plea he brings before him. The Emperor's response to Taras' pleas is to give Taras an Austrian ducat with the Emperor's image impressed on it.

Franzos, thus, acknowledges that discrepancies exist between the programmatic intentions of Austrian ideology and its practical execution; however, he does not swerve in his conviction that the German way, rooted in Rationalism and Josephinian politics, is the best. He proposes that a solution to the problem in the novel must be found in contemplation, pragmatic deliberation and the mutual co-operation of all parties involved. He suggests that the parties in the Zulawce dispute join hands in good will and warm friendship relying on patience and legal re-investigation to achieve the resolution of their problem.

To show the folly of any other means of resolving problems, Karl Emil Franzos places Taras in juxtaposition to the Austrian system, allowing him to rebel against that system, to create a separate world, and to govern it according to his own rules. This first of Franzos' manoeuvres is intended to lead Taras astray. The second manoeuvre is to place Taras in a world which is in effect patterned after the Austrian model, which is multi-ethnic and stratified, in order to impress on Taras the difficulties of governing a multi-ethnic empire and to set the stage for the evolution and obligatory solution of similar problems. Taras, like the Emperor, has absolute rule over his followers, who are representative of diverse ethnic groups: Jewish, Polish, Romanian, and Ukrainian. The only common denominator between these constituents of Taras' group is that they have sworn to live their lives according to Taras' values and imposed world order. Like the Emperor, Taras assumes: (1) that all the members of his group are motivated by those same lofty standards as he is; (2) that the order imposed by him on the members of his group is acceptable to them and that they are willing to subject their individual differences and sensibilities to those dictated by him; and (3) that his members will fulfil their duties conscientiously, never violating the integrity of their holy mission. These assumptions lead Taras, as they do the Kaiser, into: (1) believing in the righteousness and wisdom of his ways; (2) into placing his faith in the good will of individuals who were corrupt; and (3) into failing to recognise the diversity and differences between the members of his group. In the case of the Emperor, the faulty assumptions and consequently misdirected faith and lack of sensitivity led him to overlook a miscarriage of justice in the village of Zulawce, and to mishandle Taras' audience with him, thus forcing him into rebellion against the Austrian crown. In the case of Taras, the same faulty assumptions lead to similar actions. He is responsible for a miscarriage of justice. A man is unjustly accused of a crime he did not commit. Taras also mishandles and misunderstands the diverse sensibilities of the members of his band of outlaws, forcing them into insurrection against him.

At this point, then, having created parallel worlds, parallel assumptions and parallel transgressions, the author allows his characters, the Emperor and Taras, to diverge in their approaches to the solution of the problem. The Emperor, using reason, approaches the problem by deliberating and renewing his investigation of the Zulawce case. With time he is able to undo the unjustice, and thereby remove the cause for rebellion. Taras, on the other hand, is driven by emotions. His passion leads him to the rash conviction and execution of an innocent man. Had Taras taken the time to deliberate over and investigate the evidence brought against the accused man this execution could have been prevented. Similarly, had Taras been sensitive to the sensibilities of his followers and deliberated over their needs he could have prevented the insurrection against him and the eventual dissolution of his group.

These divergent resolutions to parallel problems presented here is the turning point in Franzos' novel. The Emperor's successful handling of his problem in contrast to Taras' failure serves as Franzos' ultimate proof that the German way, steeped in Rationalism, is indeed, the best. With deep remorse for his crime and a renewed reverence for the German way, Taras gives up his role as leader, and gives himself up to the Austrian authorities. He refuses to plead for amnesty, and accepts execution, as a means of purging his crime.

Franzos' novel ends with the village of Zulawce and Taras back in the fold of the Austrian Empire. It is the fulfilment of Franzos' prophecy: that, exposed to Germanisation, Ukrainians would learn not only to appreciate its merits, but to embrace it as he had.

Notes

1. Fred Sommers, ' "Halb-Asien" ': German Nationalism and Eastern European Works of Emil Franzos', *Stuttgarter Arbeiten zur Germanistik*, no. 145, 1984, p. 11.
2. Ibid.
3. Ibid.
4. Ibid., p. 12.
5. Ibid., p. 18.
6. Karl Emil Franzos in the *Vorwort* to *Der Pojaz*, Stuttgart, 1906, p. 2.
7. Adam Wandruska, *The House of Habsburg. Six Hundred Years of a European Dynasty*. Westport, Greenwood Press, 1975, p. 157.
8. Ibid..
9. Ibid., p. 159.
10. Mark Gelber, 'Ethnic Pluralism and Germanisation in the works of Karl Emil Franzos (1848–1904)', *German Quarterly*, May 1983, p. 377.
11. Robin Okey, *Eastern Europe 1740–1980*. London, Hutchinson and Co., 1982, p. 21

12.   Ibid.
13.   Sommers, 'Halb-Asien', pp. 76–7.
14.   Ibid., p. 114.
15.   Karl Emil Franzos, *For the Right*, Trans. Julie Sutters, New York, Harper and Brothers, 1988, p. 2.
16.   Ibid.
17.   Ibid.
18.   Ibid., p. 4.
19.   For a detailed discussion of the Germanisation process of Ukranians in the village of Zulawce as presented in Karl Franzos' novel *Kampf ums Recht* see: Mark Gelber, 'Ethnic Pluralism and Germanisation in the works of Karl Emil Franzos (1848–1904)', *German Quarterly*, May 1983, pp. 376–385; and Fred Sommers, ' "Halb-Asien": German Nationalism and Eastern European Works of Emil Franzos', *Stuttgarter Arbeiten zur Germanistik*, no. 145, 1984, pp. 110–121.
20.   Gelber, 'Ethnic Pluralism as Germanisation'.

14 F. D. Kniaźnin and the Polish Balloon

Nina Taylor

The successful launching of a balloon by the Montgolfier brothers at Annonay on 5 June, 1783, was greeted throughout Europe by a spate of publications: press reports, scientific descriptions, learned treatises, cartoons, epics and odes. It was perpetuated both in painting and in poetry. The balloon motif was used to decorate snuff-boxes and signet-rings.[1] It gave rise to sundry commercial games and tricks, and fashionable ephemerae such as aerostatic peaches, toy-balloons made of ox-gut, and the *coiffure à la Montgolfier*.

Two early French accounts comprise a *Lettre aux auteurs d'un journal sur l'expérience du grand Ballon de M. de Montgolfier*,[2] and the *Rapport fait à l'Academie des Sciences, sur la Machine Aéro-statique, inventée par MM de Montgolfier*,[3] giving details of the experiment, and a brief historical survey. A more frivolous item is M. Gosse's new *Almanach à la Montgolfier ou l'Amour dans le globe volant*, costing 36 sous, and containing '*pièces fugitives, légères ou galantes*' both in prose and verse, historical notes, thematic com-memorative songs and four copperplates to enshrine the experiments 'and the bewilderment of the peasants when the Balloon fell down in Gonesse'.[4]

To avoid spreading alarm among a volatile nation, the French authorities had temporarily withheld news of the event. The press expressed concern lest 'England, our rival', should get hold of the invention and perfect it to the detriment of France. Perfidious Albion retaliated with a cartoon entitled

The Montgolfier
A first rate of the French Aerial Navy,
A F–t — An Ass — A Fool — A Monkey — A Nothing[5]

In more serious vein, 'The Air Balloon or a Treatise on the Aerostatic Globe, lately invented by the celebrated Mons. Montgolfier of Paris'[6] went through three editions in 1783 alone.

Three German contributions to the topic hardly err on the side of levity.[7] In Italy, the occasion was honoured with some spontaneity by the Abate Vincenzo Monti in a thirty-five-stanza Ode dedicated '*Al signore di Montgolfier*', in which the author predictably invokes '*Il giovinetto Orfeo, D'Argo la gloria*',[8] and, somewhat belatedly, by Vincenzo Lancetti in a narrative poem of twenty cantos entitled '*Aerostiade ossia il Mongolfiero*' (1802).

Throughout the late summer and autumn of 1783, ballooning adventures remained largely the prerogative of French inventors, their followers and fans. The French aristocracy were among early volunteers for subsequent manned flights; and despite sporadic bans, by December 1783 tests and trials were being carried out in other European capitals, in The Hague, Amsterdam, Berlin and Vienna. The first official report in Poland appeared in *Gazeta Warszawska* (8 October); it was dated Paris 21 August and 8 September, and based on accounts in the European press. As from January 1784 almost every issue of the twice-weekly journal was to carry at least one news item devoted to aerostatic developments in Europe, together with the exaggerations and distortions that often embellished these stories.[9]

Indigenous aeronautic attempts were first launched in February, 1784.[10] There were further tests that year in Kamieniec Podolski on General de Witte's estate, and two years later in Czeczelnik, the estate of Prince Józef Lubomirski in the Palatinate of Bracław, culminating in the manned ascents of Blanchard, and Blanchard and Jan Potocki, in 1789 (10 May) and 1791 respectively.

The early days of ballooning were reflected in Polish literature of the time. Its impact is recorded in memoirs,[11] documented in the learned correspondence of a king,[12] or the social epistle of a Bishop,[13] not to mention the song of a blind wanderer from the Ukraine about the invention.[14] Artistic literature has made two signal contributions: an Ode, '*Gdzie bystrym tylko Orzeł polotem*' ('Where the swift-flighted Eagle') once ascribed to Trembecki, and now recognised as the work of Naruszewicz, and a mock-heroic poem in ten cantos by Franciszek Dionizy Kniaźnin, poet in residence at the magnate court of Prince Adam Kazimierz Czartoryski in Puławy, describing the founding of the Fellowship of the Balloon and the launching of an experimental airship there.

Kniaźnin states that his poem and the activity that inspired it arose 'four years ago, when balloons first came into the news in a big way'[15] – in other words, any time after October 1783, but more likely in the early weeks of 1784, concurrently with the reports in *Gazeta Warszawska* to which reference is made in Canto I.[16] There is further evidence, both textual and external. In Canto X, at the launching of the Balloon, hard by the palace and the garden, which descends by a steep embankment to the Vistula, it is snowing. 'More than one of the fleetest who ran on ahead,/Turned somersaults, and landed on the ice'.[17] Postponement of the event would preclude the participation of Princess Maryanna Czartoryska, who was shortly to be married to Prince Ludwik Wirtemberg. In the Czartoryski annals, the scientific experiment and the literary composition thus belong to a period of domestic recovery after the deaths, a couple of years previously, of Princess Teresa,[18] Prince Adam Kazimierz's eldest daughter, and of his father, Prince August, the head of the family.[19] Following the Prince's grand tour of his estates in Volhynia, Podole and the Ukraine in the spring of 1783,[20] it marks a phase of stability and rootedness after the family's permanent move from Warsaw to Puławy, as Princess Izabela devoted her energies to planning the garden and decorating the new residence.[21] In October 1783, after a two-and-a-half-year spell at the Załuski Library in Warsaw, Kniaźnin had resumed his poetic and pedagogical duties at the Czartoryski court, never to be parted from its circle again.

Kniaźnin's *Balloon* has failed to receive much critical acclaim, even from those literary historians (Borowy, Kostkiewiczowa, Guzek) who have done most to reinstate a poet all too often dismissed in the last century as 'a third-rate luminary' [22] possessing 'a narrow mental horizon'. [23] 'The bulk of his work, devoted to the transient entertainments of the inhabitants of Puławy, remains indifferent to the rest of the nation',[24] '. . . towards the end of his life (!) he wrote such poems as *Balon* merely for the amusement of the young people of Puławy'.[25] 'Here poor Kniaźnin playing the role of poet had to describe his masters' evenings and the launching of a balloon with a cat on board. ..'[26] It might however be more appropriate to say that *Balon* presents one of the most compact and at the same time panoramic pictures of life at the Czartoryski court.

Notable absentees from the epic include Julian Ursyn Niemcewicz, the painter Norblin[27] and Prince Adam Kazimierz. As chief of the Emperor's Galician Guard he had previously left for Vienna[28] where, symptomatically, he was also involved in the sponsorship of ballooning activities. Absences notwithstanding, Kniaźnin in his scientific epic deploys a cast of some sixteen characters: young princelings, pupils, wards and other dependents, with their retinue of governors, dancing masters, literati and majordomos. All belong to the extended family of Puławy and are, in the main, close associates of the poet and recipients of one or more of his poetic works. Each of these personages is given a title denoting the official role to be performed within the Fellowship of the Balloon. Faced with the difficulty of fitting them with fictitious Polish names, Kniaźnin invents Greek sobriquets that at once summarise, define, or idealise the bearer, endowing him with a super-ego. This stilted, allegorically stereotyped system of names is woven into the network of family relationships and private characteristics.

The actors in this educational charade are headed by Mme Petit, the French governess 'of many thoughts', implying perhaps mere scattiness.[29] The family nucleus consists of Princess Maryanna,[30] Prince Adam Jerzy,[31] and the nine-year-old Prince Konstanty, alias Kostuś, 'known as *Glikon* or Sweet'.[32] Further ramifications of the Czartoryski 'Familia' include Maryanna Przebendowska, alias Kleona the Nymph[33] and Princess Izabela's moral protégées, Aleksandra and Konstancja Narbutt.[34] The former appears as Kliodora, muse of History and annalist, the latter as Irys, the Rainbow, elected to chronicle events in paint. The third pupil is Franciszek Sapieha, Kallisten, alias the Handsome One, sent by the Prince Chancellor his father for his education to Puławy, where he remained only two years.[35] The two moral tutors assigned to him, freshly graduated from Cadet School, Ignacy Ciepliński,[36] known among the aeronauts as Sofronim ('cautious and provident') and Rembieliński, stayed on and became permanent residents of Puławy.

Senior retainers participating in the epic action are likewise regular members of the household. Piotr Borzęcki, 'Chryzos or the Golden One', Marshal of the Court in charge of the purse strings, was 'pockmarked and with ruddy moustaches, dressed always in the Polish style, richly and with taste'. [37] A captain of the Lithuanian Guard and adjutant to Prince Adam since 1777, Józef Orłowski is dubbed Aryston, 'the Best'.[38] Nicknamed Eufron for his deep thoughts, Stanisław Ciesielski is remembered by Niemcewicz as one of the four 'sub-brigadiers' at the Cadet School in Warsaw.[39] He was 'devotedly attached to the Prince's house, a man worthy of the highest respect; who certainly returned the affection and the trust [shown him].'[40]

While moral virtues at Puławy were inculcated by nationals, intellectual abilities and artistic talents were imparted by eminent foreigners. Simon L'Huilhier, Hypsofil, 'high-minded or of lofty thoughts', spent ten years in the Czartoryski household teaching mathematics and physics. In terms of concept and know-how he contributes most to the dynamics of the Balloon as its official Helmsman.[41] A lesser role is performed by Wawrzyniec Schmuk, a more obscure personage, known as Filon, 'l'Ami'. On the arts side, Wincenty Lessel provides the substance of his nickname 'Harmon'.[42] The last noteworthy foreigner is Dauvigny, alias Filenor, described as 'le type d'un ci-devant',[43] whom Prince Adam had brought over from the French Opera as dancing-master to the Cadet Corps in 1777.[44] He was 'the first of the really great dancing-masters'[45] and apart from his duties at the magnate court he earned a sizeable fortune from giving private tuition in town.

While technical and political tasks are performed by male agents (President, Chancellor, Marshal, Deputy Treasurer, Architect Surveyor, Weigher, and Master of Wardrobe) under the supervision of the child beadle Kostuś, the ladies appear as muses of painting and history, or enact moral and conciliatory roles: Maryanna intercedes as Grand Advocate when the juvenile beadle falls foul of his elders. Functions and characters are thus clear-cut. The system of titles and duties is further expanded in the two cantos of the 'Grand Gala', later published in the 1787–88 edition, but separated from the main body of the work. The antique names in which the characters are rigged flatter their latent qualities and set a model to emulate, whereby undisclosed foibles might be transcended in a general aspiration to excellence.[47]

The distribution of duties creates an illusion of business and activity that is belied by the poem's narrative structure: 'Extraordinarily drawn out and boring',[48] 'artificial and drawn out',[49] 'one of his less successful attempts at constructing large units of a parodistic nature'.[50] *The Balloon* consists largely of digressions that 'diverge totally from the departure point and take shape as distinctly separate digressionary fragments. Their direct connection with the sphere of events is obliterated, whereas they themselves are exposed as almost independent entities'.[51] Ballooning action is basically restricted to the initial idea (Canto I), the delegation to the feline astronauts (Canto VII) and the final launching (Canto X). Two further Cantos (III and IX) provide a pastiche of Homeric events (the quarrel and the Council) pertaining to the main narrative theme. In Canto II, a dream is more important than the building process. Four cantos are blatantly digressive: the description of paradise meant as an incentive to work (Canto IV), the heraldic dissertation offered as a relaxation or reward (Canto V), the adornment of the Balloon walls with scenes depicting aeronautic episodes (Canto VI), and a learned discourse on the properties of air (Canto VIII). There are thus instances of simultaneism (II, IV, VIII) and stasis (V). With the possible exception of the chronicle expounded in Canto V, which locates the scientific experiment within the historical context of the family tree, these canto-length asides are directly relevant to the main theme, though artistically unintegrated. The three digressional cantos (IV, VI, VIII) are moreover interlinked by a display of theme and imagery that is predominantly upwards and thrusting, connecting heavenbound longings to new scientific possibilities, and the pragmatic properties of air.

The Balloon's status as an anecdote of court life does not preclude the panegyric, or at least the laudatory. As adventure of the mind and imagination it could largely justify an epic ranking; while its scientific content implies a universal significance. The digressions introduce the lyrical element, and a pastoral dream of ideal love. The portrayal of Eden in Canto IV, and its poignant leitmotiv of escape from our terrestrial existence, has been seen as 'a deeply lyrical aside outlining [the poet's] notions about paradise and life in the other world', among other passages 'filled with his sadness, and his yearning for better lands'.[52] As the poet assumes the role of annalist,[53] the discourse element in these cantos touches on genealogy, inspired perhaps by the popular Baroque genre of armorial poetry and reflections on coats of arms; it also concerns aesthetics and science. The insight given into the process of artistic creation as the balloon panels are decorated in Canto VI is matched by frequent indications in the narrative of bardic activity,[54] his initiation in the dreams of others, and his awareness of their creative potential: 'His dreams likewise outlined to him marvels/Of which he had not heard or even thought'. The dream holds more in store: it proves to be a catalyst of action, a *deus ex machina* of discord, wherefore Canto II is described 'A quarrel over Glikon's dream interrupts the work and puts the Council at odds'.

The dream of Glikon (Canto II), an aeronautic dream, without altering the generic balance of the poem, opens it out into the world of romance and novel, as it presents a series of adventures and situations typical of prose narrative. A decade or so after the first partition of Poland (1772), Glikon's airborne departure, affording him a bird's eye view of the neighbouring countryside, offers an early sample of the poetry of partition and political lament.

> And lofty Krępak* shows him the remains
> Of Poland's eagle, banished and compelled,
> To leave defenceless her sad fledgeling nests.
> Beneath black talons small white eagles' heads
> Peer pitifully East for her return;
> From far away she soars sky-high in vain,
> And greedy guardians spite the little birds. (st.12)

* *Krępak* refers to the Tatra mountains.

This is followed by a picaresque encounter with two airborne smugglers, thought to be from Nuremberg, who slip past predatory excisemen with their freight of taffeta, handkerchiefs, gauze, fashionable *chinoiserie* and Italian pictures. Glikon is then caught up in a story or vision from the *Thousand and One Nights*.[55] He drifts to Istanbul, where the lazy tyrant reigns and a thousand beauties repine, protected by the disfigurement of the male sex. Then he watches as an aerial pirate sails in from the East and descends into the harem in his balloon, abducts his loved one and navigates swiftly away.

> He plies his oar, quick kisses are exchanged. . .
> Our Glikon is amazed and right amused
> Grasping so many scenes with greedy eyes.

This throws an interesting sidelight on the schoolroom syllabus at Puławy; while the erotic undertones of the incident, and Glikon's evident glee, are borne out by numerous anecdotes related in the memoirs of the court circle.[56] Further episodes from the dream journey derive from the genre of newspaper reporting, and reflect their general reading matter and conversational topics. As Glikon chances to fly over the Messina earthquake,[57]

> Compassion he did feel, and he thanked God
> That he by air had saved him from the earth

and witnesses the burning of the French fleet in Gibraltar by Eliot:[58] recent events, footnoted by the poet, who adds that what is seen in Glikon's dream are uses to which the balloon could be put.[59]

A further peculiarity of Kniaźnin's *Balloon* is the scholarly appendix in the form of footnotes. They emphasise the poem's scientific portent, and at the same time create the broader cultural context of eighteenth-century science, as the success of the Balloon is seen to depend on the conjoined forces of the arts – history, poetry and painting. The notes thus explicate matters linguistic (*de lana caprina* Canto III), biblical (Enoch IV, 6) and heraldic (Canto V). They discuss personal preferences within the classical tradition (*Aeneid* Canto IX, Delphi Canto X). Pope's *Rape of the Lock* is also mentioned as a literary source or model. They present topical events of general interest (the siege of Gibraltar Canto II), and trivial matters of interest to Puławy residents, less appreciable for an outside audience, such as drawing-room candles or debates about the respective merits of the seasons. About half the

notes deal exclusively with questions of science, progress and
discovery: a note on Captain Cook[60] (Canto I), on L'Huilhier's study of
the bee-hive (Canto II), on the scientific works of Osiński (Canto VI
and VIII), on the balloon experiments at the Kraków Academy (ibid.),
and on the chemists Priestley and Boerrhowe (ibid.); and comment on
the uses to which ballooning could be put (Canto II, VI). In recalling
the interdependence of arts and sciences, one might mention the prime
role of music in stimulating and harmonising human endeavour:

> The builder Harmon, both deft and willing,
> Joined up two sides and made them smooth with glue.
> Made merry melody, as though from need,
> Like famous Amfion when Thebes was being built.

Compounded all of spirit though it be, the dream of Daedalus remains
ultimately earthbound. Extremes of sublimity and degradation, set at
different tensions and pitches, ensure that the generic amalgam of
Kniaźnin's *Balloon* depends dominantly on the mock heroic vein.
Among literary historians, only Krejči has done full justice to the issue,
noting sundry Homeric reminiscences, the antique names, the heroic
pastiche of Achilles shield, and the farewell of Hector and Andromache,
likewise the mock heroic motif of the flying cat.[61] The poem's best
stanzas, it is claimed, are those that present 'the parody of knightly
sentimental feelings in the cat Filus's speech and Pstrusia's admiration
for him'.[62]

Other critics have seen *The Balloon* as 'humorous didactic',[63]
'facetious',[64] 'comical',[65] 'here and there attempting a facetious tone',[66]
recognised it as mock heroic, or rather a failed attempt at mock heroic
by a poet who was 'as unsuccessful in the mock heroic as Karpiński was
in the field of tragedy'.[67] For Borowy, the poem succeeds only in
boring, being 'fairly humourless'; the fictitious mythical gods Nudzisz
and Ziewanka (Big Bore and Yawners) 'prove even more powerful than
the author good-naturedly supposes'.[68] Kostkiewiczowa finds neither
satirical intentions nor distance, for the poet proceeds 'as though he
were singing the loftiest and most significant events'.[69] There is some
consolation, however, in being told that 'Kniaźnin knows he is writing
a trifle, and attaches no importance to it. . . . He does not even attempt
to joke, he neither parodies the heroic poems, nor imitates the mock
heroic. He writes simply without pretensions, jokingly, so that although
his *Balon* has no merit, it is not so tasteless as it could be, and indeed
should be'.[70]

The aeronautic motif had already been used by Ignacy Krasicki in *Myszeidos piesni X*, a work to which *The Balloon* more than once refers both by loan and allusion. It was likewise exploited in M. D. Krajewski's novel *The Life and Adventures of Wojciech Zdarzynski* (*Wojciech Zdarzynski, zycie i przypadki swoje opisujący*, Warsaw 1785). In Krasicki's mock epic of Cats and Mice, the King of the Mice's flight on a magic broomstick to the Witch's Bald Mountain harks parodistically back to the dark sciences of a superstitious age with whose aftermath Krasicki was polemising. Kniaźnin's status inevitably suffers in juxtaposition with Krasicki's achievement, though half a century later Zygmunt Krasiński was prepared to grant the Puławy poet 'the ease and the wit of Krasicki'.[71] Kadłubek's mediaeval chronicle had provided Krasicki with the raw material of fantasy. Questions of innate talent and individual workshop apart, Krasicki and Krajewski wrote from a combatant's position, programmatically, with satirical intent and a view to mend minds and manners.[72] Political passion informs their didactic drive. Monastic habits proved easier butts in Krasicki's *Monachomachia* than the manners of an enlightened court in the verse of Kniaźnin, whose personal situation and emotional make-up, not to mention his sentimental involvement as a fully-fledged member of the extended Familia, basically precluded a critical approach. Yet, while Krasicki's wit was a function of the reactionary world it sought to deride, Kniaźnin's presentation moves forward into a future world of experimental science.

There remains the question of the final anti-climax: in the last stanza the Cat's death in the airship is likened to that of Władysław IV at Varna. The latter's crusade against the Turks is a major symbol of Poland's commitment to the ideals of Western Christendom. While the coupling of sublimity with the tribulations of a cat cosmonaut pertains to the tricks of mock heroic, it fails to be funny, but proffers a sane recognition of historic futility.[73] Kniaźnin's poem is charged with such unresolved inner inconsistencies. An optimistic defence of science by a convinced and practising Sarmatian, its mock heroic element is counterbalanced by armorial panegyric and chronicle, its panegyric component tinged with underlying catastrophism. At the same time, through the parallel of parliamentary debate, it enunciates fundamental rules of civic duties and patriotic obligations.

Flaws notwithstanding, *The Balloon* attempts to present a composite, synthetic picture of eighteenth-century ideals, viewed from the specific angle of Puławy politics, personal affections and aesthetic affinities. It satisfies the scientist's vocation for research, the publicist's thirst for the propagation of knowledge, and the child's craving for drawing-room entertainments and sophisticated toys. The bard thus doubles up as pedagogue and artistic animator. Clearly the mock heroic still had the power to accommodate these differences.

Yet the Piławy Balloon was a fiasco. In the analogy with Władysław IV's high-minded crusade, it is sometimes tempting to see an allegory of the ship of the Polish state drifting and coming aground. As a dream of the spirit, and symbol of the Polish Enlightenment, unable to resist the brutish elements, the Puławy Balloon seems to offer a foreboding of rationalism's final collapse, and the demise of Poland at the hands of the partitioning powers – the event that reputedly triggered off Kniaźin's fits of insanity, though one might argue the case for a bard who justified his failure by going mad. It is interesting to note, here, that the visitations of his unhinged mind suggest yet another variation on the aeronautic theme. 'His madness was poetic. (. . .) Sometimes, ablaze with an unusual fire, he saw creatures flying in the clouds, conversed with them, chased after them through the air, and served them summons to the Diet. Other times he felt wings growing on him, felt himself rising in the air, could not feel the weight of his own body; and then he would escape from his keepers and run off through the gardens and fields'.[74] Thus he ended his life in madness. Although, six months after the events described in the poem, family happiness was disrupted by Princess Maryanna's marriage, there was still no call for despair on a national scale. And the Balloon remains the most cele-brated of Puławy educational games in the spirit of Krajewski's pedagogical theories.[75] It takes its place among such instructive enter-tainments as the building of fortifications,[76] and the exercise of parlia-mentary rhetoric.[77]

A register of Puławy activities, interests and standards, with its scientific baggage and panegyric overtones, its lyricism and its humour, *The Balloon* is securely rooted in old Polish values, yet remains at the pulse of the modern world, coupling eighteenth-century aspirations to progress with intimate yearnings for the transcendental, and ultimately identifying with the poetic imagination. Though widely unrecognised, it is the first serious expression of a topic that recurs obsessively through nineteenth-century Polish literature. Threading its way through the correspondence of poets,[78] the image of the balloon vacillates between the sublime and the ridiculous in the longings of Cyprian Norwid's Lord Singleworth in 'The Secret of Lord Singleworth', and Aleksander Fredro's comic hero Birbancki in *Life Estate* (*Dożywocie*) 'who dreams of escaping by balloon into the sphere of the ideal, and in the sphere of the ideal thinks of a pack of cards and a new dinner jacket',[79] hoping to rid himself of this worthless world and his creditors in one flight. Positivist heroes succumbed in turn, and the problem of steering balloons was to possess the mind of dreamer-heroes in Bolesław Prus's *The Doll* (*Lalka*).

Occupying a central position both chronologically and thematically in the poet's oeuvre, Kniaźnin's mock epic is forward-looking in yet another respect. As enlightened rationalists who became the parents and grandparents of romantics, a number of its protagonists belong to the main stream of Polish political, cultural and literary history. The most significant historical role here befalls Adam Jerzy Czartoryski, who half a century later as the leader of the Polish *emigracja* in Paris 'was the first person of an non-existent state, the king – all but the king – of the Poles'.[80] Together with young Konstanty, he exemplifies a certain typology of the Polish fate: the brothers were participants in the Kościuszko Uprising (in which fellow balloonist Orłowski also fought), then became hostages in St Petersburg. Their ways began to part when Adam Jerzy assumed office in the Russian Empire, while Konstanty (once a friend of Grand Duke Constantine), declared himself a supporter of Napoleon, and set up a regiment at his own expense; after the failure of the November Insurrection he left Poland never to return. Konstanty's son Adam Konstanty took part in the November Rising, and fought at Grochów.[81]

Prince Adam Jerzy was also the first of the Puławy balloonists to produce artistic literature, writing his Ossianistic *Bard polski* in 1795. Twenty years later Princess Maryanna produced her sentimentalising psychological novel *Malwina, or the Perspicacity of the Heart* (*Malwina czyli Domyślność serca*, 1816). Through her marriage to Józef Dembowski, Konstancja Narbutt, the Irys of the Balloon episode, became the mother of Leon Castellan, the author of memoirs, and grandmother of 'Red Edward', the radical romantic critic, theoretician and aesthetician.[82] By virtue of both inclination and rank, Prince Adam Jerzy was to act as a mediating figure in post-Enlightenment trends, pleading on behalf of the Philomaths before the Tsar, and defending Mickiewicz's ballad 'Pani Twardowska' against charges of unseemliness levelled at it by the ladies of Puławy.[83] In later years he played host to exiled romantic writers in Paris.

As characters in imaginative literature, Orłowski and Dauvigny both appear in *Rok 1794*, Władysław Reymont's prose epic of the Kościuszko Uprising. But it is Prince Adam Jerzy who has again provided literature with most stimulus and substance – as a reference in Mickiewicz's

Forefathers' Eve Part III (1833), a candidate for reincarnation in Juliusz Słowacki's *Samuel Zborowski*, a major political figure in Stanisław Wyspiański's drama *Lelewel*, and a prompt for rational intellectual debate in Wacław Berent's *Twilight of the Leaders* (*Zmierzch wodzów*). In the literary portrait gallery Kniaźnin's presentation of the adolescent Prince thus marks a 'first'.

The veracity of the likeness could perhaps be questioned. The poet Karpiński, Kniaźnin's rival and sometimes friend, complained that flattery alone paved the way to a successful career at the Puławy court. As Prince Adam Jerzy put it, 'Kniaźnin wrote best when he created from pure imagination, writing of snow in summer and violets in winter'.[84]

General relations at the Puławy court apparently call for panegyric and idealisation. Yet, despite the often tedious and heavy-handed distribution of qualities, rewards and Greek sobriquets, the pen-sketches of some of the characters are marked by a vigorous psychological realism that is substantiated by memoirs of the time and documents in the Czartoryski family archive. When, half a year after the launching, the Fellowship of the Balloon suffered its first severance through the marriage of Maryanna to Prince Ludwik of Wirtemberg at Sieniawa, the cry voiced in Kniaźnin's wedding Ode (IV, V) – 'Amarylla's ours no more' – poignantly anticipates the Princess's own, later plaintive letters to Puławy, with their messages for 'dear, good Mr Ciesielski'. As she laments, 'and I stay here like muggins; those times, those happy times, *ou nous passion notre vie ensembles* have passed, and for your poor sister will never return'.[85] All seems to justify Kniaźnin's poetic prevision of time past and of loss.

Similarly, the role in which Kniaźnin has cast Maryanna Przebendowska (1765–1799) would appear to be borne out by her second husband, Tadeusz Matuszewicz, a Horatian poetaster and translator of Homer, who describes her as 'an angel of virtue and sweetness'.[86] Praise bestowed upon the Narbutt sisters is again warranted by biographical facts: Konstancja in particular had many suitors.[87] Appointing her official painter of the enterprise was both judicious and prescient.[88] Within this context one might also point to a latent romance of two of the pratogonists, Alexandra Narbutt and Colonel Ciesielki.[89]

Three other character sketches also deserve mention. When it comes to finding an astronaut for the experiment, the dancing-master Dauvigny 'Well-versed in feline language and quick wits / Was by the call of votes unanimous / Elected human envoy to the cats'. Few, surely, could be better suited to the diplomatic task of negotiating with the cats than a maestro of entrechat and pas-de-chat; and thus snidely complimented, he proceeds from the drawing-room into the *plein air* of the rose garden. Kniaźnin's fleeting characterisation, with its discreet hint of foppery, marks Dauvigny's first entry into Polish literature. Sofia Czartoryska, later Zamojska, the youngest of the Czartoryski children, recalled her dancing-master as being 'as amusing as he was decent; his lessons entertained me enormously'.[90] In Stefan Żeromski's *Popioły* (*Ashes*) Dauvigny is no more than a youthful memory for Prince Gintułt and Piotr Olbromski; but in Reymont's *The Year 1794* (*Rok 1794*) the dandy has reverted to the basic cynicism of his type. Dauvigny's death belongs to Niemcewicz's pen: already advanced in years, a resident of Tulczyn, he took a young wife, and died on his wedding night – a harsh lesson, Niemcewicz comments, for old men.[91] Kniaźnin's evocation is but the merest cast of a shadow across the retina of future memories.

A point should also be made about the covert humour in the portrayal of Adam Jerzy. The Prince is allowed five pompous stanzas in which to expatiate, unreproved, upon the properties of gas; appearing withal to justify his mother's qualms that the boy was altogether too earnest.[92] Yet, where princes charm with tedium, hired experts are unwise to tread. Encouraged perhaps by the pupil's performance, Wawrzyniec Schmuk 'like a second Priestley or Boerrhowe' launches into a learned exposé, only to be clapped up by the sudden appearance of Boredom: the courtiers promptly drop off to sleep. 'How he inflated the Balloon remains a secret, as the bard then became overcome with slumbers.'

Finally, a word about the figure of young Prince Konstanty, who had been greeted in one of Kniaźnin's birthday Odes as the child of salvation, and whose flippancy and vigour contrast with the ramrod seriousness of his brother Adam. As overseer of the Balloon experiment, he expends his energy harassing his elders and shouting non-stop;[93] his dream is a mobile collage of schoolroom reading and newspaper cuttings. The overall portrait is much in keeping with that presented by contemporary diarists, and with his mother's misgivings. The same Kostuś who surrendered the Podolian fort and scoffed all the cakes and sweetmeats[94] is nevertheless co-opted into the sphere of visionary insight and poetic imagination. Kniaźnin has thus fully embodied the child whom Princess Maryanna addresses most succinctly of all as 'my fidgety little prankster' (*ty mój trzepiotku mały*).[95]

The humour of Kniaźnin's mock epic is thus of the family type; and further archive research would probably lead to explications of many seemingly innocuous lines. It may seem like a far cry from the magnate court of Puławy to the *drame bourgeois* then preconised in France. Yet

The Balloon might be termed in defiance of generic barriers an aristocratic family drama. Czartoryski relationships and Puławy memories were characterised by their durability.[96] Kniaźnin's mock heroic is also a celebration of friendship.

In projecting these mobile pages from the family album, Kniaźnin has captured the essence of fleeting happiness, and created a trove of reminiscences for the future. This probably accounts for the fact that the poem's only true enthusiasts are Adam Jerzy Czartoryski,[97] and Krystyn Lach-Szyrma,[98] the latter of whom was no doubt initiated into the web of family hints, allusions and jokes. Whilst taking stock of Poland's past, and anticipating future trends, the group family portrait of Puławy provides a summary of viewpoints formulated in the literature and press of contemporaneous Europe, and co-ordinates disparate voices on the most sensational event of its epoch.

Notes

1. Irena Stasiewiczówna and Bolesław Orłowski, 'Balony polskie w XVIII wieku', *Horyzonty Techniki*, 1959, No 3, (1927), p. 108.
2. Signed by 'M de la C' (that is, Mathon de la Cour) and dated Lyon, 23 January, 1784.
3. A Paris, de l'Imprimerie de Moutard, Imprimeur-Libraire de la Reine, de Madame, de Madame Comtesse d'Artois, et de l'Académie Royale des Sciences, 1784.
4. *Gazeta Warszawska*, no. 3, 10 January 1784.
5. Published by E. Duchery of St Jame's Street, and dated 25 October 1783. The 'aeronaut', coiffed in a long pig-tailed wig, borne on a globular balloon, stands astride a gun-barrel supported on the profile of 'Air', whose windswept locks end in long wing-like quills. He clutches two reins, of which one is connected to an ass's face, the other to a red jester's cap and bell. These are linked in turn to a bare-buttocked creature, which emits from its rectum six tiny balloons on strings; and a satanically bearded sheep, with curly brow.
6. It claims to show 'First – those properties of Air, which influence an Air Balloon; Secondly – The particular Construction and Methods of Filling it; Thirdly – some of the great variety of probable Uses which this important Discovery may be applied to for the Benefit of Mankind; The Whole rendered familiar to the plainest Capacity'.
7. There is a study by Friedrich Ludwig Ehrmann on the technique and history of the Montgolfier achievement; a translation of Saint-Fond entitled *Beschreibung der Bersuche mit den aerostatischen Maschinen der Herren von Montgolfier nebst verschiedene zu dieser Materie*

gehdrigen Abhandlungen von Faujas de Saint-Fond, and *Der Herren Stephen und Joseph von Montgolfier mit der von ihnen erfundenen aerostatischen Maschine Ein Auszug aus der franzosischen Beschreibung des Herren Faujas de Saint-Fond*, by C. C. von Murr; printed in Strasburg, Leipzig and Nurnberg respectively.

8. It had two editions in 1784, one in Venice, the other in Paris at Barrois's printing-press, rue des Augustins.

9. 'The story of Blanchard's ascending to an altitude of thirty-three thousand feet, whence he was abducted by an air spout from another planet is not to be credited. . . I have not read that newspaper myself, so I find it difficult to believe that stupid fairy-tale, [. . .] All these facts published in the *Courier de l'Europe* seem exaggerated, and one can certainly apply the proverb "a beau menti qui vient de loin". But nothing equals the stupidity of the claim that Mr Blanchard after exceeding that height rose swiftly to another planet. [. . .] Reduce things to reality. I have too much esteem for the sect of balloonists to tolerate the slander cast upon its patriarch, involving him in an adventure of which he certainly never even dreamt'. August Fryderyk Moszyński, *Dziennik podróży do Francji i Włoch Augusta Moszynśkiego architekta JKM Stanisława Augusta Poniatowskiego 1784–1786*. Ed. and translated from the French by Bożena Zboińska-Daszyńska (Kraków 1970) p. 480. Moszynśki was architect to King Stanisław August.

10. Okraszewski, the Royal Chemist, demonstrated a hydrogen-filled balloon in Warsaw on 12 February 1784 (*Gazeta Warszawska, no. 13. cf. Roman Kaleta 'Balony! Balony! Balony! Największa sensacja naukowa XVIII wieku' Problemy*, Vol. XVI, 1960, No. 4 pp. 302–7; and Anna Berdecka, Irena Turnau *Żvcie codzienne w Warszawie okresu Oświecenia* (Warsaw 1969), pp. 211–12). Preliminary tests were held in Kraków on 19, 21 and 24 February 1784 (*Gazeta Warszawska*, No.17; cf. Kaleta, ibid.). The first experiment by Gidelski, Korn and Bach in Warsaw on 24 February (Stasiewiczówna, *Horyzonty Techniki*) was followed by the release of a considerably larger balloon that fell some 150 km from Warsaw on 3 March 1784 (*Gazeta Warszawska*, No.23; cf. Stasiewiczówna, ibid). Three days later Okraszewski made a second attempt in Warsaw (*Gazeta Warszawska*, No.23). An experiment was carried out by Professors Jaśkiewicz, Sniadecki, Szaster and Szeidt of the Krakow Academy on 1 April (*Gazeta Warszawska*, No.29; cf. Kaleta, ibid., and Berdecka, ibid).

11. Jędrzej Kitowicz, *Pamiętniki czyli Historia Polska* (Warsaw 1971), p. 364; J. U. Niemcewicz, *Pamiętniki moich czasów* (Warsaw 1957) Vol. 1, pp. 166, 222; Antoni Magier, *Estetyka miasta stolecznego Warszawy* (Wroclaw, 1963), pp. 130–1, 227–8.

12. The sketch of a balloon by King Stanislaw August is reproduced in Maria Żywirska, *Ostatnie lata życia króla Stanisława Augusta* (Warsaw, 1978).

13. See Ignacy Krasicki, *Korespondencja*, ed. Z. T. Mikulski, 2 vols (Wroclaw, 1958).

14. Roman Kaleta, *Problemy*.

15. In the preface to *Edycja kompletna* of 1787–8, reprinted in 1820 and 1837.

140   *F. D. Kniaźnin and the Polish Balloon*

16. Stasiewiczówna and Orłowski, *Horyzonty Techniki*, p. 109. Other datings have been suggested by W. Borowy, who relates the Puławy entertainment and Kniaźnin's poem to the time 'when a general interest began to be taken in air journeys and Blanchard, the inventor of balloons, appeared in Warsaw (1782) and made an ascent above the town with Jan Potocki' (Franciszek Dionyzy Kniaźnin, *Wybór Poezji*, Biblioteka Narodowa, Wroclaw 1948 p. 10); and Władysław Smoleński, who states that 'four years after the invention, a dodecagonal balloon . . . was launched at Puławy by the mathematician Lhuilhier'. *Przewrót umysłowy w Polsce wieku XVIII*, 4th ed. (Warsaw, 1979) p. 152.
17. *Gazeta Warszawska*, no. 23, 6 March 1784 reports that the Vistula was frozen. The same issue also mentions severe February frosts in London on 27 February. Guzek has likewise noted 'The final test took place most probably in March. The inquisitive Pulawy farm hands slide on the still melting ice and sink in the snow'. Andrzej Guzek, *Twórczość liryczna Franciszka Dionizego Kniaźnina*, PhD thesis defended at the University of Warsaw. Library of the University of Warsaw manuscripts, provisional number 223.
18. She died from burns when her dress caught fire. Niemcewicz, *Pamiętniki* p. 126.
19. Ibid., p. 153. Kniaźnin dedicated to Prince August his Ode 'Cedr' ('The Cedar') in *Ody czyli Liryków IV Księgi* I, vii; hence the image of the Ode upon his death 'Runął na koniec i ów cedr wysoki!' (In the end that tall cedar also fell!'). 'Na śmierć X. Augusta Czartoryskiego Wojewody Ruskiego' *Ody* II, viii.
20. See the account in Niemcewicz, *Pamiętniki* vol. 1, p. 162.
21. Princess Maryanna describes the move: 'After the death of my grandfather (around 1782, some two years) my parents moved to Puławy with the children and whole camp, and leaving us there in winter, sometimes returned to Warsaw for a short while, but later my mother was hardly ever away; one could say that she became immersed in Puławy'. Czartoryski Archives Ew XII/608. Prince Adam Jerzy refers to the same period: 'From the time of our settling in Puławy begins my more orderly life, more organised, aimed at providing the best education which my father wished to ensure for his children. Everything was well arranged in Puławy with this aim, and carried out according to plan'. Czartoryski Archives Ew. 995.
22. W. Spasowicz, *Dzieje literatury polskiej*, 3rd ed, 1891, p. 213.
23. Piotr Chmielowski, *Historya Literatury Polskiej*, 1899, vol. 2, p. 218.
24. Jan Nepocumen Bobrowicz, 'Krótka wiadomość o życiu & &'., *Dzieła Franciszka Dyonizego Kniaźnina z popiersiem autora*, Leipzig 1837, p. xiii.
25. Julian Bartoszewicz, *Historia literatury polskiej potocznym sposobem opowiedziana*, 2nd ed, 1877, vol. 2, p. 83.
26. K. Wł. Wójcicki, *Historia literatury polskiej w zarysach*, 2nd ed, 1860, vol. 3, p. 317.
27. He had joined the Czartoryski household at the same time as Kniaźnin, in 1774, but in 1783–1785 resided at Arcadia, near Nieborów, the estate of Princess Helena Radziwiłł.

28. On 18 January, Bishop Ignacy Kraskicki wrote from Lidzbark to Ahaswer Henryk Lehndorff that 'it would appear that Prince Czartoryski intends leaving Poland for good'. Krasicki, Korespondencja, letter no. 386, p. 204 – According to a report from Vienna dated New year's Day 'Large subscriptions are being raised for the making of an Aerostatic Machine; for which His Highness Prince Adam Czartoryski has contributed 100 gold ducats, the Duke of Schwarzenberg and Aloizy Duke of Lichtenstein, 50, and the Duke of Paar 100; some people have already volunteered to go on the first air journey in this machine'. *Gazeta Warszawska*, no. 7, Saturday 24 January 1784.

29. This inference would be borne out by the memoirs of Zofia Czartoryska, later Zamoyska. 'Z pamiętnika Zofii Zamoyskiej' In Ludwik Dębicki *Puławy*, Lwów, 1887, vol. 4, p. 286. See also Niemcewicz, *Pamiętniki*, p. 126.

30. Kniaźnin dedicated to her the Posthumous Ode IV, vi 'Księżnie Wirtemberskiej' and IV xvii 'Na urodziny Ks. Wirtemberskiej'. A sprig of rosemary from her wedding wreath provides the motif for the poem *Rozmaryn, poema liryczne*.

31. Kniaźnin dedicated a number of Odes to him (II xxvii, III iv, IV iii, IV xxii; and Posthumous Odes III ii and III xxiv).

32. His birth on 28 October 1774 was celebrated in Kniaźnin's Ode 'Do J' O' Kścia Jmci Czartoryskiego, Generala Ziem Podolskich z kcajij narodzonego syna Konstantego Adama Aleksandra'. He is endowed with an aura of superiority and adulthood in 'Intryga', *Odes* IV 9.

33. Born in 1765, daughter of the Starosta of Solce; a kinswoman of the Flemmings and thereby a cousin of Princess Izabela.

34. They were the daughters of Tadeusz Narbutt, Chamberlain of Lida and squire of Sukurcz, and of Katarzyna Née Wolosiewicz. Narbutt *père*, 'about whom little is known' (Józef Szymanowski's *Listy do Starościny Wyszogrodzkiej 1792–1801*, ed. Franciszek Korwin-Szymanowski, Warsaw 1973) devoted his life to directing dietines and organising elections for the Lithuanian Tribunal, as a client of the Czartoryskis or a supporter of the King. (Bronisław Zaleski *Żywot Ks. Adama Czartoryskiego* Poznan 1881, vol. 1, p. 182). He was later deputy marshal to the Tribunal under the marshalship of Prince Adam Kazimierz Czartoryski. Niemcewicz recalls the Narbutt sisters at a feast given before the King in Wolczyn in 1777, when with other ladies of the court they dressed up as reapers. Niemcewicz, *Pamiętniki* p. 90. They lived on an equal footing with the young princesses at the Czartoryski court, where they were completing their education, and each had her 'cottage' in the hamlet at Powązki. (L. Dębicki, *Puławy*, p. 213; cf. also p. 210). The younger one in particular was Princess Izabela's favourite.

35. Young Sapieha has another aeronautic connection: his sister *en secondes noces* married Seweryn Potocki, brother of Jan, of subsequent ballooning, Caucasian and literary fame, who was however seen only once at Puławy. Leon Dembowski, *Moje wspomnienia*, St Petersburg, 1898, vol. I, p. 153.

36. Ciepliński was the recipient of an ode by Kniaźnin. 'Do Ignacego Cieplińskiego' (*Ody* III, x) 'Żalim się zawsze na to nasze życie . . . Któż

temu winien? my sami.' l.4 (We grumble daily at this life of ours. Whose is the fault? Our own). Jan Rembieliński had Ode IV, xxvii dedicated to him.

37. Niemcewicz, *Pamiętniki* p. 89. Borzęcki presided at table during the Prince's absence; the male members of court usually dined at his table. In his Ode to Borzęcki (II, 23) Kniaźnin hints at the universality of his poetic aspiration, and confides his misgivings on the decline of Poland. 'My Piotr, I work too! My task is to explore the air,/The earth and sky; and all that flies,/And crawls, and shines'. ('Pracuję i ja, moj Pietrze!/ Celem tej pracy powietrze,/Ziemia i niebo; co leci/Pełza i świeci.') Borzęcki was also a correspondent of the poet Józef Szymanowski. Szymanowski, *Listy* p. 107.

38. Orłowski was later commander of Kamieniec. 'Beneath a gloomy exterior (he was) cheerful, honest and kind'. Niemcewicz, *Pamiętniki*, p. 137. In 1789–91 he accompanied the young Adam Jerzy and Princess Izabela on their tour of England and Scotland. In 1800, in the latter-day loneliness of Puławy life, Princess Izabela wrote 'there is no one here, apart from Major Orłowski, who sometimes comes in the morning or for dinner'. *Listy Księżny Izabelli z hr. Flemmingów Czartoryskiej do starszego syna Ks. Adama* sebrała Seweryna Duchińska, Kraków 1891. Letter dated 10 April 1800. Kniaźnin dedicated two Odes to him, 'Do Józefa Orłowskiego' (II, v and III, 15). The second of these is a meditation on the durable fame of the Argo, whose aim was conquest and theft. Similarly, Europeans head for America, like a band of mercenary thugs, seeking not sun worship, but the glitter of gold.

39. Niemcewicz, *Pamiętniki*, p. 56. After a spell in the Lithuanian Guard Ciesielski was appointed steward to the young princes, and he also taught history to Adam.

40. He is referred to in family letters as 'your best friend'. 'Stay always with Mr Ciesielski, you owe it to us, you owe it to him'. *Listy Księżny. . .* Letter from Warsaw dated 8 May 1785. He accompanied young Adam to Karlsbad, a journey on which Kniaźnin also went, and later on to Prague and Weimar. In the late summer of 1787 he took his pupil to observe the military exercises at Belgard in Pomerania. His namesday was celebrated at Puławy even in his absence, and gifts of ices, oranges and preserves were sent to his nephew at Cadet School. Kniaźnin addressed him an Ode 'Do Stanisława Ciesielskiego, rotmistrza Kawalerii Narodowej' ('Czy miły tobie głos mój, Stanisławie?') ('Is my voice sweet to you, Stanisław?'), *Ody* IV, 16).

41. An exact contemporary of Kniaźnin's, Simon L'Huilhier (1750–?1810), was a member of the Prussian Academy of Sciences, the Royal Academy in London, and a Correspondent of the Imperial Academy in St Petersburg. During his sojourn in Poland, he produced a number of arithmetic, geometry and algebra text-books for the palatinal schools, sponsored by the Commission for National Education. *Arithmétique pour les écoles palatinales Warsaw,* 1778. His primers were used for almost half a century. Other publications include *De relatione mutua capacitatis et terminorum figurarum geometrice considerata, seu de maximis et minimis pars prior elementaris,* Warsaw 1780–92; 'Quelle est la notion claire et précise qu'il faut se faire de l'infini mathématique' which was

awarded the Prize of the Academy of Berlin, 1786; 'Principiorum Calculi Differentialis et Integralis Expositio Elementaris ad normam dissertationis ab Academia Scient. Reg. Prussica anno 1786. Praemii Honore Decoratae Elaborata auctore Simone L'Huilier etc'; *Exposition elementaire des principes des calculs superieurs*, Berlin 1787. He later settled in Geneva, where he taught mathematics at the university and published textbooks at his own expense both in Tubingen and Geneva (1789, 1795, 1797, 1801, 1804, 1809). This last, entitled *Eléments d'analyse géometrique et d'analyse algébrique, appliquées à la recherche des lieux géometriques, par Simon L'Huilier etc* was dedicated to Prince Adam Jerzy in the hope it would be adopted as a text-book in those educational establishments of the Russian Empire that came under the Prince's jurisdiction. See entry in the *Grand Dictionnaire Universel du 19e siècle*, Larousse 1873, vol. 10. In a footnote to Canto II Kniaźnin mentions a learned paper of L'Huilhier's entitled 'De cellulis Apum'. The dodecagonal design of the Puławy Balloon was based on the model of the bee-hive.

42. Born c. 1750 in Germany (Magier, *Estetyka*, p. 111 and footnote p. 339), Lessel came to Poland in 1780 and joined the Puławy court in the following year as composer and *kapelmeister* in residence. As a freemason, he made frequent visits to Warsaw, where he gave public lectures to popularise science at meetings of the Ladies' Lodge. See Władysław Smolénski, *Przewrót*, p. 216.

43. See Dębicki, *Puławy*, vol. 4, p. 288.

44. Niemcewicz, *Pamiętniki*, p. 55.

45. Magier, *Estetyka*, p. 110.

46. Niemcewicz, *Pamiętniki*. Adam Jerzy Czartoryski mentions that Dauvigny had also been ballet-master of the Prince of Wurtemberg in Stuttgart. Adam Jerzy Czartoryski, *Początek Pamiętników*, Mss. in the Czartoryski Archives, Ew. 995 f. 5.

47. Cf. Teresa Kostkiewiczowa 'In this way [by using names] the person depicted and the activities that person performs gain as it were a higher dimension, are made more lofty, as they are related to some concealed, higher meanings revealed in the poems'. 'Poematy Kniaźnina wobec tradycji gatunkowej' *Pamiętnik Literacki* LXI, 1970, z. 2, p. 219.

48. Roman Pilat, *Historia literatury polskiej*, 1908, vol. 4.

49. Mieczysław Klimowicz, *Oświecenie*, Warsaw, 1977, p. 319.

50. Ibid.

51. Kostkiewiczowa, 'Poematy Kniaźnina' p. 216.

52. Felicyan Suryn in *Tygodnik Ilustrowany*, vol. XI, 1 January–30 January 1881, p. 363.

53. Kniaźnin taught history to Princess Zofia, who comments: '. . .for various reasons the course was interrupted. I only reached the beginning of the Jagiellos, who absorbed my attention as it was said that our family descends from them'. *Z pamiętnika Zofii Zamoyskiej*, L. Dębicki, *Puławy*, p. 287.

54. See Teresa Kostkiewiczowa, 'Koncepcja poezji i poety we wczesnej twórczości Kniaźnina', in *Prace z poetyki poświęcone VI Miedzynarodowemu Kongresowi Slawistów*, 1968, pp. 196–219.

55. Galland's collection of Arab tales was translated by Lukasz Sokołowski and published as *Awantury arabskie lub Tysiąc nocy i jedna*, T. I-XII 1767–69; Mme Petit probably had her own French digest.

56. Several incidents are related in Gabriela Pauszer-Klonowska, *Pani na Puławach*, Warsaw 1978.

57. Niemcewicz, who left Prince Adam and Vienna for Italy at about the time the Puławy balloon was being launched, visited the ravaged scene after the Messina earthquake, and heard guitar and sad Sicilian songs inspired by the disaster. Niemcewicz, *Pamiętniki*, p. 207. The work he recommends on this subject, Deodat de Gratet de Dolomieu's (1750–1801), *Mémoires sur les tremblements de terre de la Calabre pendant l'année 1783*, came out in Rome in 1784.

58. Montgolfier had projected his design with the idea of bringing supplies to the besieged inhabitants of Gibraltar. It would be interesting to date the compilation of this note. The Prince of Nassau, a hero of the Siege of Gibraltar, visited Puławy in 1786, a year and a half before Kniaźnin's complete collection was printed.

59. These thoughts were inspired by a reading of Osiński's *Robota machiny powietrznej pana Mongolfier*, przez X. J O Scholarum Piarum, Warsaw 1784. It illustrates principles of construction, and numerous calulations. The most original part puts forward the idea of an iron flying vacuum machine, and proves the possibility of realising this. Such an Aerostat would be used for the transportation of goods (a horse would be harnessed for lack of favourable wind), ferrying people across rivers, marking straight roads, and making topographical maps. It presented no danger of fire and unforseen changes of altitude. 'It is a project in which nothing is impossible, nothing opposed to reason. [. . .] but were it to be realised withall, it could be useful, for it seems that flying balloons made of paper or taffeta will be of no benefit'.

60. Together with Shakespeare, Bacon and Newton, Cook was one of the English figures whose likeness King Stanislaw August ordered of Vincent de Leseur, his favourite court miniaturist.

61. Karol Krejči, *Heroikomika v basnictvi Slovanu*, Prague 1964. Krejči erroneously attributes the decoration of the Balloon to 'Jedne z knežen'. The only princess in the *Balloon* is Maryanna Czartoryska.

62. P. Chmielowski, *Historya*, p. 218.

63. Dębicki, *Puławy*, vol. 5, p. 852.

64. Borowy, *Kniaźnin, Wybor Poezji*.

65. V. V. Witt, I. S. Miller, B. F. Stakheev, V. A. Khoreyev, eds., *Istoriya pol'skoy literatury*, Moscow 1968, vol I, p. 139.

66. Stanisław Pałuchowski, 'Kniaźnin i Sabłocki w stosunku do siebie i dworu Czartoryskich', in *Sprawozdanie dyrekcyi C. K. Gimnazyum V we Lwowie za rok 1907*.

67. Chrzanowski, *Historia literatury niepodległej Polski*, PIW 1971, p. 710 (1st edition c. 1920).

68. W. Borowy in *O poezji polskiej w wieku XVIII*, Warsaw 1978, p. 247.

69. Teresa Kostkiewiczowa 'Poematy Kniaźnina' (as in n. 47) p. 210.

70. Stanisław Tarnowski *Historia literatury polskiej*, 1904 (2nd ed.), p. 373.

71. Zygmunt Krasiński 'Lettre sur l'état actuel de la littérature polonaise

addressée à M. de Bonstetten' in *Dzieła literackie*, ed. Pawel Hertz, Warsaw 1973, vol. III p. 210.

72. The tone of the narrator stranded on the moon is relaxed in the extreme. 'As the Sielans know neither pate en croûte, nor second nor third courses, nor broth, nor jellied consommé, I could never have assembled enough cattle membranes to make a Balloon'. M. D. Krajewski, *Wojciech Zdarzyński...*, Warsaw 1785 p. 140–1.

73. There was a family connection here. Władysław IV, descended from Grand Duke Giedymin of Lithuania, issued in Buda in 1442 a privilege, 'in which he calls the Princes Czartoryski his cousins'. Dembowski, *Moje wspomnienia*, p. 174. The youthful king was restored to a more conventionally heroic role by Niemcewicz, who made his literary début three years after Kniaźnin's *Balloon* with a historical tragedy entitled *Władysław pod Warną* 1787). See Niemcewicz, *Pamiętniki* p. 421. Niemcewicz's earlier exercise in the mock heroic genre, entitled *wojna kobiet* (*The War of Women*), written when he was sixteen, was 'corrected' by Prince Adam Kazimierz who 'ticked off' two lines as good. The manuscript was subsequently lost. Ibid, I, p. 82. Niemcewicz also translated Pope's *The Rape of the Lock*.

74. A. J. Czartoryski, 'Życie Kniaźnina. (Z manuskryptu pisanego w r. 1817)', *Przegląd Poznański*, vol. XVI, 1853, p. 125.

75. Krajewski was also the author of *Gry nauk dla dzieci służące do ułatwienia ich edukacji przez które łatwo nauczyć się mogą poznania liter, sylabizowania, czytania w polskim i francuskim języku, formowania charakteru pisma, języków ze zwyczaju, historii, geografii i początków arytmetyki*, Kraków, 1777. See Irena Łossowska, *Michal Dymitr Krajewski. Zarys monograficzny*, Rozprawy Uniwersytetu Warszawskiego. Wydawnictwo Uniwersytetu Warszawskiego, 1980, pp. 94–108. One statement in particular (quoted in Łossowska, p. 107) could serve as a motto to Kniaźnin's *Balloon*. 'Czegoż nie można dokonać w dziecięciu wesoły humor, gdy kształnie ukryjemy przed nim imię nauki, a wszelką przykrość zabawą, i rozrywki słodyczą ułatwiać staramy się' (What may a merry humour not achieve with a child, when we skilfully conceal the name of science, and endeavour to make all unpleasantness easy with amusement, and the sweetness of entertainment').

76. Niemcewicz has left the following account of their tour of Prince Czartoryski's Eastern Borderland estates in the spring of 1783. 'We were accompanied on this journey by the Prince's young sons, Adam and Konstanty, with their steward, Colonel Ciesielski, and their numerous teachers. The elder, today most eminent for his civic conscience, was thirteen, the younger barely nine [in fact eight and a half, his birthday being six months later, after the events described]. They were both of them possessed by the martial spirit; the elder was studying fortifications. Having nothing to do in Miedzyboż, they had the idea of building a fortress, and dividing the youngsters who were with the Prince in two camps. One was to lock itself in the fortress, the other to take it by storm. As a pupil of the cadets, I was chosen as general of artillery and entrusted with digging the entrenchments. (. . .) Young prince Konstanty and I had to defend the fortress, Prince Adam and Molski were to take it

by storm; it was decided that no weapons would be used other than sand and clods of earth. When we had already nicely entrenched ourselves, the enemy army appeared in the distance. Molski, who assumed for the occasion the Spanish name of Don Inigo Henriko di Molo – sat on a splendid steed. . . We began throwing clumps of earth, then fistfuls of sand so thick and fast from both sides that we could not see each other; the trench was easily passed (. . .) we would not surrender to the bitter end, so the fortress was taken by storm; the victors did not find much loot, as all the sweets and cakes during the assault had been eaten by our commander, little prince Konstanty, and his young play-mates'. Niemcewicz, *Pamiętniki*, vol. 1, p. 162. Another account is to be found in Adam Jerzy Czartoryski, *Pamiętniki i memoriały polityczne*, ed. Jerzy Skowronek, Warsaw 1986 p. 89–90.

77.   'Another type of fencing we also liked to exercise ouselves at was the parlimentary kind. A subject was proposed, discussion followed. One day, I recall, it had to be proved before an audience whether society had more to gain from the régime of liberty such as we then conceived it, or from that of a strong central authority'. Adam Jerzy Czartoryski, 'Sketch to my Memoirs', Czartoryski Archives Ew. 995 f. 22.

78.   See J. U. Niemcewicz, c. 25 August 1834, 'The Balloon burst, you must have known about it. I much regretted it'. ('Balon pękł, musisz Pani o tym wiedzieć. Bardzo go żałowałem'); Adam Mickiewicz's letter (no. 378) to Klaudyna Potocka about 'a dirigible balloon' ('balon sterowiec') – '30 oars with gas able to move in different directions' ('30 wioseł z gazy mogących się poruszać w różne strony'); Zygmunt Krasiński's letter to Stanislaw Małachowski of 15.iv.1843 concerning the success of 'the air-machine'. In a letter to Jarosław Iwaszkiewicz dated 20 December 1930, Czesław Miłosz refers to one of his ancestors who reputedly 'flew about in a balloon'. See Grażyna Martenko-Obrąpalska, 'Skamandryta i Żagarysta', *Poezja*, 1981, no. 7.

79.   Jarosław Marek Rymkiewicz, *Aleksandr Fredro jest w złym humorze*, Warszawa 1977, pp. 262, 249.

80.   Ibid., p. 58. At the end of 1839, the Czartoryski party created the Towarzystwo Monarchiczno-Insurekcyjne and iproclaimed Prince Adam Jerzy king *de facto*. See programme in J. Woronicz's brochure *Rzecz o monarchii i dynastii w Polsce* (1839). Their press organ, entitled *Trzeci Maj*, is referred to in Adam Mickiewicz's letter. Mickiewicz wrote to Ignacy Domeyko from Paris on 23 or 24 December 1840. 'In émigré circles the struggle is still going on for the reign of Czartoryski, who is violently supported by a new party, while his old supporters, perturbed and estranged, have left him. The Prince is noble-minded, not always diplomatic, and has allowed medals to be issued with the inscription "God, give us back our king", which infuriates his opponents. I love the Prince as I ever did, but do not understand and support all his steps.'

81.   See the entry in *Polski Słownik Biograficzny*.

82.   Edward Dembowski (Konstancja Narbutt's grandson) 'Nowe odkrycie w dziedzinie przyrody', *Przegląd Naukowy*, 1842, vol. III. Reprinted in E. Dembowski, *Pisma*, vol. II, Warsaw 1955, pp. 272–279. Dembowski is the hero of a socialist realist *biographie romancée*.

83.   Adam Jerzy Czartoryski, Diary.

84. Adam Jerzy Czartoryski, *Przegląd Poznanski*.
85. The original text reads as follows: 'a ia jak gab tu siedzę; minęły te czasy te szczęsliwe czasy ou nous passion notre vie ensembles minely i dla twoiej bidnej siostry nigdy sie wiecej niewruco'. She further writes: 'Muj Panie adamie, extra mi tęskno extra extra po Pulawach okrutnie et je vous dis en confidence qu'il n'y a que la (que) je puis etre heureuse' (My Lord Adam I am ultra homesick for Pulawy ultra ultra, terribly' etc. . .). Princess Wirtemberska's Letters to her brother, Prince Adam Jerzy Czartoryski. Czartoryski Archives Ew XVII/823.
86. Szymanowski, *Listy*, p. 147. Przebendowska died in 1799. Her infant daughter Zofia was brought up by Izabella Czartoryska, and became albeit briefly a prospective bride for Adam Jerzy (See Diary of Adam Jerzy Czartoryski, p. 126; also Natalia Kicka, *Pamiętniki*, ed. Józef Dutkiewicz and Tadeusz Szafrański, Warsaw 1972), only to be married off to Ludwik Kicki; she died of tuberculosis in the autumn of 1822 after giving birth to two daughters. Ibid, pp. 345–347.
87. These included a German count, Orłowski, Niemcewicz and the poet Szymanowski.
88. Her daughter Cecylia took private lessons with the painter Norblin at his *atelier* in Warsaw (1801), and illustrated Adam Jerzy's *Bard Polski* (1795) in the Ossianic manner. A copy was deposited in the Temple of Sybilla by Princess Maryanna Wirtemberska in 1803. Czartoryski Archives, Ew XVII/712.
89. In a letter to Konstancja Dembowska dated London 10 January 1790, Princess Izabela writes, 'I feel terribly sorry for Aleksandra. Why is that man so cold, you know ever since reading your letter I have been angry with Ciesielski, and if Alexandra is not cured, and he does not warm up (*rozgrzeje sie*), I shall find him obnoxious. I shall do my utmost to console her when I come back'. Czartoryski Archives Ew. XVII/1094, Letters of Izabela Czartoryska. . . Another ten years went by before Alexandra married her companion of the Balloon. Alexandra could also draw and paint well, but, writes her nephew, 'in all her hundreds of sketches I never saw anything other than the sea at sunset, Cupid sailing away from the shore, and a damsel on the shore leaning on an anchor, her arms stretched out to him in longing. Aunt Alexandra's Cupid was none other than old Colonel Ciesielski. Hymen finally crowned these long and lasting amours, providing the artist with a new theme – two hearts burning on an altar, by which a flower-decked Cupid lay in repose'. Dembowski, *Moje wspomnienia*, pp. 16–17.
90. Dębicki, *Puławy*.
91. Niemcewicz, *Pamiętniki*, p. 55.
92. Princess Izabella Czartoryska, *Listy*,.
93. Though all work hard, he spurs them on the more
    Sometimes endearing, others he upbraids;
    His gaze full both of thunder and of charm;
    Weary at last, like a young colt let loose,
    Frolicking for a time, he now seeks rest;
    He leant upon a stool, and rubbed his brows,
    Half shut one eye, fell blissfully asleep.
94. Cf. note 76.

95. Princess Maryanna Wirtemberska, *Listy*.

96. Referring to the battle game of the Podolian journey, 'Thirty-four years later, returning from Odessa, I stopped deliberately in Miedzyboż to visit the place of our youthful games. Alas! My fortress had sunk into the earth, though it was still possible to distinguish its shape'. Niemcewicz, *Pamiętniki*, vol. 1, p. 162.

97. '(*The Balloon*) became one of the dearest works of his pen' Adam Jerzy Czartoryski, *Przegląd Poznański*, p. 126. 'When their still fresh memory becomes veiled in the mist of the passing years, Kniaźnin's works will assume a new charm, and will be read by our grandsons with increased curiosity and sadness'. Ibid, p. 128. It is perhaps symptomatic that Adam Jerzy Czartoryski wrote his biographical outline of Kniaźnin in 1817, a year of deep stock-taking as he deliberated upon his marriage to Princess Sapieha's daughter (Adam Jerzy Czartoryski's Private diary).

98. '. . . besides this, his principal poem' (. . .) is 'esteemed the best of his writings (. . .), which by its length and dignified flow, borders on the epic, immortalising the enterprise, and the individuals concerned'. Indeed, in his longer poems Kniaźnin 'excelled more than in the short ones'. K. Lach Szyrma, *Letters, literary and political, on Poland, comprising observations on Russia and other Sclavonian nations and tribes*, Edinburgh 1823, pp. 217, 216. Lach Szyrma was what one might call a co-opted member of the Puławy set. For ten years he was tutor to Konstanty's son Adam, and was presumably initiated in the collective memories of the family. He accompanied his pupil when the latter was sent to study at Edinburgh University. Szyrma is an interesting bridge-figure; in the literary field he contributed to the development of the ballad and the *dumka*, and later on as a political émigré promoted the Polish cultural cause in the United Kingdom, where he launched translations of Mickiewicz, M. Czajkowski, and Ewa Felińska's *Siberian Revelations* (1852). See also Nina Taylor, 'Krystyn Lach-Szyrma. A Pole's Impressions of Nineteenth-century Scotland', *Scottish Slavonic Review*, 10, Spring 1988, p. 135–153.

15 Karel Čapek and English Writers
Bohunka Bradbrook

Karel Čapek's 'Englishness' may surprise many, if one considers how little contact there was between Britain and the Czech lands before his time. Situated in the heart of Europe, his fatherland has always been exposed to the influences of neighbouring Germanic cultures and, at the beginning of this century, the French *fin de siècle* style fascinated and quite strongly influenced Czech artists of all kinds.

Čapek was no exception. In addition to attending the University of Prague, he studied also in Berlin and at the Sorbonne, but there, instead of studying French, he enrolled as a student of English literature.[1] Having interviewed Čapek in Prague, the English Slavist Lawrence Hyde reported in the *Manchester Guardian*[2] that 'English literature is his favourite study and he reads English with perfect ease'. Even more importantly, Čapek himself declared to an English journalist[3] that 'as far as outside literature is concerned, I myself have been under the influence of the Anglo-Saxons'. By this, however, Čapek does not mean to say that his preference for English literature excluded other influences and experience: he acknowledged his debt to Czech literature and tradition, and was surprisingly well read in the French, German, Russian and other great classics as well as contemporary writers.

Čapek's contact with English literature can be traced back to his childhood: his father's enthusiasm for knowledge brought Shakespeare, Dickens, Scott, Swift, Defoe into the family library, as well as Marryat who made Čapek wish to become a sailor. After he had grasped the philosophy of pragmatism[4] during his university studies, the world and mind of the 'Anglo-Saxons' were firmly rooted in his subconscious and one can see that he himself possessed the qualities he most admired in them – namely, common sense, empiricism, politeness, social finesse and fair play. When he visited Britain in 1924, the country seemed to him quite familiar, as he commented in his speech to the London PEN Club.

His link with Britain was also strengthened through his friendship with Professor Otakar Vočadlo who was in the 1920s a lecturer at King's College, London. He encouraged the shy Čapek to accept the invitation of the London PEN Club and became Čapek's 'guardian angel' and companion during his London visit as well as on his travels through Britain. It was through Vočadlo that Čapek came and subsequently wrote his charming *Letters from England*; the fact that this work is the best among his seven travelogues only supports the strength of his 'Englishness'.

Before coming to London, Čapek wrote to Vočadlo that he would like to meet his most admired writers, Shaw, Wells and Chesterton.[5] He named them in this sequence, but his preference was in the reverse order.

His favourite has always been Chesterton. In Shaw he saw an almost superhuman being and in Wells, above all, a wise prophet. Like Čapek, the three were journalists, too, . . . and they had one basic quality in common, namely, humour. Čapek liked Chesterton's humour best, as it was kindly and exuberant. He appreciated the delightful sparkle of his countless paradoxes and he also praised his poetic democracy and genial optimism. He did not mind Chesterton's Victorian conservatism, nor his bias towards the idealised Middle Ages, nor his Bellockian Catholic view of life.[6]

Whenever Čapek asked his friend Vočadlo to send him English books, those of Chesterton were the first priorities.[7]

Although Chesterton admired Čapek as a dramatist, it is, sadly, rather obvious that he resented the fact that Čapek and his liberal country did not belong to the same conservative, Catholic flock as Poland: the reserve with which he treated Čapek seems to indicate this clearly. Chesterton did not usually attend PEN dinners, but he made an exception when one was arranged in Čapek's and the Romanian Queen Mary's honour; later, however, he proved himself not to be a very good correspondent. Čapek's letters to him[8] abound in admiration and affection and yet Chesterton failed twice to answer. Confessing eventually[9] 'what a muddle I make of my life and letters', he did not visit Čapek in Prague in 1926 or later, as he seems to have promised.[10]

In 1927 Chesterton dealt a blow to Čapek by printing in *G. K.'s Weekly* Dudley Heathcote's article 'The Slovak Problem' instigated by Hungary which resented the loss of this territory to the newly created Czechoslovakia. it was a fierce and direct attack on the young Republic of which Čapek was so proud. He protested, painstakingly explaining point by point, the problem which Chesterton may not have fully understood. Čapek had spent long periods of time in Slovakia when his father lived there as a doctor, and knew the people well; the more reason now for repeating his invitation to Chesterton who could have repaired the damage by visiting Czechoslovakia and seeing things for himself. Chesterton printed Čapek's reply, adding an editorial note[11] that 'it seemed good to have various opinions about European policy' and that 'the appearance of such an article (i.e. Heathcote's) does not imply that the paper can vouch for the accuracy, or support the policy, of such an article'. A letter from Mrs R. J. M. Witton, supporting Čapek, is printed in the same issue, but, on 4 February, a long letter defending Heathcote's argument against Čapek's analysis of the true situation was published. Although disillusioned and deeply hurt, Čapek never ceased admiring 'The good Chesterton', as he entitled his obituary in the Czech press.[12]

Wishing to enrich Czech literature with the introduction of new genres, Čapek found good sources in English literature. He read Chesterton's essays with great enthusiasm, liking particularly the form of the brief, witty article which he himself developed into the 'little column', as he called it. Čapek's interest was taken by Chesterton's defence of penny-dreadfuls, nonsense, useful information, ugly things, farce, slang as well as detective stories in *The Defendant*, because 'it does me good to find pleasant things in the realms of bad reputation.'[13] It has also led him to explore other primitive literary forms, such as popular poetry, proverbs, sayings, urban songs, novels for maid-servants. In the application of serious methods of literary theory to the light forms of popular literary creations, Čapek's irony resembles Chesterton's; in fact, direct reference to Chesterton[14] suggests that *The Defendant* inspired his *Marsyas* (1931).

Chesterton's *Tremendous Trifles* may have indirectly influenced Čapek. Not so much by its paradoxical title, but by the attention the author paid to little, insignificant things. Čapek did so, too, in most of his works, more in the essays, but examples can be found also in the novels and plays. Essays on dreams, melancholy, the barrel-organ, names, post, cats, matchboxes, candles and other matters in *Intimate Things* were followed by many similar ones on trifles in the later collections, *The Calendar, How they Do It, About People*.

Coincidences when two writers use the same subject may well serve to show their similarities, but also their differences: Chesterton's charming essay 'The Ethics of Elfland',[15] although using the language of literary theory, sticks strictly to its title, human ethics, while Čapek's three essays on the subject in *Marsyas*, 'Towards the Theory of Fairy-Tales', 'A Few Fairy-Tale motifs', 'Some Fairy-Tale Personalities', are concerned with purely literary-theoretical interest. Their essays on leisure, Chesterton's 'On Leisure'[16] and Čapek's 'In Praise of Idleness'[17] show more than just the two writers' interest in human 'affairs', although they start in an almost identical manner: Čapek's piece was published in 1920, eight years before Chesterton's who could hardly have read it before it was translated into English in 1935.

Like the essay, the detective story had no tradition as a genre in Czech literature. As a journalist, Čapek would have found enough material in newspaper law court announcements for developing this literary genre, but he seems to have learnt from Chesterton in this field, too. Father Brown, Chesterton's unprofessional detective with a vast knowledge of human character gained through his priesthood, and gifted with an exceptional share of intuition, wit and common sense, has distant relations in Čapek's two lay detectives, Dr Mejzlik and Mr Janik in *The Tales from Two Pockets*. Their knowledge of human nature comes from their collaboration with the police; they too, are witty, but their intuition and ability lacks the touch of miraculousness of Father Brown's; in that sense they are more realistic than their Chestertonian colleague: they are unable to be on the spot at the very moment or even before a crime is committed, like Father Brown, who can be in England one moment and in America the next; they seem to have enough to do in their own small country. However, their intuition is supplemented by sheer good luck. Moreover, against Father Brown's seriousness, there is Mr Janik's amusing paradox: at the moment he decides to accept an offer from the police to join them professionally, he finds that – for all his success in detection – his own clerk has been cheating him of money for years.

Dealing with justice, law and order, both Chesterton and Čapek believed that there is something good in every human being and have, therefore, some sympathy with offenders:

> . . .burglars and bigamists are essentially moral men; my heart goes out to them. They accept the essential ideal of man; they merely seek it wrongly. Thieves respect property. They merely wish the property to become their property that they may more perfectly respect it.[18]

For Čapek,

> a criminal is something like a hero: he is shrouded with romanticism, he is an outcast, an outlaw: pulling the henchmen's noses as well as those of the court and of the law, he enjoys secret popular sympathy.[19]

Both Chesterton and Čapek believed in conquering evil and crime by kindness rather than by legal justice: some of Father Brown's repentant criminals (Flambeau, Bohun) are offered a helping hand and the secrecy of the confessional, just as Čapek's Mr Janik can solve his case when a murderer, Basta, shows him his victim buried in the woods, after Mr Janik has addressed him politely as 'Sir' and offered him a bun out of pity. However, Čapek-the-pragmatist also relies on the common sense of his trespassers against the law: so the murdered Kugler ('The Last Judgement') accepts his damnation without a protest, or the matrimonial swindler ('The Misadventures of a Matrimonial Swindler') can be left unguarded at the railway station: after his return, the detective finds him in the same place, ready to be taken into custody.

Among all criminals and sinners, the sympathies of both Chesterton and Čapek go especially towards artists. In 'The Ghost of Gideon Wise'[20] Chesterton excuses a murderer: 'Horne is a sneak and a skunk, but do not forget that, like many other sneaks and skunks in history, he is also a poet.' And Čapek writes a tale about the disappearance of the actor Benda who led an immoral life. His friend finds the murderer, but, unable to prove him guilty, threatens to be his living conscience: 'Till your dying day I'll keep on reminding you: Remember Benda the actor. I tell you, he was an artist, if ever there was one.'[21]

Some themes in Chesterton may have inspired Čapek, although he always created original stories. In 'The Hammer of God' and 'The Record' respectively, both writers use the theme of an incredible physical achievement possible only through the stimulus of moral indignation, leading to crime, although the culprits could be reprieved: conscience-stricken, Chesterton's murderer gives himself up, while Čapek's, in a charmingly comic situation, claims credit for his sporting record even if it means his going to jail.

This example also shows how the two writers used the serious and the comic for different purposes. Murder is a serious matter and Chesterton's priest, God's representative on earth, is the proper person to deal with it; on the other hand, Čapek-the-pragmatist preferred to use lighter offences in comic rather than tragic situations.[22]

Passionate collectors of rarities can be found in both Chesterton's and Čapek's stories, but here, again, Čapek's collectors are ridiculous and harmless when compared to Chesterton's maniacs.[23]

Another example of the two writers using a similar theme for different purposes are the stories 'The Mistake of the Machine' and 'The Experiment of Professor Rous': in the former, Chesterton proves guilt by means of a psychometric machine, while in the latter Čapek ridicules journalistic clichés.

Two of Čapek's God-like characters, one in the novel *Krakatit*, the other in the story 'The Last Judgement', resemble Chesterton's Sunday in *The Man who was Thursday*; their similarity lies in their large size but also in the aura of the supernatural which surrounds particularly the character in *Krakatit*. He is an almost superhuman, underdefined figure who appears at critical moments, as if by chance, to give the hero a lesson in humility. Even so, compared with Sunday, he is much more terrestrial, appearing at times as an old peasant of great wisdom experience and common sense.

In some of his tales, Čapek used paradox very cleverly; he may have learnt this art from Chesterton, but he never developed it into a literary mannerism as the English writer did. Occasional paradoxical conceptions as well as some other stylistic devices, like bathos and oxymoron, occur in Čapek where Chesterton can be felt behind them but the similarity of their wit and humour may account for this. Although Čapek was an admirer of Chesterton, he was certainly not a mere imitator. His essays have the same lightness as Chesterton's and in their use of colloquial language one can, at times, hardly distinguish one from the other: 'On, yes, I saw the Escorial. Yes, thank you, I visited Toledo',[24] 'Before I forget: of course, I went to look at Baker Street.'[25]

The great Czech critic F. X. Salda called Čapek 'a Chestertonian conservative' before he fully understood and appreciated his art. Chesterton's influence on Čapek was beneficial and did not impair his originality. It was Chesterton's wit and humour which attracted Čapek to him; serious matters of religion and their differing political views divided them.

In H. G. Wells Čapek found a true friend. The English writer could have easily resented the fact that, during his stay in London, Čapek unable to cope with all the invitations he had received, had to postpone his visit to H. G. Wells more than once, but he was very patient and understanding. He could put the shy Čapek at his ease and even allow him a glimpse into his private life: when Čapek accepted a separate invitation from Rebecca West, he knew about her close friendship with H. G. Wells, but did not suspect anything more; astonished by seeing a leisurely-looking Wells in her flat, he reacted: 'Fancy, I ring the bell and the door is opened by Wells – in shirtsleeves!!!'[26] When he was eventually able to spend a weekend at Wells's country residence Easton Glebe, he enjoyed the visit very much. H. G. Wells proved to be a

excellent host, especially when some more guests arrived, John Galsworthy with his wife and the Countess Daisy of Warwick among them.
Although physically not too energetic, Čapek even joined in a dance in
a reconstructed barn on the estate. Praising the beauties of English
homes, he described Easton Glebe:

> Briefly, the English home is the English home, and therefore I have
> drawn it for you as a souvenir, with the cuckoo and the rabbit; inside,
> there lives and writes one of the wisest men in this world. Outside the
> cuckoo calls as much as thirty times in succession; with this I
> conclude the fairy-tale about the best things in England.[27]

Like Chesterton, Wells was not a good correspondent, but his wife
acted as his reliable secretary, so that Čapek did not lose his valued
contact. With great pleasure he welcomed H. G. Wells to Prague in the
late 1920s and again in 1938 when the International PEN Club met
there. In 1935 Wells suggested that Čapek should succeed him as
President of the International PEN. In a letter to the PEN Secretary
Hermon Ould[28] the modest Čapek was willing to accept, provided that
H. G. Wells definitely wished to resign and that the executive committee
would agree to it. Unfortunately, the election failed because Čapek
could not make the journey as far as Buenos Aires where the Congress
was held.

Čapek's library and his reviews of Wells's works in the Czech press
indicate that he knew his writings well; it was his science fiction and
stories of adventure which inspired him most. In his childhood he had
read Verne avidly but, apart from J. Arbes's fantastic pieces which he
called 'the romanets', there was hardly any science fiction in the true
sense in Czech literature. Unlike Wells, who was a trained scientist,
Čapek was only a well-informed layman, fascinated by progress in
science which stimulated his imagination.

It is possible that the hero of Wells's story 'The Country of the Blind',
marooned in a place of no escape, helped Čapek to put his protagonist
of the early story 'The Island' in a similar situation, but the climaxes of
the respective stories differ: the two characters encounter people with
whom they find it difficult to communicate, and only the love of a
woman in each case makes their lives tolerable; Wells's hero even
goes so far as to consent to conform with his blind co-citizens by
sacrificing his sight, but flees, risking his life, when the critical moment
approaches. Čapek's hero could be saved by a passing boat; he
promises to join the crew, but at the last moment, conscience-stricken,

he cannot leave the woman who has devotedly served him.

The two writers can be compared more positively in relation to their common source in Swift. Wells himself confesses to his early, profound and lifelong admiration for him[29] and the relationship between his Morlocks in 'The Time Machine', Martians in *The War of the Worlds*, spiders in 'The Valley of Spiders', man-beasts in *The Island of Doctor Moreau* and giants in 'The Food of the Gods' and Swift's creatures that Gulliver meets, is obvious. Swift's repulsion at the ugliness of human nature also appears in Wells and the setting of some of his stories against the background of contemporary events may also derive from Swift.

The last two devices, whether Swiftian or Wellsian, play an important part in Čapek's novel *War with the Newts*; but choosing newts for the main characters seems rather Wellsian. Although they are black and Wells's Morlocks 'of a half-bleached colour of the worms and things one can see perserved in spirit in a zoological museum',[30] both of them are slippery, and the cold, wet bodies, chinless faces and great lidless eyes of the Morlocks suggest creatures of the salamander family. Both of these ugly, disgusting animals personify bad human qualioties, although Čapek's newts are originally good, but learn their bad habits from people. This is Čapek's accusation of mankind in a novel full of wit and humour, its apocalyptic forecasts making it topical even nowadays, in relation to the warming of the earth: it is flooded when the supernewts take over from men.

Most of Čapek's scientific romances belong to his early works and it is possible that he, like H. G. Wells,[31] considered them as exercises in imagination. Both writers wished to entertain their readers, but Čapek's message was usually more serious than Wells's who himself admitted[32] that his scientific romances – unlike Verne's – do not aim to project a serious possibility of invention or discovery. Yet, in the age of space travel, some of his forecasts did come true. And so did Čapek's: he wrote about the splitting of the atom as early as 1922 in his *The Absolute at Large* and two years later in *Krakatit*. In the same year Čapek met Professor Blackett in Cambridge, but, presumably, the information the nuclear physicist could give him then must have been only rudimentary; yet Čapek was quite correct in warning about the disastrous effects of nuclear devices. Admittedly, the deity which his Absolute emits as a biproduct is absurd, but the treatment of this part of the novel is reminiscent of the Wellsian sense of social comedy which, in general, was more prominent in Wells than in Čapek.

As for other predictions: Čapek's robots (*RUR*) serve as computers and people do live longer, not as a result of an elixir of life (*The*

Macropulos Secret), but because they live on better, scientifically controlled food; cancer is consuming mankind just as Čapek's white plagues (*Power and Glory*) and one can only hope that a less obstinate inventor who would *not* allow himself to be smothered to death by a crowd of ignorant people, will soon emerge out of the host of researchers.

Both Wells and Čapek realised that the absurdity of the invention must be camouflaged, that the reader's curiosity about its substance must be drawn to its effects, in order for their story to be credible. Wells commented in the Preface to *Scientific Romances of H. G. Wells* that:

> For the writer of fantastic stories to help the reader to play the game properly, he must help him in every possible unobtrusive way to *domesticate* the impossible hypothesis. He must trick him into an unwary concession to some plausible assumption and get on with the story while the illusion holds. And that is where there was a slight novelty in my stories when first they appeared.

Čapek may have learned this technique from Wells, and Václav Cerny has pointed out[33] his skill in using it. If we compare Wells's quite elaborate effort to explain scientifically the cause of his Invisible Man's condition with Čapek's mere hints, the latter emerges as the more skilful of the two. Čapek simply describes *an* invention or *a* drug and develops the plot around its influence on human life: the Absolute is produced by *a* machine, in *The Macropulos Secret* there is *an* elixir of life, the robots are made of *a* colloidal material; the external appearance of the newts is described quite vividly, but when it comes to giving exact anatomic details in his scientific report, Čapek admits frankly: 'anatomical details follow, which in our case we laymen would not understand'. Or, in one of his late tales, 'Removers' Business', inspired possibly by Wells's *The Time Machine*, he writes about carriages travelling into time, not the future, but the past: 'true, I do not yet know how to do it technically; but a technical solution can always be found if there is an idea promising a good profit.'

A comparison of the two inventors, Wells's Invisible Man and Čapek's hero in *Krakatit*, Prokop, will show Wells's greater concern with the invention which causes invisibility, while Čapek's attention is directed more towards the effects: both are surrounded by test tubes and bottles, but when Prokop's Krakatit starts exploding, its substance becomes less relevant in the novel and the interest is directed towards the chances of Prokop's escape from the place of destruction; Wells, on the other hand, feels that some scientific proof must be offered to justify the hero's (or, rather the villain's) invisibility. Hence there are lengthy passages of scientific argument in the middle of the book, while Čapek's reader is carried away by a more captivating narrative. Both the inventors are titans whose exceptional position excludes them from the fellowship of society; fear of their power breeds hatred towards them and shapes their character accordingly. Čapek's Prokop is more realistic, as he has room in his heart for human affection, while Griffin's emotional life is reduced to one single feeling, hatred of people. This makes him a more conventional protagonist of science fiction than Prokop who appears quite small and humble when disaster strikes in the end. Yet both Wells and Čapek agree that fame, power and glory are not enviable.

Wells's megalomaniac creation may have inspired Čapek more directly in his story 'The Mountain' and once can agree with A. Matuska[34] that the similarities are too numerous to be coincidental. Yet these similarities are mainly ones of detail in a particular situation affecting the two protagonists; the plot and 'message' differ greatly from each other. While Griffin turns out to be a real villain and efforts to catch him resemble a chase in a detective story, Čapek's pursuers of the 'megalomaniac' are more concerned with the mystery of both the murderer and the murdered man, the unknown and mysterious which baffles them. 'One takes one's soul into consideration only when one is confronted with a mystery', wrote Čapek to S. K. Newmann[35] in 1917 when 'The Mountain' appeared in *Wayside Crosses*: this explains why Čapek's protagonist is deliberately less clearly defined even if he behaves in a similar way to Well's Invisible Man.

The large footprints of a man who 'slid down the wet soil' reminded Matuska of Griffin's slowly drying footprint that has resulted from a puddle in Tavistock Square, a footprint as isolated and incomprehensible as Crusoe's solitary discovery'; Čapek's inspiration could, therefore be Wells or Defoe. However, apart from 'The Mountain', two other 'footprint stories' are included in *Wayside Crosses*, 'The Footprint' and 'Elegy'. All three were written at the time of Čapek's painfully intensive philosophical search for the truth and, as Hume's mysterious single footprint is directly mentioned in 'The Footprint', this would seem a more direct influence that either Wells or Defoe. Hume's mysteriousness provided a greater challenge for Čapek, while Wells's and Defoe's footprints lend themselves more easily to a rational explanation.

Taking their work as a whole, there is a fundamental difference between Wells and Čapek: Wells wished human nature to change. For him, invention was a means of reconstructing the world, while for Čapek it is an instrument to display his philosophy of life: man is capable of interfering with the development of the world through the power of his brain, he is able to a certain extent to correct and rule it, directed by his sense; yet ultimately his innovations usually have a negative effect upon the welfare of mankind, because man is incapable of seeing their consequences to the very end. On the other hand, Wells had more faith in modern technology than Čapek, whose scientific romances are much more subjective and symbolic.

In structure, Čapek's novel *The Absolute at Large*, describing the action of an explosive in different places and observed by different people, is strongly reminiscent of Wells's technique in his *The War of the Worlds*, as well as in *The Invisible Man*. This may be just a coincidence due to Čapek's liking for the form, the result of a common outlook with a similar sense of system and order. The serial publication of his work in newspapers may have directly led Čapek to use this method.

Two more short stories could be included among Čapek's fantastic pieces, 'Glorie' and 'The Man who Knew how to Fly', but they are not Wellsian and have little in common with science fiction, in spite of their fantastic subjects. The halo in 'Glorie' which appears on the head of a man who knows how to pardon his neighbours when they hurt him, but disappears when he begins to feel hatred, is only symbolic – and the man who knew how to fly achieves his skill by training, just as a child learns how to walk; he loses his ability when his amateur methods are criticised by experts in physical training.

The story is therefore related to the 'Record' in *Tales from Two Pockets*, about incredible actions which untrained people can perform in individual cases when they are stimulated by an unusual emotional state.

Wells's biographer Vincent Brome concludes[36] that H. G. Wells exercised comparatively little influence on his contemporaries or younger writers. If Čapek paid a small tribute to him in his work, he admired his ideas, his common sense, and loved Wells – the man and the pacifist. Both writers were ardent spokesmen for democracy, both of them saw the dangers of dictatorship and warned people against it, both of them tried to persuade the world by the same means to prevent war – by common sense and humanity.

Čapek's charming sketch of George Bernard Shaw in his *Letters from England*, with his forefinger in a warning position, indicates his respect, almost awe, of the older, more experienced and famous playwright. His initial shyness, though, was soon overcome when he saw Shaw's encouraging interest. Shaw entertained Čapek for lunch,[37] played the clavichord for him and kept him till after tea. Shaw's comment on Čapek's premature death in 1938 best expresses his appreciation:

> It is absurd. It should have been my turn this time. Karel was far too young to go like that. He had at least another forty years to give so much to the world. His plays proved him to be a prolific and terrific playwright.[38]

As far as Shaw's influence on Čapek's writing is concerned, there appears to be no more than he had on any playwright of the 'Shavian age', in spite of the fact that *Back to Methuselah* and Čapek's *The Macropulos Secret* appeared a short time after each other and the younger writer could have been accused of plagiarism. Yet clearly Čapek's play had been written before he heard about Shaw's.[39]

It was Professor Metchnikov's topical ideas about possible longevity that roused the imagination of the two dramatists to use their art for a discussion of the subject. They did this in very different ways. Shaw's large-scale rational metabiological pentateuch (as he called it) with its span of five evenings allows more scope for details and philosophical analysis than Čapek's romantic three-act play, but, dramatically, the latter is much more effective, the former being described by Desmond McCarthy as 'rather wonderful but distinctly boring.'[40]

Perhaps the tedium is caused by the lack of one central character, as the *dramatis personae* in *Back to Methuselah* are more like people taking part in a public discussion; on the other hand, Čapek, so successful in his novels without a central hero (*The Absolute at Large, The War with the Newts*), concentrates the action on a beautiful and accomplished singer: what a dream to live long and achieve perfection in art! For Čapek, however this is merely a thesis; after a time, his heroine feels tired of her luxurious and glorious life and she reaches the stage of depression when nothing matters and life becomes sheer boredom.

Fame, property, love, admiration cannot give anything to the weary soul whose art has reached perfection, but whose life has become comfortlessly miserable. Her callous reaction to a young man's suicide for his unrequited love of her is the crowning point of Čapek's refusal of longevity as a blessing.

Shaw's characters provide a similar argument: the Ancients forgot how to laugh, how to speak, read and think in the usual way; they, too, lose their sense of beauty, love and everything that contributes to the happiness of mortals. Through his 'elderly gentleman' Shaw seems to agree that a short life, lived honestly and usefully is worth living:

I accept my three score and ten years. If they are filled with usefulness, with justice, with mercy, with good will: if they are the lifetime of a soul that never loses its honour and a brain that never loses its eagerness, they are enough for me.[41]

Shaw's more optimistic view is, however, developed through his deeper philosophical argument which, to the detriment of the play's stage effectiveness, leads to the discussion of a higher morality which could be achieved through longevity. His mature Ancients, free from all bodily passions, reach a higher degree of responsibility and honour; long life would not allow anything dishonest because the punishment and shame of offenders would be too long to bear. The long-lived do not know how to lie because all lies will be found out eventually; there cannot be secrets between two opposing parties, therefore secret diplomacy may be abolished.

As in science fiction, both writers feel that they must explain how longevity can be achieved. An elixir of life or some supernatural power? Čapek's romantic spirit looks into the past, when the Emperor Rudolf II alive in the late sixteenth and early seventeenth centuries surrounded himself with scientists who hoped to find the former; the fictitious personal doctor to the Emperor, the Greek Macropulos, tries his invention on his daughter Elina. Again, for Čapek, the effect of the invention is more important for the momentum of the play than its substance, while Shaw discusses the subject in his usual brilliantly intellectual manner which was criticised as being less dramatic by Leo Tolstoy, among others. In his 'thank-you' letter to Shaw for a copy of *Man and Superman*, he commented:

In your book I detect a desire to surprise and astonish the reader by your great erudition, talent and cleverness. Yet all this is merely unnecessary for the solution of the questions you deal with, but often distracts the reader's attention from the essence of the matter by attracting it to the brilliance of the exposition.[42]

So, in the course of the pentateuch, various kinds of elixir of life are discussed: sour milk, lemons, soya beans; in the fifth part, Pygmalion admits the existence of an elixir called the 'breath of life'; yet the philosophical basis of the whole pentateuch is concluded by Shaw's thesis that imagination is the beginning of creation, that long life can be achieved by a mere wish.

As far as the dramatic effect is concerned, a comparison of how the two writers have linked the past with the present is interesting. Čapek's law-suit lasting several generations in which the singer is involved proves her identity and true age after eye-witnesses of her early existence are long dead; a link smooth and credible for the spectator who is still keenly expecting the proof of longevity, but perhaps Shaw's new people reincarnated are even more acceptable, even if, as a link, they are less dramatic. However, they show some of Shaw's iconoclasm and humour: Eve in the first part appears later as the socialist, modern, but still rather feminine, Savvy; two politicians, Burge and Lubin, in the second part act as one character, Burge-Lubin in the third and the elderly gentleman Bolge-Bluebin-Barlow in the fourth part; the first killer Cain has his descendant in Napoleon; the clergyman Haslam is reincarnated as the Archbishop and the maid as the Home Affairs minister. Shaw-the-evolutionist speaks through the last two who are the only elect, the long-lived; they must marry and populate the earth.

The task of setting the long-lived among normal mortals needed some consideration from both writers. Čapek relies on the flow of the play, which should prevent the spectator from questioning how the beautiful singer who keeps on changing her name, is unobserved from one country to another, even if this happens only once in a generation. Shaw's characters also change their names, but Haslam also pretends to be drowned, leaving his clothes on the shore; appearing in another country, he professes loss of memory to be accepted by his new fellow-citizens.

Both dramatists seem to expect human life to be extended to some 300 years. How then do these long-livers die? Shaw believes in a fatal accident, such as the death of a fawn in the first part of the pentateuch, while Čapek's heroine dies simply because the manuscript containing the elixir formula has been destroyed and she cannot rejuvenate herself any longer.

Yet the 'pessimist' Čapek (as he calls himself in the Preface to the play) allows life to celebrate its victory: 'If we were to think of birth. . . rather than death. . . life is not short. As long as we can be the cause of life. . .'[43]

Shaw, of course, took this into account, as Adam and Eve are among the characters of the pentateuch.

If Shaw offers some hope of a better long life and Čapek does not consider it a blessing, both dramatists show dissatisfaction with man: could artificially created people be better? Neither Shaw's Pygmalion (fifth part of *Back to Methuselah*) nor Čapek's Adam in the play *Adam the Creator* gives a satisfactory answer nor do the robots (*RUR*). In fact, the idea seems to them all almost blasphemous, as Pygmalion dies after being bitten by one of his creations, and in the end Čapek's robots practically destroy man.

In his thoroughness Shaw devoted one part of the pentateuch to each of the main areas of thought: religion, politics, philosophy, nationalism, and the arts and sciences, working new plots around them. Yet, in spite of his play's brevity compared to Shaw, Čapek, too, incorporated important ideas and aspects of life. This is achieved by the characters representing them, such as Vitek-the-socialist, the Nietzschean-Darwinian Baron Prus, the pleasure-seeking senile Baron Hauk and the lawyer Kolenaty who represents the practical side of life (pensions, contracts, insurance and economy). They present theses, unlike Shaw who tries to offer solutions.

A comparison of *Back of Methuselah* and *The Macropulos Secret* shows how the two playwrights caught hold of a contemporary idea and that, on the whole, Čapek succeeded more effectively in expressing it. If the idea of mutual influence does not arise, one can see not only Professor Metchnikof, but perhaps also Swift's Struldbruggs (in the third part of *Gulliver's Travels*) as a common source. Also, it is almost certain that Čapek knew his friend F. Langer's short story 'Eternal Youth', written 1910–1911. Although inspired by the superstition of ritual murder, Langer's beautiful heroine also moves from one country to another, changing her name. But there is little doubt that Čapek's living model was the famous Czech singer Ema Destinova.

Contemporary events may have brought another coincidence in 1938 when Shaw's *Geneva* and Čapek's *Power and Glory* were written. Dictators were too much in the public eye, but it is typical how a member of a small nation in the centre of Europe felt the danger for his nation and tried to warn against it, while Shaw, the iconoclast and *enfant terrible* of the time, could, even at that late hour, write his 'political extravaganza' as he subtitled *Geneva*.

The question of Shaw's influence on Čapek, seems, then, to lead to a quite negative conclusion and yet are not, perhaps, Čapek's brisk dialogues, like the one in the first act of *RUR*, reflections of Shaw's 'tennis-ball' technique? Or were these dramatists simply equally sharp? In his study of Shaw Desmond McCarthy reminds us in retrospect of the age of Voltaire and suggests that the first half of the twentieth century should be called the 'Shavian Age'.[44] The influence that Shaw exercised on the cultural life of Europe was great, especially after the production of *Man and Superman*, he became the spokesman of the generation to which Čapek also belonged. Shaw's outspokenness, irreverence for all the solemnity of old traditions, his dissatisfaction with man and deep interest in human nature, his vitality, sense of humour and original style were inspiring, admired and warmly accepted by his contemporaries who looked beyond the boundaries of their own countries and tried to participate in cultural life on a broader scale.

Apart from Chesterton, Wells and Shaw, Čapek met other writers in England, Galsworthy, James Bones, Ivor Brown, Hermon Ould, and he knew Edwin Muir in Prague. They were all good friends and admirers of the Czech dramatist, who, even if they did not influence his work, encouraged him and strengthened his own 'Englishness'; in the best sense.

Notes

1. O. Vočadlo, *Anglické listy Karla Čapka* (Prague: Academia, 1975) p. 329.
2. Ibid., p. 327.
3. Ibid., p. 327.
4. One of his longer university essays came out later as *Pragmatismus*, 1918.
5. B. R. Bradbrook, 'Letters to England from K. Čapek,' *The Slavonic and East European Review*, XXXIX, 92, December 1960, p. 62.
6. O. Vočadlo, *Anglické listy K. Čapka*, p. 239. My translation.
7. Letter from O. Vočadlo to B. R. Bradbrook, undated, Spring 1955.
8. B. R. B., 'Letters to England from K. Čapek', as above, p. 69.
9. B. R. Bradbrook, 'Chesterton and Karel Čapek: A Study in Personal and Literary Relationship'. *The Chesterton Review*, IV, 1. Saskatoon, 1978, p. 94.
10. Vočadlo, p. 279.
11. *G. K.'s Weekly*, 14 January 1928, p. 902.
12. *Lidové Noviny*, 16 June 1936. Reprinted in *Ratolest a vavřín* (Prague: Borovy, 1947) p. 255.
13. *Marsyas*, transl. as *In Praise of Newspapers* (London: Allen and Unwin, 1954), p. 122.
14. Ibid., p. 9
15. *Orthodoxy*, 1908.

16. *Generally Speaking* (London, 1928).
17. *O nejbližších věcech* (Prague: Aventinum, 1920) transl. as *Intimate Things* (London: Allen and Unwin, 1935).
18. G. K. Chesterton, *The Man who was Thursday*, 1908 (Penguin, 1938) p. 46.
19. *In Praise of Newspapers*, p. 108.
20. *Father Brown Stories*.
21. *Tales from Two Pockets* (London: Faber and Faber, 1932) p. 151.
22. 'Mr Havlena's Verdict', The Misadventures of a Matrimonial Swindler', 'Record', 'The Secret of Handwriting'.
23. K. Čapek, 'The Stolen Cactus', 'The Troubles of a Carpet Fancier'; G. K. Chesterton, 'The Arrow of Heaven', 'The Curse of the Golden Cross'.
24. G. K. Chesterton, *Autbiography* (London: Hutchinson, 1952), p. 315.
25. K. Čapek, *Letters from England* (London: G. Bles, 1925) reprinted 1941, p. 25.
26. O. Vočadlo, p. 106.
27. *Letters from England*, p. 83.
28. Dated 6 October 1935. In the archives of the London PEN.
29. Preface to *Scientific Romances of H. G. Wells* (London: Gollancz, 1933).
30. *The Time Machine* (Penguin, 1946) p. 59.
31. Preface to *Scientific Romances of H. G. Wells*.
32. Ibid.
33. V. Černý, *Karel Čapek* (Prague: Borový, 1936) p. 15.
34. A. Matuška, *Člověk proti skaze*, (Bratislava, 1963) pp. 30–1.
35. *V. Dyk-S. K. Newmann-Bratři Čapkove*, korespondence z let 1905–1918, (Prague, 1962), pp. 190–191.
36. Vincent Brome, *H. G. Wells* (London: Longmans, Green and Co, 1951) p. 236.
37. O. Vočadlo told me about this visit before he wrote his book *Anglické listy K. Čapka* where this event is recorded on pp. 102–105. Cf. also B. R. B. 'Letters to England from K. Čapek', note 5.
38. *Daily Express*, 27 December 1938.
39. In a letter of 22 November 1956 O. Vočadlo drew my attention to Dr Port, Čapek's colleague at the Vinohrady theatre, who confirmed this fact which Čapek himself states in the preface to the play.
40. Desmond McCarthy, *Shaw* (London: MacGibbon and Kee, 1951), p. 139.
41. *Back to Methuselah* (Penguin, 1954) p. 248.
42. A. Henderson, *Bernard Shaw* (London: D. Appleton, 1932) p. 522.
43. The last scene of *The Macropulos Secret*.
44. D. McCarthy, *Shaw* preface, p. VIII.

Index